FOREWORD BY JV CRUM III

INTERNET

LESSONS LEARNED AND STRATEGIES USED BY

BUSINESS

101 SUCCESSFUL INTERNET-BASED ENTREPRENEURS

INSIGHTS

CHRIS NAISH AND BUCK FLOGGING
+100 OTHER ENTREPRENEURS

Developmental editing and consulting by
Loretta Crum of EBookSalon.net

Publishing services provided by

Archangel Ink

ISBN-10: 1548142859

ISBN-13: 978-1548142858

DEDICATIONS

CHRIS NAISH

To my daughters Kisha and Natisha: This book is what it's all about, girls. It's my hope you don't wait as long as I did to finally start waking up. This is for you two most of all!

To my beautiful wife Rowena: Thank you for having faith and standing behind me while I sank the last of our money into this project. And for your patience while I sat hunched over a computer for eight months.

Mum: You've always been there to encourage me and tell me you're proud of me even in the lowest of times, and no matter how many times I "fail." I inherited the will to keep at it from you!

Finally, to my Auntie Jeanette: Everybody misses you, the world lost a good 'un. I will always remember your tales of me and my brother in the bath as kids, when he took a shit and ruined my day when I spotted it floating past me. Rest in peace, I'm so sorry I couldn't come to say goodbye.

BUCK FLOGGING

I'd like to say a very special thank you to the most important person in my life. This person taught me everything I know, has been with me through all my failures and successes, and is ultimately the best person to walk the face of the earth ever. Certainly the smartest and best-looking. You mean EVERYTHING to me, Buck Flogging. You are the man.

Oh, and Chris Naish. Thanks for doing ALL of the hard work putting this book together while I chased hot Latinas all over Central and South America. I look forward to taking all the credit for its inevitable success.

SPECIAL THANKS TO OUR CONTRIBUTORS

Adam Rotman

Adam Sicinski

Akshat Choudhary

Al Spath

Amanda Turner

Amy E. Smith

Annie Grace

Barbara Findlay
Schenck

Beate Chelette

Ben Tristem

Bill Burniece

Brad Wilson

Brandon Carter

Britt Malka

Chris Guthrie

Christina Nicholson

Cody Barbo

Connie Ragen
Green

Damon Freeman

Daniel Knowlton

Dave Fuller

David Huckabay

David Perdew

Davide De Guz

Debbie Drum

Dennis Becker

Derek Doepker

Derek Murphy

Derric Haynie

Dominic Wells

Emily Gowor

Fred Stutzman

Gail Gardner

Grant Cardone

Holly Casto

Dr. Ian Dunbar

Jacob Cass

James Heller

Jamie Lewis

Jamie Stenhouse

Jason Little

Jason Treu

Jeff Brown

Jeff McMahon

Jeff Sanders

Jess Larsen

Jesse Krieger

Jimmy D. Brown

Johannes Voelkner

John Bura

John Lagoudakis

John Pollock

John Ruhlin

Josh Hoffman

Jyotsna Ramachandran

Kary Oberbrunner

Kate Erickson

Keith Blount

Kwame Christian

Kyle James

Lise Cartwright

Lisette Sutherland

Lynne Goldberg

Mark Goblowsky

Mark Messick

Mark van Stratum

Matt Bodnar

Matt McWilliams

Merrymaker Sisters (Emma and Carla)

Michael Bungay Stanier

Michael Sliwinski

Michelle Dale

Mind Pump Media (Sal Di Stefano, Adam Schafer, Justin Andrews)

Nicole Dean

Patrick King

Patrick McGinnis

Quinton Hamp

R. Michael Anderson

Rachel Pederson

Rich Latimer

Rick Smith

Ryan Kulp

Sammy Davis

Sarika Kharbanda

Scott Ginsberg

Sergey Kotlov

Shawn Manaher

Sherry Thacker

Stephanie Locsei

Stephen Guise

Steve Alcorn

Stuart Walker

Sujan Patel

Suzanne Vennard

Talita Estelle

Tyler Wagner

Whitney Nicely

Yaro Starak

Yvonne DiVita

Zac Johnson

CONTENTS

FOREWORD

It's 2017 and we are experiencing the fastest shift in history away from brick and mortar retail to online retail. According to CNBC, online retail sales show almost two straight years of monthly gains!

By contrast, traditional malls and shops are dropping share at an incredible rate. A third of the growth in retail sales is now online. This means more and more dollars are finding their way to the online marketers. And, this spells opportunity for YOU!

Moreover, because of the proliferation of internet business subscription services, the exact tools that internet based marketers and internet retailers like you need to be highly successful, it literally becomes easier each month to stake your claim as an online marketer.

Although we think of the gold rush as having been an unparalleled opportunity for anyone with determination, a pick and shovel, and a means to go west, in reality it was a very limited opportunity.

By contrast, the rapidly expanding internet marketing opportunity is a global phenomenon that anyone with a computer, an internet connection, and the commitment to learn and become successful can participate in, from any place at any time.

In fact, as I write this, I'm embarking on a potentially 18-month long "adventure-experiment" to run my organization, host multiple syndicated radio shows, podcasts, web TV shows, coach my VIP private clients, run masterminds, and oversee a global nonprofit—all while traveling the world and "landing" for a month or longer in various countries and cities.

This is the lifestyle that becoming an internet marketer affords both you and me. I believe that it's not only the best way for anyone to build a full or part-time business, coaching practice, or product marketing business, but it can also be the grandest adventure of your lifetime!

Unfortunately, not everyone will be successful. Please read that sentence again.

Many will waste their life savings and years upon tireless years of trial and error before they even become successful, if ever. I sincerely do not recommend this route to success, whether it is online, as an entrepreneur, or any other solo or small business endeavor!

If you want to maximize the probability of your success, then you need the right information, pre-organized, and easily accessible—ready for you to apply as an internet marketer.

Now, I've made millions in business, around $30 million to be more precise. One of the most important lessons I've learned through more than three decades of being a serial entrepreneur is this:

Constantly decrease the time it takes to execute,

while constantly increasing your impact and profits!

The information in *Internet Business Insights*, combined with its easy to access organization, is the precise type of resource you need now, whether you are eager to birth your first internet marketing business, or are a seasoned internet entrepreneur seeking to up your game and play on an entirely new level.

It's time for you to consciously choose how you want to help others and the big difference you want to make with your life. Whether that's to be an online coach, create a worldwide podcast, or develop products and services that positively impact others, use the information in *Internet Business Insights* to market them faster and better online!

– JV Crum, III, MBA, JD, MS Psychology

Founder, ConsciousMillionaire.com and FirstMillionAcademy.com

Host, ConsciousMillionaireShow.com, syndicated radio show & podcast

Author, *Conscious Millionaire: Grow Your Business by Making a Difference*

INTRODUCTION

No nonsense, no fluff, no "inspirational" stories that read like an infomercial in the introduction.

Let's cut right to the chase...

This book is a huge compilation of insights from 101 different people who have had real, lasting success on the internet.

Each of the contributors took the time to write a couple pages or more on their biggest successes and failures and what really made their internet businesses work.

This book is an absolute gold mine of advice and ideas for those looking to earn a full-time living from an internet-based business of any kind—from aspiring authors, bloggers, coaches, YouTube stars, freelancers, and much, much more.

In addition to the stories, we've compiled charts and a huge summary (at the end) of the core themes that were repeated again and again. It gives some organization to what appear to be universal principles of success online.

If you feel a strong desire, like so many do, to earn some money without having to go to work or answer to a boss, you should read every word of this book. You won't find a more concise or exhaustive resource for learning from such a wide variety of experts than this.

Sure, you can find plenty of interviews and courses and books about ONE person's success, but 101 all in one place? This is the only thing of the sort in existence. It took a monumental effort on our part (about eight months of grueling work) to put it all together for you. Identifying and tracking down 101 busy professionals and getting them to share their inside secrets to success is no small feat! We hope you put it to great use, absorbing lesson after valuable lesson like a sponge.

To learn more about who we are, why we created this book, and the most reliable and replicable methods for building a successful enterprise online, please visit our website: QuitN6.com

Happy reading!

– *Chris Naish & Buck Flogging*

Chapter One

TEACHERS AND COACHES

TEACHING TECHNOLOGY: GAMES AND APPS

JOHN BURA OF MAMMOTHINTERACTIVE.COM

HOW DID YOU COME UP WITH THE IDEA FOR YOUR BUSINESS?

I started freelancing and other entrepreneurial activities in high school. In 2009 I seriously started to publish my own software and other projects. It was a different development world back then. Software was way harder to produce. I wanted to produce an Xbox 360 game and there were literally no classes I could take in C# at the time. The only option was to purchase a DVD set. I did exactly that and the following year I published my own Xbox 360 game. For the next year, I would release iOS game after iOS game. The income was okay but I still needed a part-time teaching job to sustain myself. I remember working 14 hour days between both jobs. It was really starting to wear me out. In 2011 I quit my teaching job to focus on app development full time. I literally cannonballed into being a full-time entrepreneur.

WHAT WAS YOUR FIRST MAJOR BREAKTHROUGH?

When I told people about my games and apps that I have developed, everybody was interested in how to make the games and the apps versus the actual apps that I have created. Somewhere and somehow I heard of this startup called Udemy which was a marketplace for online courses. I decided to put together a comprehensive 35-hour course on HTML5 game development. On Boxing Day in 2011, my course went on sale and sold several thousand copies. I realized that I had stumbled across something people really wanted. Finally, after all of that work, I had my first breakthrough!

The next year I went on to make six figures working from home creating courses. That's when Mammoth Interactive truly began. It's been upward ever since.

HOW LONG DID IT TAKE YOU TO REACH 100% DIGITAL FREEDOM?

I had saved up enough money when I quit my job so that I could live and still not be in any debt. This is good advice for any entrepreneur who wants to make the leap into full-time entrepreneurship. I also purposely set up my day so in the mornings I could work on my business, and my safety job was at night. It's very easy to go out with friends in the evening or get distracted. This way, I maximized my productivity.

When the sales of my HTML5 game development course rolled in, I had exhausted a lot of my savings and was starting to run out of money. When I finally got a sales boost, it was literally at the last moment. In January I was going to look for a job or go back to school.

WHAT WAS YOUR BIGGEST MISTAKE?

When you decide to purchase a service such as lead generation or marketing, make sure you don't spend too much money. Test with smaller amounts.

Generally, try very hard to not spend money. I spent a lot of time when I first started trying to do things for free instead of paying. It's really hard to get money back, so try and hold on to it as long as possible.

WHAT IS THE SINGLE MOST EFFECTIVE TACTIC YOU DISCOVERED?

My whole company has been built with simple email marketing. Basically, we give away a free product and upsell a larger one. If you do this, make sure the free content is amazing and has useful information. People are more likely to want more if you give away a good product to begin with.

You also want to diversify your income streams as much as possible. The more diversified your income streams are, the higher chance you have at holding on to your business. In the past, I had most of my money come in from one source. I realized one day that if that source of income were to dry up, I would be out of business. I am constantly trying to diversify my business; that way I can stay in the game much longer.

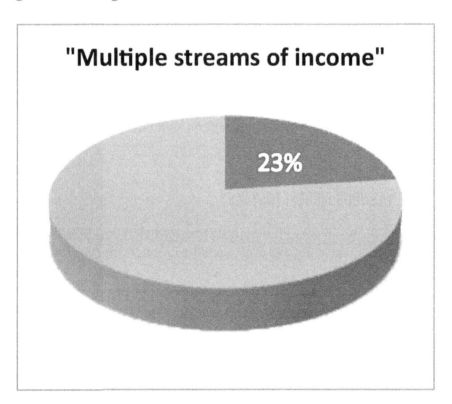

WHAT ADVICE WOULD YOU GIVE SOMEONE WANTING TO ACHIEVE SIMILAR SUCCESS?

If you want to make digital products, get in the habit of releasing often. Sometimes you don't know what will be a success. This has happened to me on more than one occasion. If you want to create online courses, then I would suggest releasing on a schedule. For example, you could release a one hour course once a week for a year. That way in one year you have 52 hours of produced content. With each new course you produce, the better you will get at making courses and the quality will go up. Ultimately you will get to test what works early and often.

Lastly, try to do something different that you are not used to doing. I love locking myself in a room and working on projects. For me, I always need to push myself to go meet people at events. Other people have the opposite problem, they are way too social and need to lock themselves in a room and get things done.

LEARN MORE ABOUT JOHN'S BUSINESS:

Go to MammothInteractive.com for a free course on how to code. You can go there and find all of the interesting projects we are working on. We do occasionally have Kickstarters for new and exciting projects. Check us out on Kickstarter to get in on the ground floor of some ground breaking projects. Check back regularly for daily deals. You can also follow us on:

Twitter: Twitter.com/MammothCompany

Facebook: Facebook.com/MammothCompany

Thanks for reading and I hope to see you in one of our courses!

BEN TRISTEM OF GAMEDEV.TV

HOW DID YOU COME UP WITH THE IDEA FOR YOUR BUSINESS?

I came up with the idea of teaching people computer game development because I could not find the sort of quality instruction online I needed when I first wanted to learn the subject. There were a lot of free YouTube videos, but the quality was relatively low and there was no structured course I could find. Furthermore, by just watching others and following along I didn't feel I was learning. In other words I was serving a personal need.

WHAT WAS YOUR FIRST MAJOR BREAKTHROUGH?

My first major breakthrough came when I launched a Kickstarter campaign with a friend. This was done without too much thought or preparation. To my delight the campaign funded over 1000%, giving me the confidence, audience and funds to start work. I put the campaign success more down to luck than judgment. I hit upon a common need and the campaign showed this. If you have a business to consumer product idea, I encourage you to test it in its simplest form using crowdfunding.

HOW LONG DID IT TAKE YOU TO REACH 100% DIGITAL FREEDOM?

Within three months of starting my online business I was able to live comfortably from the income. I should qualify that before that I had made three unsuccessful online courses. However once I hit upon a pain many people have, that I was uniquely qualified to solve, things really took off. Since then we have focused on listening to our customers and improving the courses on a daily basis in response to feedback.

Our entire production process is continually improved to be as "lean" as possible. We want to make sure we can respond to customer feedback as fast as possible, and we continually aim to remove as much friction as possible from this process. When a student has an issue with understanding or following something, our ideal response is "thank you, we have improved this content, now take a look."

By continually working on the root cause of issues, we ensure that as many students as possible stick with the courses and have a good experience. By turning one person's criticism into a benefit for everyone else, we can effectively provide one-to-one support even though our courses are affordable to everyone. This sounds like a sales pitch, but it's an important combination of service and scalability which I encourage you to engineer into your business.

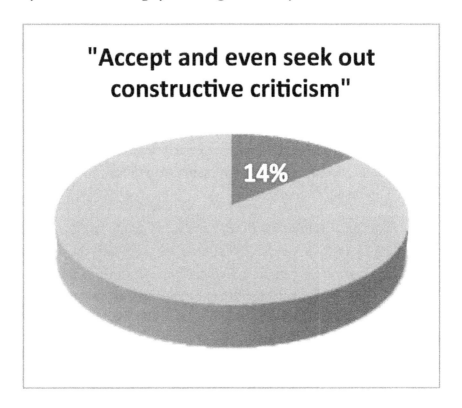

WHAT WAS YOUR BIGGEST MISTAKE?

The most embarrassing mistake I made was in the Kickstarter campaign, where I referred to the wrong programming language. I then shared the campaign with a group of seasoned professionals on Facebook, who quickly pointed out my mistake. I listened to their feedback, apologized, and even changed the direction of the product in response. This earned their respect, and that Facebook group are now avid supporters of our work.

The fact the communities were so forgiving is a testament to human nature. If you can be vulnerable enough to make mistakes in public, and humble enough to accept them and immediately act upon them, then your mistakes actually create value. That is, you give yourself the opportunity to push the boundaries, while making space for great customer service when things do go wrong.

WHAT IS THE SINGLE MOST EFFECTIVE TACTIC YOU DISCOVERED?

The most effective tactic I have found to grow my business is listening to my customers, and rapidly responding to their feedback. Having a digital product allows me to be extremely lean about the way I create content, and I make improvements in response to customer feedback on an almost daily basis.

I have mentioned lean a few times here. I encourage you to investigate the principles if you haven't already, starting with the Toyota Production System. Lean is extremely counterintuitive to most people at first, as the factory era has entrenched us all in a batch mindset. However once you practice it daily, it will soak in and transform the way you think. Hire a lean consultant for a while if you can't do it alone, and trust me you probably can't.

WHAT ADVICE WOULD YOU GIVE SOMEONE WANTING TO ACHIEVE SIMILAR SUCCESS?

When thinking about what advice to give someone wanting to achieve similar success, I'm aware of the pitfalls of giving generic solutions to specific problems. I would say keep doing what you love, keep learning, stay humble, stay open minded, challenge yourself and when the time is right your moment may come.

A lot of this is getting used to acting despite discomfort, and incomplete information. The fear will never go away, but the opportunity will. Building the habit of acting despite discomfort is like building a muscle: the more you do it the better you'll get.

LEARN MORE ABOUT BEN'S BUSINESS:

If you would like to know more about what I do, you can see our portfolio of courses at udemy.com/u/bentristem or GameDev.tv.

TEACHING PERSONAL DEVELOPMENT: BE ALL YOU CAN BE

R. MICHAEL ANDERSON OF RMICHAELANDERSON.COM

HOW DID YOU COME UP WITH THE IDEA FOR YOUR BUSINESS?

I was in the second year of my master's program for the Spiritual Psychology school, and I thought, "how can I create an awesome life for myself?" I thought, "what do I love to do?" I always loved to facilitate and speak, and entrepreneurs and business owners are my tribe. That's who I really enjoy hanging around and being with. I really enjoy deep, deep conversations, and I love helping people heal, whether it's myself or other people, heal at the deepest level possible—and to me, that's the subconscious, the emotional, and the spiritual level.

Because I was going through so many learnings and transformations myself, I thought, why don't I become a professional speaker and an author and an educator, and basically teach other business owners and high-achieving people the same type of skills and transformation that I went through?

So I sold my companies and I did exactly that. Some people say, "Hey Michael, you have such an awesome life." I'm like, "Thank you. I do have an awesome life, but I'm not lucky. It didn't come lucky. It came very intentionally."

WHAT WAS YOUR FIRST MAJOR BREAKTHROUGH?

To me, it wasn't about breakthrough. Again, mine was intentional: "I want to live this type of life, so what do I need to do to do it?" I guess my major breakthrough was setting an intention and following through on that intention. I'm what they call intentional: when I want to do things, I basically focus on a few things. I don't try to do everything in the world. That's why I get things done. I am, to be honest, a very accomplished person, and that's because I don't try to do too many things.

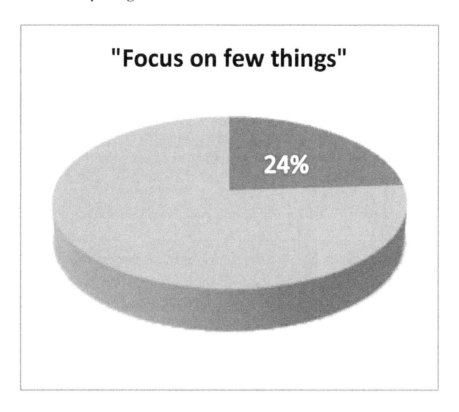

HOW LONG DID IT TAKE YOU TO REACH 100% DIGITAL FREEDOM?

Again, I sold companies, and I sold my companies probably—I'm 46 now, started selling them when I was about 42. I really liked my companies when I was in San Diego, and I had an office-based company there, but I also evolved, and then I realized that I wanted to get back on the road—because even before that, I lived in six different countries before starting my business, all in my adult life.

WHAT WAS YOUR BIGGEST MISTAKE?

That's always a tough one. The biggest mistake I've made and I see other people making are bringing on partners when I'm not absolutely 100% sure that they're the right partner for me. I've had one that ended up in a really nasty lawsuit, which was very expensive, and another partnership that almost did. When I look back, I forced those partnerships. And I see so many other younger people, early in their entrepreneurial career—sometimes they're not even young people; they're older people—but they bring on partners for the wrong reasons.

To me, a partner is like a romantic partner, where you're probably going to have to live with them for the rest of your life, or for a long time. Really just make sure that however many parties you have in the partnership are crystal clear on their roles and are crystal clear what's going to happen as the business, for example, gets larger. You can always renegotiate those, but it's just good to make sure expectations are rock solid and to have that on paper.

There's two aspects to having it on paper. One is don't start anything until you have an operating agreement that has different types of outs in it. You hate to go through that, but as companies grow, oftentimes it doesn't always grow with everybody else's vision, and it's really important to have. Basically if people want to get out because not everybody agrees, that's okay, and give them the facility to do that.

The second thing is—maybe you might even have an informal document to say "Hey, in 1 year, 2 years, 5 years, 10 years, if we go to this revenue, if we do these, this is how we're going to expand. These are going to be your roles and my roles," so at least you have a baseline to work from. Again, that can be changed, but too many times I see people say "we're going to figure it out when we get there," and then once you get there, there are so many differences in people's expectations that it's really difficult.

WHAT IS THE SINGLE MOST EFFECTIVE TACTIC YOU DISCOVERED?

Again, that's focus. To be really good at one or two things. I see so many people that have this fear of missing out (FOMO), or they want to spread their risk around and they do one or two or five or ten things, and none of them are that good. What I really believe in is doing one or two things really, really well and figuring that out, and then life's much more simple. We don't get addicted to all this busyness, and that makes life much better. That's, to me, where greatness is achieved in this world: when we do one thing really great, not a hundred things "okay." And it takes sometimes months or years to really get great at something—in fact, it often does.

WHAT ADVICE WOULD YOU GIVE SOMEONE WANTING TO ACHIEVE SIMILAR SUCCESS?

I'd be honest to yourself. I look at these boards, especially of people creating online sales funnels, and they're advertising "Hey, earn $100,000 a month"—when the person who is actually creating that has never earned $100,000 a month. So many times we'll read a book or do a course on how somebody else has done it, and it's just so unauthentic, and to me that's really a turnoff. There's so many ways you can add value in this world; I think you want to be of service to people and add value in this world, and to be true to yourself and other people. That's, to me, how I want to go through life ethically and spiritually.

LEARN MORE ABOUT MICHAEL'S BUSINESS:

I'm pioneering something called Soul-Centered Leadership. There is a lot of leadership stuff out there—and when I say "soul-centered," it's nothing really to do with religion, but if you do believe we're all connected or you do believe there's a Higher Power, I've come up with this system. It's really great because it's based on love and compassion, it's based on being of service, it's based on adding value to other people. How do you lead other people, and how do you lead your life from that place of love and compassion and connection to other people? There's a lot of psychology in it, some emotional intelligence, and some spirituality. It's not just some woo-woo type of thing, but it's hard nuts and bolts of how you do that.

You can go to my site, RMichaelAnderson.com, and there's a lot more on Soul-Centered Leadership. Grab the book. I'm developing a community around soul-centered leaders, and I'd love to have you on board.

CODY BARBO OF INDUSTRY.CO

HOW DID YOU COME UP WITH THE IDEA FOR YOUR BUSINESS?

I went head first into the startup world with my first startup right out of college, and when it didn't quite become the next Snapchat, I decided to take on a temporary role within the restaurant industry. It was the archaic process of seeking out a job in a restaurant, and the lack of usage of LinkedIn within the service and hospitality industry, that inspired me to start the business. It just blew my mind that Craigslist and a paper resume were somehow the best way to seek out most employment opportunities in the service industry.

WHAT WAS YOUR FIRST MAJOR BREAKTHROUGH?

It's one thing to have an idea, and it's an entirely different ballgame to execute on that idea. It wasn't until we met the first user who got a job on Industry that we knew we were on to something. We were randomly checking in with some of our businesses the first week after launching our beta, and we happened to speak with a bartender who was hired on Industry. Her enthusiasm was radiating as she described how our solution made it much easier for her to get her job compared to the old way of doing things. That small instance (now happening at scale) is the fuel to our fire.

HOW LONG DID IT TAKE YOU TO REACH 100% DIGITAL FREEDOM?

It wasn't until a year in, that we raised our angel round of $200k and finally went all in on Industry. It was a major commitment, especially to my partners and I that have significant others, to take the leap like that.

WHAT WAS YOUR BIGGEST MISTAKE?

There are too many to name! If we could go back, I would say that working with a PR firm in the early days was a waste of time and money. If you are a great founder, you can knock out most of the PR yourself with much more success. My most embarrassing moment goes back to the early days of meeting with investors, and not knowing "investor-speak," the terms and metrics that matter to them the most. I remember the first time I was asked about our LTV to CAC ratio and thinking "WTF did this guy just ask me..." that's when I knew we needed to step up our game.

WHAT IS THE SINGLE MOST EFFECTIVE TACTIC YOU DISCOVERED?

Find amazing mentors and surround yourself with highly motivated individuals. There are so many people who are willing to lend a hand or help guide you in the right direction. We would be lying if we didn't share our success with our advisors, investors, team, friends, family, and of course, our industry. We like to surround ourselves with people who complement our strengths and strengthen our weaknesses.

WHAT ADVICE WOULD YOU GIVE SOMEONE WANTING TO ACHIEVE SIMILAR SUCCESS?

Don't ever let the haters get in the way of your opportunity to succeed. I can count too many times where we would meet people, investors, etc. that immediately turned to criticism or the lovely "this will never work" line. To that hear that as a young, passionate entrepreneur sucks, but it ultimately lit the fire under our asses to prove them wrong. I will tell you this, there is no better feeling in the world than those haters coming back to praise you, and those investors wishing they would have invested. Be so dedicated to the vision and mission of your company that nothing can stop you from making your dream a reality.

LEARN MORE ABOUT CODY'S BUSINESS:

If you or anyone you know works in a restaurant, bar, club, or hotel, please send them to Industry.co where they can sign up for free and find their next great opportunity. Check us out on Instagram Instagram.com/Industry, and feel free to connect with me directly @ codybarbo on all social networks.

MATT BODNAR OF SCIENCEOFSUCCESS.CO

HOW DID YOU COME UP WITH THE IDEA FOR YOUR BUSINESS?

My podcast, The Science of Success, began after several kitchen table conversations with a friend of mine who suggested that I take all of the knowledge and wisdom I had learned from reading and studying some of the smartest and most successful people in the world (Warren Buffet, Charlie Munger, Ray Dalio, etc.) and turn it into a podcast. At the time he owned a small science news website named Red Orbit and we partnered up to launch the podcast on his site. We created a joint venture where I was responsible for content and he was responsible for audio production and marketing.

WHAT WAS YOUR FIRST MAJOR BREAKTHROUGH?

The first major breakthrough was partnering with Red Orbit (my friend's website) and launching through their site. This gave me immediate access to a much larger audience than I would have had if I had started totally on my own. This also helped fill gaps in my skillsets to help get the show launched. This initial launch helped propel the podcast to #1 New & Noteworthy with listeners in over 100 countries and now more than 750,000 downloads.

HOW LONG DID IT TAKE YOU TO REACH 100% DIGITAL FREEDOM?

I'm a bit unique in this regard. Out of school I worked on Wall Street at Goldman Sachs for a number of years, and after that left to become a partner in an investing firm (where I still work and very much enjoy what I do). The Science of Success is a project that I use to help learn, sharpen my thinking and decision-making, and make myself smarter so that I can continue to be successful as an investor.

That said, if I were to fully monetize the podcast with ads, affiliate revenues, and proprietary products, I could make a very comfortable living just doing the podcast. My number one goal right now is continued audience growth, so I have stayed away from monetization for the risk of any friction it may create until I have built the audience to be even larger.

WHAT WAS YOUR BIGGEST MISTAKE?

One of the hardest things for me was having to take over The Science of Success full time when my friend sold Red Orbit out of the blue one day. We had an agreement that I could take complete control if he ever left the company, so it was a great opportunity, but also a very challenging one as I had to learn how to take over audio production, editing, marketing, distribution and many other aspects that my previous partner had handled. I learned how to do all of that, streamlined the operations with the help of a virtual assistant and several great services, and now the podcast runs more smoothly than ever while I control 100% of the show.

WHAT IS THE SINGLE MOST EFFECTIVE TACTIC YOU DISCOVERED?

Growing my podcast audience has been a combination of several strategies. The most basic strategy is just to try and create great content. Over a long time frame, if you keep putting out great content, your audience will grow and slowly more and more people will hear about you, share the show, and build your audience. As Casey Neistat said about being successful on YouTube, "Never stop uploading."

Another strategy is interviewing guests who already have a built-in audience, and getting them to share with their audience helps build and expand yours.

Third, doing other interviews, being on other people's podcasts, doing guest posts, etc., also helps reach a wider audience and get more listeners.

Finally, recombining and repurposing content has been huge as well. Things like taking episode transcripts, turning them into articles that we then pitch to websites like Entrepeneur.com, turning quotes from the articles into Instagram posts, adding the audio to videos and putting them on YouTube, etc. Once you have a piece of content, there are lots of things you can to do repurpose it and generate more audience, more listeners, and more viewers from different channels.

WHAT ADVICE WOULD YOU GIVE SOMEONE WANTING TO ACHIEVE SIMILAR SUCCESS?

Launch with a partner who already has an audience. Find clear audience buckets that fit the type of content you want to create, figure out where those audiences live, and see how you can partner up to access them. It's really really hard to create an audience from scratch. Its much easier to piggyback off of an existing audience, someone who has built up a following, an email list, etc. Find a way to do a guest post or add value to them and their audience, and connect that back to your show or idea. Find a website or platform that is aligned with what you want to do, and see if you can launch in partnership with them. This was critical to the audience growth of The Science of Success.

LEARN MORE ABOUT MATT'S BUSINESS:

The best way to learn about me is to listen to The Science of Success! You can find our latest episodes at ScienceOfSuccess.co You can also chat with me on Twitter Twitter.com/MattBodnar or shoot me an email (I give out my email address at the end of every episode of The Science of Success).

You can also find The Science of Success on iTunes, Stitcher, or by searching in your favorite podcast app.

iTunes Link: itunes.apple.com/us/podcast/id1059509178

Stitcher Link: stitcher.com/podcast/the-science-of-success

I would love to hear from you and I am always happy to share insights or ideas with listeners!

JEFF BROWN OF READTOLEADPODCAST.COM

HOW DID YOU COME UP WITH THE IDEA FOR YOUR BUSINESS?

My main source of income is derived from my podcast of coaching and mentoring-related activities. This includes digital products and services, along with group and one-on-one coaching.

It wasn't until someone else suggested it that I seriously gave thought to helping others learn how to do what I'd done. It made perfect sense, as I would be leveraging my 26 years of experience in radio along with what turned out to be a successful and well-regarded podcast launch of my own just six months earlier.

I likely would never have ventured into this space if not for the encouragement and near insistence of those in my mastermind group. They, better than I, were able to quickly identify my true gifts, many of which I'd discounted for years. It was their encouragement and prodding that convinced me to take the leap.

This past month was my most successful yet, so I'm glad I did.

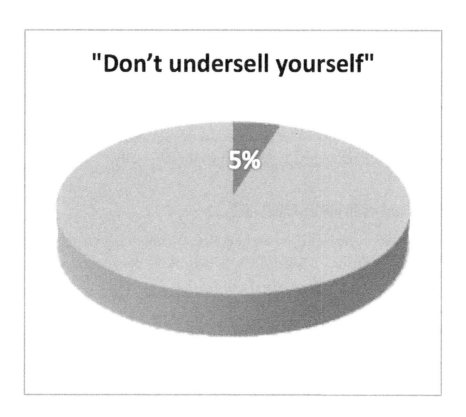

WHAT WAS YOUR FIRST MAJOR BREAKTHROUGH?

I hinted at it earlier but, for me it was the realization that I didn't see my gifts as true gifts that others would not only value, but value highly. It's the best argument there is for surrounding yourself with people who are where you want to be. When they're also people, like those in a mastermind group, who have agreed to invest in you, challenge you, and encourage you, then all the better.

HOW LONG DID IT TAKE YOU TO REACH 100% DIGITAL FREEDOM?

I had to do this virtually from day one as I didn't quit my job. My job quit me.

Thankfully, because of a side hustle I'd cultivated in the margins of my life for two or three years, I was able to jump into that side hustle head first and give it everything I had. It became my full-time gig overnight.

Because the groundwork had already been laid—I started it before I truly needed it—I was able to hit the ground running to the point that, within a month of being let go at my previous job, I'd invoiced clients an amount equal to double my monthly salary.

WHAT WAS YOUR BIGGEST MISTAKE?

For me, it was creating something before confirming there was a viable market for it. Fortunately, it only takes doing this once to ensure you're not likely to do it again.

WHAT IS THE SINGLE MOST EFFECTIVE TACTIC YOU DISCOVERED?

Dovetailing with the last answer, it's selling the idea of something and getting literal buy-in for it first, before investing all the time necessary to create it. Are people willing to pay you for it based solely on the promise or description of what it will be?

Set a specific threshold goal for pre-sales that, once surpassed, is the confirmation you need to get busy creating. I did this with my first-ever podcast course several years ago, and again recently with my members-only book club as part of my Read to Lead Podcast.

WHAT ADVICE WOULD YOU GIVE SOMEONE WANTING TO ACHIEVE SIMILAR SUCCESS?

There really isn't a shortcut for a willingness to do the work. The single best decision I ever made was to launch a podcast. Doing so put me on the map. Doing one thing consistently, more than anything, has allowed me to leverage it in so many other ways, from sponsorships, to keynoting conferences, products, services, membership sites, and more.

I see so many launch a blog, a podcast, or whatever, and then quit before it's had the chance to gain a foothold.

LEARN MORE ABOUT JEFF'S BUSINESS:

My main home on the web is at ReadToLeadPodcast.com.

Those who desire to go deeper, who want to be more consistent with putting into action what they're learning, choose to join our members-only community called Read to Lead University (ReadToLeadUniversity.com) where the main focus is our ongoing book club.

MICHAEL BUNGAY STANIER OF BOXOFCRAYONS.BIZ

HOW DID YOU COME UP WITH THE IDEA FOR YOUR BUSINESS?

Jim Collins (of "Good to Great" fame) talks about "firing bullets before you fire cannon balls." In retrospect, I can see that's what I did. I tried out a bunch of different things, and the one that happened to feel most interesting, most different, most sellable (our different approach to giving busy managers practical coaching skills) was the one we double down on.

WHAT WAS YOUR FIRST MAJOR BREAKTHROUGH?

I've found that success is more an accumulation of a lot of small things, rather than one big thing. Even the "big" things I've done—Rhodes Scholar, books published, etc.—have not had the same impact as the daily work.

HOW LONG DID IT TAKE YOU TO REACH 100% DIGITAL FREEDOM?

For my first year, I had a two day a week contract that covered my financial needs. It gave me a year and three days a week to experiment. By the end of that year, I was good to go.

WHAT WAS YOUR BIGGEST MISTAKE?

I've never "gambled the farm" and I'm relatively cautious about money, so no big financial failures. And honestly, in line with my answer above, I tend to think that it's a lot of small actions—some forward a bit, some back a bit—that get you where you're going. So I don't tend to look at things that didn't work as embarrassing or a waste of time. Just, in Edison-esque fashion, I've found out what doesn't work so I'm closer to what does.

WHAT IS THE SINGLE MOST EFFECTIVE TACTIC YOU DISCOVERED?

Focusing on one thing. We don't, for instance, do "leadership." We offer busy managers the practical tools so they can coach in 10 minutes or less. That makes us distinctive and allows us to be efficient.

WHAT ADVICE WOULD YOU GIVE SOMEONE WANTING TO ACHIEVE SIMILAR SUCCESS?

Be wary of advice. Try stuff out. Take time to reflect on what's working and what's not. Buy in as much support as you can afford as early as you can. Know that hiring people is really hard, so you'll get it wrong.

LEARN MORE ABOUT MICHAEL'S BUSINESS:

My bestselling book, *The Coaching Habit*, can be found at TheCoachingHabit.com, and information about our programs can be found at BoxOfCrayons.biz

KWAME CHRISTIAN OF AMERICANNEGOTIATIONINSTITUTE.COM

HOW DID YOU COME UP WITH THE IDEA FOR YOUR BUSINESS?

My business is a consulting firm called the American Negotiation Institute. It took me about eight months to fully flesh out this idea. I came up with the idea of the American Negotiation Institute by following my passion. I knew that I loved negotiating and resolving disputes and I loved teaching these skills to people. We are never taught how to effectively resolve disputes in school. Although 90 to 95% of our communication would qualify as persuasive in nature, we are never given the tools in formal education to create a persuasive argument. I see this as a huge gap in our system of education.

So I asked myself, what kind of business would allow me to do both of those things? When I looked around, they was no other business that would allow me to both utilize these skills in practice and teach them to others. That's why I decided to build it myself.

WHAT WAS YOUR FIRST MAJOR BREAKTHROUGH?

I was working at a public policy research institute right after I graduated from law school in 2013. After about a year, I decided that I would open my own law firm to serve the needs of entrepreneurs. I started to build up the firm on the side while still working full time. The whole time I was building up the law firm I knew that this was just a temporary fix because my ultimate goal was to start a negotiation consulting firm. However, since I didn't know the path at the time, I decided to start the law firm because I knew it would give me the opportunity to negotiate and develop more experience.

HOW LONG DID IT TAKE YOU TO REACH 100% DIGITAL FREEDOM?

I was finally able to build up enough business to leave my job in February of 2016 and pursue the law firm full time. This is when I had my first major breakthrough on my path to success. I always thought that I would have to practice law for five to 10 years before I would be "qualified enough" to serve as a negotiation consultant. After spending some time in introspection, I decided to challenge that assumption. That's when I decided to create the American Negotiation Institute and build that consulting firm while building the law firm. This was the best business decision of my life.

My strategy with the Institute was to focus first on building my reputation and exposure in the business community. To do that, I launched Negotiation for Entrepreneurs, a weekly podcast that teaches business professionals how to be more persuasive. The response has been overwhelming! After only eight months, the show is now the top ranked negotiation podcast on iTunes, has over 30,000 downloads, was featured on the homepage of iTunes, and has listeners in over 60 different countries.

One of the best parts about this is that during this first year, I wasn't anticipating making much money through the Institute. However, listeners started to reach out to me to ask if I could serve as a negotiation consultant on some of their projects.

WHAT WAS YOUR BIGGEST MISTAKE?

I would say that my biggest failure throughout this process was the fact that I doubted myself so long and it took so long to pursue this path. Creating a podcast was something that I always wanted to do. I was always passionate about teaching people how to negotiate. It was the obvious option and I failed to pursue it for years because I didn't think I was good enough. Self-doubt cripples execution, and it wasn't until I saw some of my good friends take the leap and get started that I decided to throw my hat in the ring.

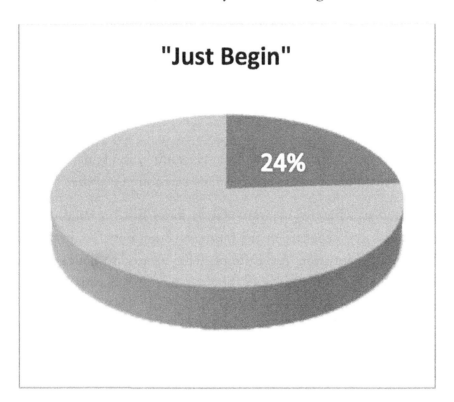

One of my favorite sayings as an entrepreneur is "fail faster." Failure is going to happen. We need to embrace it, learn from it, make the necessary adjustments and try again. The number one characteristic of successful entrepreneurs is grit—the resolve to push through obstacles and dedication to a singular goal.

WHAT IS THE SINGLE MOST EFFECTIVE TACTIC YOU DISCOVERED?

The most effective tactic for me in business has been the organic growth that has been earned through the constant creation of high-quality content. When you are starting a blog or a podcast, you have to become comfortable with the fact that you will be talking to yourself for the first few months, and that can be incredibly discouraging. However, it's important to recognize that people aren't willing to commit to you until you show that you are willing to commit to yourself. Most podcasts end after six episodes because the host simply couldn't keep up. He or she got discouraged and quit. If somebody sees that you are constantly producing content, they feel comfortable committing to you because they know you won't leave them.

WHAT ADVICE WOULD YOU GIVE SOMEONE WANTING TO ACHIEVE SIMILAR SUCCESS?

To other people who are interested in following the same path, I would say your first step is to first seek to establish your credibility through the creation of high-level content. I chose to do this predominately through my podcast, but you could do it through a blog, guest posting, or presenting in person. The single best thing I did to develop my clientele locally was speaking engagements. There are local business organizations that are constantly looking for speakers. Reach out to them and offer to give a presentation. This will give you great practice speaking in front of people and might set you up for paid speaking engagements in the future. When people go to the presentations, they will identify you as an expert and will feel more comfortable retaining your services.

LEARN MORE ABOUT KWAME'S BUSINESS:

Go to AmericanNegotiationInstitute.com/prep for a free negotiation preparation guide. If you would like to learn more about me and my journey, please connect with me on LinkedIn: linkedin.com/in/kwamechristian/. I respond to everybody that reaches out to me with a personal message. This has been one of the most important things for me as I grew the podcast because it helped me to get to know my audience and it allowed them to give me input and feedback, which improved the quality of the content.

Finally as an entrepreneur, it's important to recognize that the ability to negotiate may be the single most important skill you have. A negotiation is any conversation where you or the other person wants something. With that definition, it is easy to see that the majority of our conversations classify as a negotiation. It is completely unavoidable. As such, you should take the steps to improve these skills whenever you can. The Negotiation for Entrepreneurs podcast is a great place to start!

YVONNE DIVITA OF LIPSTICKINGSOCIETY.COM

HOW DID YOU COME UP WITH THE IDEA FOR YOUR BUSINESS?

The concept of The Lipsticking Society—teaching smart women better leadership skills to grow stronger, more successful businesses—began over 10 years ago. I wrote a little book in 2004 about marketing to women who shop online. The book, which advised folks to step out of that old Dick and Jane world of the 20th century and join us here in the 21st century, was titled, *Dickless Marketing: Smart Marketing to Women Online*. It got a lot of attention! And it jumpstarted my consulting business, working with women entrepreneurs. Here's a big lesson learned—the concept was marketing *to* women, as I recognized the lack of marketing online to those of us with money to spend and little time to go to the mall to spend it! However, over the first year of publication, the book, the blog, and the business, began to change. It became marketing *for* women, as so many women were starting new businesses and didn't have a clue how to manage or grow their business online.

We, my husband and I (he is my PIAT: Partner in All Things), took Chapter Two of the book—"Lip-sticking"—and created a blog, then a business, using the advice in that chapter. The advice? To be serious about your marketing to a growing audience that has money to spend online—women with a purse! In order to be serious and successful, you need to talk to us as human beings, not children! Lip-sticking your message is critical to your online marketing success!

WHAT WAS YOUR FIRST MAJOR BREAKTHROUGH?

My first major breakthrough was writing the book. I was desperate to get that message out—the message that women were flocking to the internet to shop. And I knew it was timely—I knew it had to be a print-on-demand book as I did not want to wait for a traditional publisher to take a whole year to publish it. Working on the book, researching women's shopping habits, and talking to brands that catered to women online was a big awakening. I knew how powerful the subject was, but I soon learned it was much larger than I'd imagined, and I learned that women were not only shopping online, they were beginning to build businesses online— businesses that needed help with marketing!

You need to understand that I am a writer at heart. I love the written word. I am devoted to it. Words are powerful tools and yes, "the pen is mightier than the sword" as demonstrated by Edward Bulwer-Lytton, in his play *Richelieu: Or the Conspiracy.*

True, This! –

Beneath the rule of men entirely great

The pen is mightier than the sword. Behold

The arch-enchanters wand!—itself is nothing! –

But taking sorcery from the master-hand

To paralyse the Cæsars, and to strike

The loud earth breathless!—Take away the sword –

States can be saved without it!

Because of my love of words, I have spent years studying not only creative writing, but copywriting. I've watched and learned from the giants of the marketing world online, from Brian Eisenberg, Andy Sernovitz, and Peter Shankman, among others. The thing that strikes me to this day is that women are underrepresented in this industry. The amazing women of BlogHer—Lisa Stone, Elisa Camahort Page, and Jory Des Jardins—were pioneers in the blogging industry focused on women, but even they have not yet proven that "women are the architects of society", as Harriet Beecher Stowe said so long ago in the 19th century. There is still much work to be done.

So, that breakthrough in 2004, when my book came out and garnered so much attention because I, a woman, was brave enough to give it that provocative title, I began a journey that I know will never end. It's a journey not only of discovery, but of fascination, of community, of connectedness, and of storytelling. Women are, if nothing else, remarkable storytellers—they just don't know it. My job now is to gather those stories, drag them out of the women if need be, and get them online. That's how you market a business today. You tell a good story.

HOW LONG DID IT TAKE YOU TO REACH 100% DIGITAL FREEDOM?

This is an interesting question. I am a risk taker. I didn't wait to earn enough money to quit my job. Quitting the job came first! After many years working for other people, mostly men who held me back, who would not let me take my innate creativity and push their businesses online, I realized I needed to shuck all that baggage and go it on my own. I met my husband shortly after and together, we forged a new path, we began a new journey, and, of course, we made money.

The money came quickly because I didn't waste time pushing the ideas I wanted—I went where the opportunities were, and I took my writing skill and sold it to the right people. In the background, I worked on Lipsticking (now TheLipstickingSociety.com); I took my focus on the road to national networking events, where I met amazing people in marketing. I interviewed women and began to embrace the idea that my path wasn't marketing to them, it was marketing for them. And now, it's brought me to an amazing place of community, working with women, for greater success all around.

WHAT WAS YOUR BIGGEST MISTAKE?

I have to laugh at this one. It's the same mistake so many new business people make. My most embarrassing mistake... a big waste of time and money...was creating an elaborate brochure. Oh, it was beautiful! And oh, we never used it. Thousands ended up in the dump.

WHAT IS THE SINGLE MOST EFFECTIVE TACTIC YOU DISCOVERED?

In a word, the most effective tactic for growing any business is *networking*. Real, in-person networking. You can meet people via social media and yes, they become friends, but there is no substitute for face-to-face meetings. When you sit with someone over lunch, or coffee, you learn so much more about them. The way they smile, the way they sit and sip their coffee, the coffee they order, and the actual physical contact—a hug or a handshake—make all the difference in the world. I have advised this for over 10 years, and will continue to say it, get out of your house and away from your computer. Your business needs you to be visible in real life.

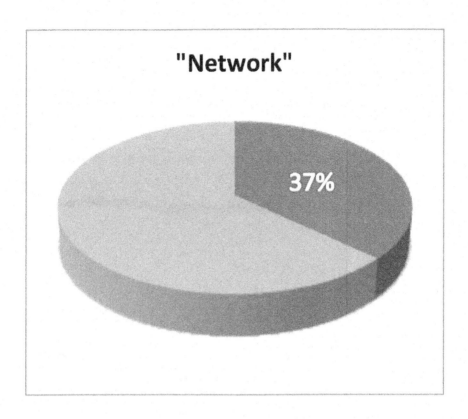

WHAT ADVICE WOULD YOU GIVE SOMEONE WANTING TO ACHIEVE SIMILAR SUCCESS?

My advice to those looking for success on the internet is this. Research your industry—trust me, your "original, fantastic, new" idea has been thought of by someone else, somewhere. Find them. Learn from them. And remember, tangential businesses count as competition. Invest in yourself. Stop whining about not having the cash to get online, or travel to networking events, or buy a new computer. Money follows those who aren't afraid to use it wisely. Oh, don't forget about time. Time is the biggest investment you will make. Use it wisely. Give back. Give something back every single day. Time or money or effort—the more you sow, the more you reap.

LEARN MORE ABOUT YVONNE'S BUSINESS:

TheLipstickingSociety.com is a growing community of smart businesswomen who want to get to that next level, and beyond, right now. Let me rephrase—smart women and the men who love (work with) them! First, sign up for The Lipsticking Insider to stay abreast of the amazing opportunities we have in store for next year. If you're working on a book, or thinking about sharing your remarkable story, contact me—I want to help! Yvonne@lipstickingsociety.com

MARK GOBLOWSKY OF MARKGOBLOWSKY.COM

HOW DID YOU COME UP WITH THE IDEA FOR YOUR BUSINESS?

Both businesses are rooted in the question of, "What would I do, if I had all the money I would ever need?" My answer was, "I would help others live a better life." Then I asked myself, "How can I, Mark Goblowsky, do that? How can I help others live a better life?" Initially the answer was through sharing the life changing and empowering teachings of Kung fu with people, which I have done for nearly 30 years at this point.

This current business I created came from the same questions. However, my life had changed dramatically in recent years due to my son getting hurt in 2005. He suffered a massive traumatic brain injury during a hit-and-run collision with two semi-trucks. He was three and a half years old at the time and was left, as the doctor put it, "neurologically devastated."

I felt utterly alone going through this experience and the pain of it was overwhelming. I decided to create a platform to help others who found themselves struggling to find a way through adversity in any area of their lives—personal or professional. To that end, I created a podcast, Strength Through the Struggle, where I interview others who have had to navigate adversity for any number of reasons. It could be health, financial, relationships, business. You name it, I cover it on the podcast. I've also written a book and blog to help others create perspective, maintain hope and build momentum.

The listener or reader can expect to be encouraged in the content I create. I let them know I believe they have what it takes, they are not alone, there are tools available and skills they can develop to handle anything and everything life has to offer. Of course there are coaching and masterminds available for more in depth solutions.

WHAT WAS YOUR FIRST MAJOR BREAKTHROUGH?

It was getting connected to a consulting company at the beginning of my teaching journey. It put me in proximity with people who were further along the path of success who could coach me. Once connected, my revenues doubled year after year for five years. It was all due to the advice I got and then putting it into action.

HOW LONG DID IT TAKE YOU TO REACH 100% DIGITAL FREEDOM?

I choose to maintain a brick and mortar business along with my online work. I've been in business for myself full time since 1990, and it has provided for me in a wonderful way, allowing me the time and resources to take care of my son. It also feeds my soul because I see my students experience tremendous growth and know their lives are better because of what I'm teaching.

WHAT WAS YOUR BIGGEST MISTAKE?

Hmmm... Can I skip this one? There are too many to pick from! There was a time when I wanted to throw in the towel on my martial arts business. I stopped setting goals and growing both personally and professionally. I started to coast and become complacent. It affected my mind but I didn't realize what was going on. I believe the people contributing to this book and reading the stories need momentum in life. I know I do. When I stopped creating momentum, I started to backslide and mistakenly thought it was the business that was the problem.

It wasn't the business, it was me. Me and my stinking thinking that got me in trouble. Momentum is going to occur. Negative or positive.

We have to be conscious about creating it and maintaining it in the direction that serves us best.

WHAT IS THE SINGLE MOST EFFECTIVE TACTIC YOU DISCOVERED?

The best thing for growing my business is getting connected with other people who are on a similar journey. You have to get out there and build relationships with other people who are getting things done. I've found many people who have experienced success are incredibly generous with their ideas and their time. Successful people want to help others. That's one of the reasons they became successful. And definitely don't limit yourself to only your industry. It becomes an echo chamber from time to time. Look at other industries occasionally and bring freshness into yours.

WHAT ADVICE WOULD YOU GIVE SOMEONE WANTING TO ACHIEVE SIMILAR SUCCESS?

This is a mantra I try to remember whether with my ongoing business or creating something new: Patience, Perseverance, Perspective.

Patience—Things really do take time. Let time work for you. Impatience brings grief and frustration. Getting in a hurry creates mistakes—costly, time robbing mistakes.

Perseverance—You have to push through mental, physical and emotional resistance on a daily basis. When things are going well that is easy. When they aren't or you aren't seeing results you think you should, you have to keep pushing forward with your dream. Nothing will replace perseverance.

Perspective—Maintain a healthy perspective. Keep things in a healthy perspective by not comparing yourself to others, and don't "should" all over yourself. When we get out of balance mentally or emotionally with our thoughts and feelings, we start making bad choices. The best solution is to get a mentor (paid or not) who has real wisdom to help keep you accountable and thinking clearly.

LEARN MORE ABOUT MARK'S BUSINESS:

The best way to stay connected is to opt in at my website. If you go to MarkGoblowsky.com/InternetBusinessInsights and opt in there, I will send you a chapter from my book for free.

Follow me on:

Facebook: Facebook.com/MGoblowsky

Twitter: Twitter.com/MarkGoblowsky

Instagram: Instagram.com/MarkGoblowsky/

Private message me on Facebook if there is a way I can serve you.

LYNNE GOLDBERG OF OMGMEDITATE.COM

HOW DID YOU COME UP WITH THE IDEA FOR YOUR BUSINESS?

I had been teaching meditation at schools in my community, and the teachers were always asking if I had any recordings that they could use on their own. My husband was in the technology business, and so I asked him if he could help me record them. We decided to turn them into an app, and that was the beginning of OMG. I Can Meditate!

WHAT WAS YOUR FIRST MAJOR BREAKTHROUGH?

We didn't really experience any major failures but, as always, not everything went smoothly. We had the usual technology glitches and marketing mishaps that most startups experience. Each set back gave us time to readjust and adapt. I would say that the first major breakthrough was being featured globally by Apple as one of the top apps in the app store. This really set the tone for us and its been growing steadily since then.

HOW LONG DID IT TAKE YOU TO REACH 100% DIGITAL FREEDOM?

Luckily for my husband and me, we both had successful businesses prior to launching this business. My husband had a business creating and distributing content for mobile phones even prior to the iPhone. To give you an idea, the company's most successful product was the fart ring tone. I guess we were both looking for something that was a bit more meaningful this time around.

WHAT WAS YOUR BIGGEST MISTAKE?

That's an easy one. By far my most embarrassing moment was when my phone went off with a blaring loud ring in the middle of a private meditation session with Leonardo di Caprio. I was mortified, as I always make sure to turn it off. He was really cool about it though.

WHAT IS THE SINGLE MOST EFFECTIVE TACTIC YOU DISCOVERED?

It may sound a bit cliché, but the most effective tactic we've used to grow our business is to keep our app relevant to the practical aspect of people's lives and to keep it easy to use. This has lead to amazing word of mouth growth that is far more efficient than any other marketing strategy we've tried. When people use something that results in meaningful benefits to their lives, they become our best salespeople. They get really motivated to share it with friends and family.

WHAT ADVICE WOULD YOU GIVE SOMEONE WANTING TO ACHIEVE SIMILAR SUCCESS?

Follow your heart and listen to what your passion is. Don't get caught up in data or all the "should's." This business came from a place of real passion and need. The idea to develop an app came from real people asking us to make one, and meditation was a passion for everyone involved in this project. Financial success is important but it shouldn't be the ultimate motivation.

LEARN MORE ABOUT LYNNE'S BUSINESS:

We love to have people be a part of our online community. They can tune in every day for a morning meditation on the web or by downloading the app, at OMGMeditate.com. Follow along on social at @OMGMeditate

ANNIE GRACE OF THISNAKEDMIND.COM

HOW DID YOU COME UP WITH THE IDEA FOR YOUR BUSINESS?

I was the global head of marketing at the time—looking after 28 countries and flying all around the world—when I realized the corporate drinking culture had snuck up on me and I was drinking more than I ever intended. I set out to free myself from an increasingly unhealthy relationship with alcohol and the result was my book, *This Naked Mind*. The business grew out of the book. I didn't expect to make a living out of this; in fact I published a book just because I felt others could benefit from what I had learned, but the method I developed was so well received that I was able to leave the corporate world and pursue this newfound passion.

WHAT WAS YOUR FIRST MAJOR BREAKTHROUGH?

Once I had a first draft of my book, I was so convinced that the material would help other people as well as myself that I put it online for free download. I made a rookie digital entrepreneur mistake, however, and did not get email addresses in exchange for the download! In hindsight I know the importance of an email list and can't believe that I didn't realize I should be collecting emails. At the time my passion was certainly greater than any internet marketing skills and I felt strongly that I wanted to get the draft into people's hands and start to get feedback. Ironically this was a huge breakthrough because within the first few weeks more than 20,000 people downloaded the book! It was nuts. Feedback poured in from all over the globe and I was able to tweak and improve the book and method to be so much better than I would have been able to alone.

It was an amazing and humbling experience. A few weeks into it I actually had a reader suggest I put the download behind and opt-in page and collect emails—and my list was born!

HOW LONG DID IT TAKE YOU TO REACH 100% DIGITAL FREEDOM?

I had a unique situation where my company asked me to move to the UK. Since I wanted to publish the book and take a chance on an entrepreneurial lifestyle, I decided that instead of moving my family overseas I would take a severance package. That packaged allowed me a three month runway to get the business up and running. My last day in the corporate world was on Oct 1st and my book was published on Oct 15th. In the first three months I was able to generate enough income from book sales that my 'runway' could be extended to six months. Then by six months I was able to make the savings stretch to a year's worth of expenses. By the one year mark I was no longer flirting with the idea of finding a corporate job, and I started turning down corporate interview requests.

WHAT WAS YOUR BIGGEST MISTAKE?

Oh so many!! The entire process was a huge learning curve (and still is). Instead of investing in courses and tools from people who knew what they were doing, I tried to figure things out on my own, and I regret that. There is a saying that yes, as an entrepreneur you can figure it all out, but your business will grow much slower than if you look to others and invest in your own education. Ironically I have a master's degree and didn't think twice about investing $100,000 in a degree, yet when it came to spending money on an internet course I was gun-shy. I've since learned and invested in education to get me where I need to go. Not doing that sooner was huge waste of time and also a big waste of money I could have been making.

Also, once I had an English book selling well, I decided to invest in translating it into another language. That was a mistake. I hadn't really figured out the English market, so trying to market a book in a foreign language was a disaster. I invested almost $2,000 in translation, design, etc., only to sell five books! It was a mess but a good lesson learned.

WHAT IS THE SINGLE MOST EFFECTIVE TACTIC YOU DISCOVERED?

Online communities. Finding people who are gathered together who might be interested in what you have to say and then spending the time and effort to be part of the community as a real human, with stuff to share, rather than as a person who is just there to promote their products. I joined a half-dozen communities as part of my own journey and to get feedback from others who were also looking to drink less. I always gave away my book for free (never trying to pitch it) and offered as much as I could in terms of sharing articles, advice and good content. It was a 100% giving activity. In fact, I didn't even realize that I was marketing at the time! Now it is these communities that recommend my book—and 100% of my sales are word of mouth. I would never have that type of traction if I hadn't been in the communities making friends and building authentic relationships.

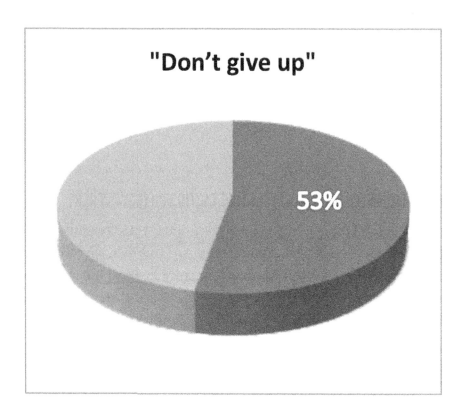

WHAT ADVICE WOULD YOU GIVE SOMEONE WANTING TO ACHIEVE SIMILAR SUCCESS?

Learn as much as you can. I thought that since I was a marketing executive and had a master's in marketing I had it all figures out. Yet the online world is so different from the offline world. You can't learn this stuff in universities; you must learn from people who are doing it—right now—and being successful. The market changes all the time and if you make a commitment to always learning and implementing stuff you can't go wrong. I would also say to be persistent in trying new things. It is easy to get discouraged when something doesn't work but you don't have a chance of success if you give up. As long as you keep pushing forward, you always have hope that your dreams will come true. Finally, I would say give as much as you can as often as you can. It seems counterintuitive but it's not. If you give away as much as you can, people will want to get to know you more and will talk about your services. This is so important.

LEARN MORE ABOUT ANNIE'S BUSINESS:

Speaking of giving! You can get a free digital copy of my book here: ThisNakedMind.com/free-tnm-book or learn more about me here: ThisNakedMind.com

SARIKA KHARBANDA OF MINDSPACES.COM

HOW DID YOU COME UP WITH THE IDEA FOR YOUR BUSINESS?

This question takes me down my memory lane, where I've seen way too many purely financial transactions when it came to coach and consult teams. Built-up or self-painted success stories of partnering and working as one team, focus on only running the billing meter but no real value-add for customers, not walking the extra mile for a customer or colleague even in dire times was such a put-off—such are a few others to highlight along the way.

An obvious dire need for a personal touch to consulting, coaching and driving change and a cry for help, not just in the IT world but a horizon of domains, triggered me to think and remind or ask myself:

» Is it time again to do what I did in the year 2000? Start my own business that delivers high value to customers but with newer variables in the market today?

» Time and again inspiration and reminders from ex-colleagues and customers who had seen me run my own business in 2000 and other close friends who believed I could add value where others were failing to deliver the value customers expected made me think even harder—is this already the right time to begin this journey?

» How can I deliver value differently given the different variables today compared to 2000?

» Should I experiment to test the waters or jump in directly?

And then one day as I watched *Kung Fu Panda* (the movie) with a few kids on the block, Master Oogway's point connected with me instantly—"One often meets his destiny on the road he takes to avoid it." That brought up my realization and it was then easy to decide and start to plan next steps—go for it and be the difference!

How better to say this than as Mahatma Gandhi put it—"Be the change you want to see in the world."

WHAT WAS YOUR FIRST MAJOR BREAKTHROUGH?

For me it is not easy to put my finger on something and say this was it—the very first major breakthrough. But I would highlight my co-working with an international partner—a partner who was true to the word "partner," who saw the value of my work and offered me an opportunity to work together but also independently. That set the stage for many new things to follow.

HOW LONG DID IT TAKE YOU TO REACH 100% DIGITAL FREEDOM?

Well, like all startup entrepreneurs, I looked at my sustainability in terms of finances and time, weighed the pros and cons, did SWOT analysis (strengths, weaknesses, opportunities, threats), etc.

Did I really put so much detail into all of that—nah, I really didn't! I did a very quick assessment of finances and time and weighed that with the growing passion within me to deliver high value and change for and with customers—value and change as co-defined or co-created with customers. And viola—I jumped in once that was in place.

It took me close to a year's worth of sustainability to be built for a good balance of both business and personal life. And I am grateful for that, as it has now allowed me to focus on delivering value which in turn allows the financial wheel to move forward.

WHAT WAS YOUR BIGGEST MISTAKE?

I do not really consider anything on my journey to be a waste of time or money or an embarrassing mistake. I have learned along the whole way—celebrated learning and learned from each failure.

Trust and integrity are extremely high and critical values for me. But to my surprise or even shock at times, I found that being honest and working transparently to build trust was not inherent in many individuals whom came across during my journey.

I had a handful of bitter experiences to learn where actions betrayed the words of portrayed trust. So it would be only fair for me to say that working with partners whose value systems, ideologies and work ethics didn't align has been a learning experience for me along the journey so far.

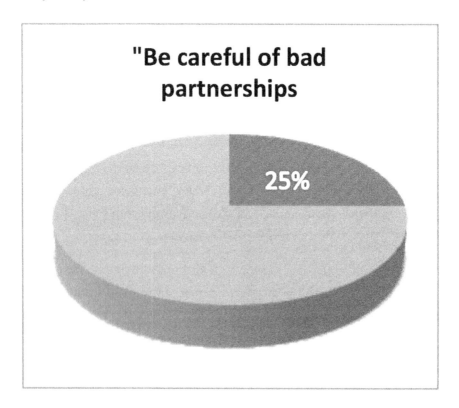

WHAT IS THE SINGLE MOST EFFECTIVE TACTIC YOU DISCOVERED?

When I started out on this journey, my existing connections and word of mouth referrals were the only way to grow my business. Over time I learnt that would not be sufficient or sustainable in the long run. I would need to adopt other means to grow my business and make that a sustainable model.

With several approaches that I heard from people applying in their business models, I figured what worked best for me was building and nurturing my existing connections and building networks in the global professional world. This has worked wonderfully for me so far!

WHAT ADVICE WOULD YOU GIVE SOMEONE WANTING TO ACHIEVE SIMILAR SUCCESS?

I have three key points of advice:

1. As in *Kung Fu Panda*, I truly believe and advise others too, "If you only do what you can do, you'll never be better than what you are."

2. If you want to make a change, be the change yourself, listen to your heart and go for it with all your passion.

3. Keep and nurture your growth mindset and be open to learning at every step. There's always something new you'll find that allows you to adapt your actions and do even better than what you do today.

LEARN MORE ABOUT SARIKA'S BUSINESS:

Find out about me and my services by visiting my website: MindSpaces.com or at my Twitter handle @SarikaKharbanda Twitter.com/SarikaKharbanda

Reach me directly over email at sarika@mindspaces.com for any additional information, queries or elaboration about services. Soon to be published (hopefully in June 2017): my very first book that will add more value and information on my experience and services.

PATRICK KING OF PATRICKKINGCONSULTING.COM

HOW DID YOU COME UP WITH THE IDEA FOR YOUR BUSINESS?

Here's the thing—I'm a social skills and conversation coach and writer—I definitely did not come up with the idea right at the outset. That would have been simply impossible, and it's impossible for nearly anyone.

I believe that's one of the biggest mistakes that people can make. They try to think of the end product and result before they've even started, which of course causes massive analysis paralysis because no one has any clue where they are going to end up. If you fixate on one goal, you're going to shoot yourself in the foot because you'll ignore what the market and your experiences are telling you to do.

The path to my business and its current incarnation (important distinction here) was a pretty winding path. And that's okay, because the important part is to just start doing something, and once you're in that world and learning and soaking things up, only then will opportunity and chance become apparent to you. If you can seize what comes your way, that's how your business idea will truly be determined.

I started as a run of the mill dating coach because it's something I was good at, and online dating especially. I can write a profile and messages that would pretty much guarantee dates—I had a marketable skill that I was above average at. That's where everything starts. I dove into the industry and eventually received a lot of feedback about what people were looking for and truly learned about the needs of my clients and this market. Turns out there was a pretty big demand for social skills and conversation skills, so I headed there as I was more interested in that versus traditional dating and online dating anyway.

You can't figure out the end form of your business on day one.

WHAT WAS YOUR FIRST MAJOR BREAKTHROUGH?

My first breakthrough was publishing my first book on online dating back at the end of 2013. I had been coaching for months before, but this was early in the self-publishing movement, and I was able to simply put it up and the book began to sell without my really understanding how. I got extremely lucky.

For a couple of years, my books would pop up first if you typed "online dating" into Amazon, and that was a pretty big boost because I gained many clients from there and saw the instant positive feedback that told me that I was doing something right. It encouraged me to keep going, and that I was onto something.

HOW LONG DID IT TAKE YOU TO REACH 100% DIGITAL FREEDOM?

I was working full time as a startup lawyer while I was doing a lot of these things initially. It wasn't until about six months on the side that I felt like I had a comfortable cushion from which I could scale, and then three months later I quit to go full time on my own business.

I do want to make this point clear: it wasn't some sort of courageous choice or leap of faith. I built something viable on the side (by accident and purely for fun at first), and I hated my day job as a lawyer. When you combine those factors, there was simply no choice for me but take the leap because I needed a change in my life.

WHAT WAS YOUR BIGGEST MISTAKE?

Luckily I've been able to escape *massive* failures, but I can tell you that at a certain point, I felt that I 100% understood my audience, when in reality I began to lose touch with it. I got too cocky, and that's what initial success does to some. They don't quite understand why the success came, and they focus on the wrong bits. I wrote and published on things they really didn't care about, and they let me know that I was incredibly wrong.

Point being, never think that you fully understand your audience, and keep striving to discover what makes them happy or sad. It will indirectly and directly affect your bottom line.

WHAT IS THE SINGLE MOST EFFECTIVE TACTIC YOU DISCOVERED?

I've got a pretty boring answer here and it's not quite a tactic per se. Copywriting.

Copywriting is essentially the art of writing for sales, but it's not limited to sales pages or advertising. It should affect 100% of your messaging and branding, and in reality, it's the psychology behind why people should care about you.

It helps you understand the market, your customers, why people buy, and what you're selling. Overall, if you are trying to run any type of business without copywriting knowledge or experience, you're selling yourself massively short and leaving a lot of money on the table. I'm not exaggerating.

WHAT ADVICE WOULD YOU GIVE SOMEONE WANTING TO ACHIEVE SIMILAR SUCCESS?

It's all about skill acquisition.

You can't be a one-trick pony and depend on others to do things for you, or constantly outsource everything. You simply need to step out of your comfort zone, not categorize yourself as a "X" person, and learn as many relevant skills as possible. Roll up your sleeves, don't be lazy, and just dig in. It's not supposed to be easy, and that's why most people don't start their own business.

For example, for an online business, skills might include copywriting, email service providers, autoresponders, WordPress, basic design, writing, editing, negotiation, building funnels, paid traffic, cold emailing influencers, website design, hiring and firing contractors, basic accounting and finances, reading and understanding contracts, and so on.

There's a lot to do, and you need to be able to do or understand almost all of it. There is something to be said for outsourcing things that are your weaknesses, but you must at least understand them at first.

LEARN MORE ABOUT PATRICK'S BUSINESS:

You can find out more about me or read more of my writings at PatrickKingConsulting.com—and I've also got a pretty cool and nifty Conversation Cheat Sheet for you there with some easy and counterintuitive ways to build better rapport and avoid awkward silences.

MARK MESSICK OF TORCHTHERULES.COM

HOW DID YOU COME UP WITH THE IDEA FOR YOUR BUSINESS?

Well, my first tiny step in the giant world of online business was to publish a book. And at the time my only desire was to become a successful author. But I quickly realized that if I wanted to hit the top of the bestseller lists, I had to treat my book like a business. As time went on I grew to love the business side of things just as much as I loved the writing. Until eventually I decided to start a full-fledged business of my own.

After a few embarrassing failures ("Epic Productivity", "Daily Diets Deluxe", and "Deranged Brilliance" were a couple of my early businesses) ,eventually I just decided to follow my passions. I didn't do any market research, I didn't test anything, I didn't come up with a specific marketing plan. I broke all of the rules.

The result? It quickly became my most successful business venture of all time. It's (appropriately) called "Torch the Rules", and it's my baby. I love that sucker more than anything. I've already been able to help loads of people break free from the imaginary rules holding them back from their true potential. And I absolutely can't wait to see what the future holds.

WHAT WAS YOUR FIRST MAJOR BREAKTHROUGH?

In 2015 (two and a half years after I published my first book) one day everything just clicked and my books took off. I was instantly propelled to the top of numerous bestseller lists, and I started making more money than any teenager should be allowed to have. (Oh yeah, I'm 17 years old. Just FYI.)

I honestly don't think there was any one thing that contributed to my success. But if I had to pick a #1 deciding factor, it would be my stubborn attitude. I never would have been successful if I was a wimp and gave up when the going got tough. But instead I was just so darned stubborn that eventually the universe just got tired of trying to keep me out of the "bestselling author club."

HOW LONG DID IT TAKE YOU TO REACH 100% DIGITAL FREEDOM?

Two and half years after I published my first book, five years after I first started seriously writing.

WHAT WAS YOUR BIGGEST MISTAKE?

Oh man. I made just about every mistake that is possible for a self-published author to make. I made my first cover myself in Microsoft Paint. (It was wretched.) I didn't hire an editor (rendering my book virtually unreadable). I didn't have a marketing plan (which is why my first book only sold six copies, five of which were to people I knew).

But if I had to pick my *biggest* failure, it would be trying to write books and start businesses in niches I wasn't truly interested in. I need to truly care about what I'm doing in order to get it to succeed.

You can't fake passion. You either have it or you don't. And if you're not passionate about what you're doing...dude, just stop. You're being stupid. Get your act together.

WHAT IS THE SINGLE MOST EFFECTIVE TACTIC YOU DISCOVERED?

Traffic + Conversion = Sales.

As soon as I understood this basic formula, it allowed me to engineer a specific marketing strategy for my business. Beforehand I was just kind of doing whatever. One day I'd try to book some guest posts, and the next day I'd work on my website, and the day after that I'd network with an authority. But I didn't have a unifying strategy. My business was super messy and awkward and unstable. But the moment I realized that traffic and conversion are all it takes to be successful...things just started to click for me.

WHAT ADVICE WOULD YOU GIVE SOMEONE WANTING TO ACHIEVE SIMILAR SUCCESS?

Want it.

You absolutely have to want success more than anything else. You need to be willing to work for it. You need to want it more than you want Netflix. Because if you want something bad enough, you'll find a way to get it. Humans are amazing. We can do practically anything. When I think about where we started (rocks and loincloths) and where we are now (spaceships, supercomputers, heart transplants), it just blows my mind.

And the "great" people from history (Albert Einstein, Ben Franklin, The Wright Bros...you get the idea) are just normal people. Just like me and you. They weren't give a special magic potion as a child.

There's no reason you can't do anything just as amazing as any of history's heroes. But you have to want it. More than anything. I truly believe that *desire* is the strongest emotion humans are capable of experiencing. Use that to your advantage!

LEARN MORE ABOUT MARK'S BUSINESS:

My baby is a business called Torch the Rules, where I inspire people to break free from the chains of mediocrity and live life bold, loud, and unapologetically. My website has all sorts of awesome stuff, including 5+ hours of inspirational videos, 1,000 pages of self-help books, and a newsletter that will teach you how to torch the rules that are holding you back from achieving your full potential. You can check that out here: TorchTheRules.com

You can also get my books on Amazon (most of which are free) by visiting: Amazon.com/author/MarkMessick

And finally, I absolutely love to hear from people individually! Please feel free to shoot me an email at any time. I always take the time to personally respond: Mark@DerangedBrilliance.com Can't wait to hear from you!

JEFF SANDERS OF JEFFSANDERS.COM

HOW DID YOU COME UP WITH THE IDEA FOR YOUR BUSINESS?

I studied many great entrepreneurs, authors, speakers, podcasters, online content creators, and coaches for years in order to develop the business I now run. I am a big fan of modeling, meaning that if I can find an expert doing something that I would also love to do myself, I will then study and reverse engineer their success. Over time I have been able to find my own voice and customize my offers, but everything was based off of the work of others. They paved the way and showed me what success would look like as an Internet entrepreneur.

WHAT WAS YOUR FIRST MAJOR BREAKTHROUGH?

Launching my podcast was easily the first big breakthrough that put me on the map. I have a background in theater, so I was experienced in the world of performance and production, which made podcasting a natural fit with my talents and interests. Within a few months of launching my weekly show, The 5 AM Miracle, I was getting noticed and growing my audience quickly. My podcast has led to millions of episode downloads, a book deal, speaking engagements, coaching clients, and many product sales. Podcasting is very hard work, but the payoff is enormous when you can consistently produce a high-quality show.

HOW LONG DID IT TAKE YOU TO REACH 100% DIGITAL FREEDOM?

I had been planning to quit my day job for years, but never quite had all the pieces together. Ironically, the company I worked for went bankrupt and closed their doors before I was ready, or so I thought.

I had been building my online business for a few years and making some money—just not enough to go full time. When my day job disappeared, I had a choice to either find another job or attempt to turn my little business into a full-time gig. Within a few months I was able to get more coaching clients and launch a product, both of which generated just enough revenue to pull it off.

WHAT WAS YOUR BIGGEST MISTAKE?

Easily my biggest mistake was spending too much time on the fluffy parts of online business (social media, graphic design, excessive content creation) and not enough time on revenue generation. The story of my life has been one of avoiding making money to do things I enjoyed. What I have realized over the years is that you really can have both. You can do work you love *and* get paid well to do it. I just had to make a mental pivot to begin focusing the vast majority of my efforts on growing my business instead of my vanity metrics.

WHAT IS THE SINGLE MOST EFFECTIVE TACTIC YOU DISCOVERED?

Sell the dream. You have to sell people what they want, not what they need. I have a terrible tendency to create products and services that sound great to me, but that don't necessarily appeal to real people who buy real products and services online. The key is to sell the dream, or paint a beautiful picture of the desirable end result, not the work to get there. Most people are very willing to buy the promise of six-pack abs and million-dollar business ideas—though they may or may not do what's required to actually achieve that result. Additionally, it's a great idea to develop solutions that cause a visceral emotional response in your customers. If your customer sees your offer and immediately has a gut reaction that he or she "has to have it" then you are on the right path.

WHAT ADVICE WOULD YOU GIVE SOMEONE WANTING TO ACHIEVE SIMILAR SUCCESS?

Find the intersection of what you love to do and what the marketplace is willing to buy. When you can spend your time getting paid well to do things you're great at, success comes faster and you can work less to achieve more. However, this is still a long-term game. Many people jump into Internet business with the hopes of making millions overnight. That doesn't exist. What does exist is traditional business norms—working hard for many years to solve real problems for real people.

LEARN MORE ABOUT JEFF'S BUSINESS:

You can find me and what I'm working on at JeffSanders.com.

My podcast, The 5 AM Miracle, is on iTunes: itunes.apple.com/us/podcast/id668541939

You can also pick up a copy of my book, *The 5 AM Miracle*, on Amazon: Amazon.com/dp/1612435009

ADAM SICINSKI OF IQMATRIX.COM

HOW DID YOU COME UP WITH THE IDEA FOR YOUR BUSINESS?

As a student in high school I was fairly average. I got average grades, had an average memory and struggled to stand out from the crowd. I was interested in learning, but just didn't know how. Nobody ever taught me how to learn most effectively. While at university I came across a mind mapping book written by Tony Buzan. This book showed me how to use mind maps to improve my memory, recall and study technique. It worked so incredibly well for me that I very quickly fell in love with mind maps and literally started building my entire life, study routine and schedule around them. My other passion was of course self-development, which is how I got into life coaching a few years later. While undertaking my life coaching studies I created mind maps to help me to better learn and understand the information I was working through. Initially I created these mind maps for my own purposes. However, when I started coaching clients, I discovered that my clients loved these mind maps as well and wanted to use them as reference posters. I thought it was a pretty good idea, and very soon afterwards IQ Matrix (originally branded as Study Matrix Art) was launched.

WHAT WAS YOUR FIRST MAJOR BREAKTHROUGH?

I wouldn't say that there was any one major breakthrough. Things never happened quickly for me. It took consistent effort over time to persist with the development of these mind maps and to refine my creation process. Many times in the early years it would have been easy to quit. The sales were not very good and at best very inconsistent, and I really wasn't sure whether these mind maps would gain any real long-term traction with my website visitors. Mind mapping was kind of a niche interest area. People either loved them or absolutely hated them. However, I believed in what I was doing and persisted with my efforts to keep developing more mind maps over time. What kind of kept me going was my own journey of self-development. I wanted to create these mind maps not just for my clients, but selfishly also for myself to help me along my own personal journey of growth and transformation. Eventually though you reach a certain point in your business where the scales suddenly start weighing in your favor, and all the work you put in finally pays off. However, consistency and persistence are the key ingredients that helped bring me that outcome.

HOW LONG DID IT TAKE YOU TO REACH 100% DIGITAL FREEDOM?

It took about five years to transition to a full time passive income online (2008-2013). For a period of time, my full time job was life coaching, although that wasn't really a full time gig in the beginning stages. It was actually a big struggle. I worked a casual job on the side, and tried to earn the best living I could by coaching as many clients as possible. I eked out a living, but it was really tough. Over time things of course got easier as I gained more experience. With experience came competence, and with competence came self-confidence. I reached a point where life coaching became my full time work, and that is when I started spending more time on developing mind maps. I ideally wanted to sell digital products online. I wanted to earn a passive income and not rely on exchanging time for money (coaching clients). As I created more maps over the years, I started to generate more sales from the digital sales of these maps. I therefore progressively began taking on fewer coaching clients and spent more time working on my online business. Again, this was a very progressive process that took time. Initially creating these maps felt like a waste of time from an income earning perspective. However, I looked at it as a long-term investment and opportunity. If I could get hundreds of mind maps onto my website, I was confident that I could sell enough to generate a full time income. And that's what eventually happened.

WHAT WAS YOUR BIGGEST MISTAKE?

The first two years of the online business were good from an awareness perspective. A lot of people were enjoying what I was doing; however, not a lot of sales resulted from all the buzz. I think at that stage my branding and positioning was very confusing. I wasn't quite sure myself where I wanted to take my online business. Yes, I had these maps that explored personal development topics, and yes I thought they were brilliant tools for life coaches and/ or for self-coaching purposes; however, there just wasn't a clear enough direction. I was kind of stuck and stagnating. Then out of the blue my website got hacked and all the content I had worked on for two years was deleted. What's worse, is that I had never done a proper backup of the content on the website, which meant that everything was literally lost. It appeared to be an absolute disaster and it took me several days to gain some proper clarity about what just happened. However, what came out of this mess was a complete brand makeover, new website security and platform, and a very clear direction and purpose that drove my online business forward. It was as though I needed a setback like this to spur me to action in a more optimal direction. Out of the dust came the IQ Matrix brand, and I said goodbye to Study Matrix Art.

WHAT IS THE SINGLE MOST EFFECTIVE TACTIC YOU DISCOVERED?

To successfully grow an online business you need to be consistent for an extended period of time. Consistency is the key to absolutely everything that eventually turns out to be successful. Yes, you hear all the time about people becoming overnight successes. However, things are never really that easy. A lot of work, thought, experimentation and failure goes on behind the scenes. In fact, it typically goes on for many years—possibly not in the area where the person eventually succeeded, but in other areas where they struggled to gain traction over time. They used these experiences and lessons to adapt their approach, which eventually led to their current breakthrough. Yes, this latest breakthrough might have been an overnight success, but it was the persistent and consistent effort they put into their work and the lessons they learned from their results that brought them to where they are in their life right now.

WHAT ADVICE WOULD YOU GIVE SOMEONE WANTING TO ACHIEVE SIMILAR SUCCESS?

Developing a successful online business isn't easy. It takes consistent work and effort. What worked in the past will probably not work today. And what worked for someone else, possibly might not work in your situation or for your type of business, niche or brand. It's of course important to learn and develop yourself in ways that help you grow your business over time, however it's also important to be very flexible and to adapt whatever you learn to your specific situation and business. Don't just accept that something will work. Question absolutely everything, be willing to experiment, and adapt what you learn to what you're doing. Then of course measure your results and make adjustments until you figure out the best course of action for your business moving forward.

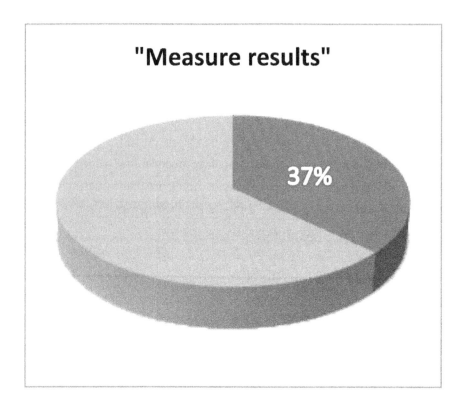

LEARN MORE ABOUT ADAM'S BUSINESS:

I welcome readers to visit IQMatrix.com/free-maps and download 30+ free self-growth mind maps. On the website I condense and simplify personal development topics and turn them into beautiful reference posters that people can use for guidance and inspiration. There are now over 350 mind maps that can help people succeed in any field of endeavor. It's like having an entire library of knowledge on a single sheet of paper available for easy reference at any time. What makes these mind maps so effective is that they are built upon life coaching principles that provide people with the impetus they need to maximize their results and optimize the way they live their lives.

Mind maps, doodling and visual thinking of course go hand-in-hand and can become a potent combination for long-term growth and transformation. I would therefore also recommend IQDoodle.com where readers can learn how to doodle and use visual thinking principles to optimize their lives.

MICHAEL SLIWINSKI OF NOZBE.COM

HOW DID YOU COME UP WITH THE IDEA FOR YOUR BUSINESS?

It was mid 2005 and I was running a small Internet marketing consultancy, helping my customers sell their stuff on the Internet. And I wasn't bad at it… so when my client list started growing and the number of my commitments increasing, I had hard time keeping up and had to figure out a system to manage it all.

I read the book by David Allen, *Getting Things Done. The Art of Stress-Free Productivity*. I loved the book and wanted to implement the GTD Method right away in my life… but being a geek, I wanted to implement it digitally as I was spending most of my day in front of a computer anyway.

I searched for a tool that would help me implement GTD and there weren't that many back then, so I started working on making my own GTD system.

WHAT WAS YOUR FIRST MAJOR BREAKTHROUGH?

I was discussing my tool on GTD blogs and forums with other productivity geeks like me… and one of them happened to be a blogger for ZDnet. His name was Marc Orchant. Without telling me anything, he wrote about Nozbe on ZDnet and it started everything. Gina Trapani wrote about Nozbe on Lifehacker. Other blogs followed… and my server almost crashed. Nozbe.com appeared on the home page of Delicious, which was the top social bookmarking site at the time. Everybody praised Nozbe's simplicity. I was completely blown away and started working even more to improve the app as user suggestions kept coming in.

HOW LONG DID IT TAKE YOU TO REACH 100% DIGITAL FREEDOM?

I was still working as an Internet marketing consultant for my clients and had previous commitments. I just worked a lot. And I was a one-man-shop. Until about 4 pm every day I'd work for my clients and then I'd literally put on my "Nozbe CEO" badge and from 4-9 p.m. I'd work on Nozbe. I didn't have kids then and my wife was working for a top law firm, which basically meant she'd work long hours anyway. I had plenty of time to work. And I did.

After about three months of beta phase, around 5,000 users had signed up for Nozbe. I knew I was on to something and decided it was time to start charging for Nozbe's premium plans. I got my first 100 paying customers within the first week. It wasn't much, but a lot more than what I had hoped for initially. I gradually started finishing my client work and finally in January 2008 I decided to work on Nozbe full time. The rest, as they say is history.

WHAT WAS YOUR BIGGEST MISTAKE?

Greg McKeown's book *Essentialism* says that when you achieve a certain level of success, you know it doesn't matter what the world thinks, but you think you have success. When you reach success you start seeing all these opportunities and without thinking too much about it you start taking them and then you lose focus on your main thing. And each time for me it was a failed product. Each time it was months of wasted time and each time my main product suffered. I would have been further along with my main product if I hadn't done this, but now I know better. So now if anyone is saying to me, "Michael I got this idea, maybe we can do this together?" and then I'm like "Thank you, but no thank you."

WHAT IS THE SINGLE MOST EFFECTIVE TACTIC YOU DISCOVERED?

I think the biggest tactic for me personally was to have me as an ambassador of our brand. So to have me as the productivity guy because we're not only providing the tool, we are also spreading the message of productivity, giving away our productive magazine, my e-books, things like that. These are things that we do for content marketing but it's not content marketing for us— it's spreading the message. I think teaching customers has been the most effective way for us because this way people learn why they need the tool. Often people just think, "I can get organized, I can get by, I have just a few things I have to do!" which is of course not true but you know they cheat themselves. Over deliver on teaching; in this way you know people will be grateful to you that you have taught them a few things for free and then they will be happy to pay for the software. And by seeing me behind this, seeing a real person, somebody who's real flesh and blood is also helpful, because they are not buying from some anonymous company somewhere.

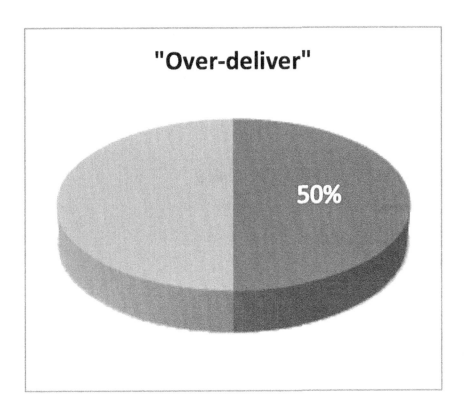

WHAT ADVICE WOULD YOU GIVE SOMEONE WANTING TO ACHIEVE SIMILAR SUCCESS?

I failed several times before I launched Nozbe so I know what failure means, and for me Nozbe was successful because it solves my own problem. I was solving my own problem and I knew that other people had the same problem because when I was building Nozbe I was very active in the discussion forums and blogs about getting things done and I saw people searching for a similar tool like Nozbe. I saw that it is not just me that needs the tool but there are other people who are searching for similar things.

So I would say there are so many problems, so many solutions that need to be found for so many things. I think if you build something useful, it will stay useful for a long period of time.

Also, don't be afraid of the competition. You solve things your own way and the pie is so big. You know the Internet is so big that if you find just a few people who just like the way you're solving this problem you've already got a few customers and from there you can build your business.

LEARN MORE ABOUT MICHAEL'S BUSINESS:

Nozbe.com

ProductivityCourse.com

Sliwinski.com

AMY E. SMITH OF THEJOYJUNKIE.COM

HOW DID YOU COME UP WITH THE IDEA FOR YOUR BUSINESS?

Like many digital freedom ambassadors, I found myself in my mid-20s, well on my way up the corporate ladder, and dying a slow death. I had an epic quarter-life crisis and I realized that the company car, the assistant, the travel, the faux clout were all leaving me unhappy and downright miserable.

Amidst this misery, my adoring husband came home one day and said, "I heard this person on the radio who does a job you need to do. He was called a life coach."

I was like, "What is this life coach you speak of?" And I was off and running. I devoured self-help books and personal growth conferences like a carnivorous beast—well, maybe that's a bit dramatic, but I did immerse myself in the work and ultimately decided to get my coaching certification through the Coaches Training Institute. There's a long story of what my practice looked like over the next decade, but I ultimately realized that my super power was helping people find their voice and actually use it. I teach people how to actually tell their in-laws what they think about their incessant meddling (while still being kind), or how to ask for a divorce without being a goddamn banshee. I essentially help people untangle all the inner shit that arrests them from really going after what they want, locks them into fear, and has them constantly concerned about what everyone else thinks. I realized that the internal component was paramount, but the external component of what to actually say was lost on many, so I also realized that people needed to know what it really sounded like to set a boundary or say "no," or humbly request something.

WHAT WAS YOUR FIRST MAJOR BREAKTHROUGH?

Going back to the fucking basics. I shit you not. I wish I could say it was a book deal or a rad affiliate alliance, but it was seriously pulling myself up after damn near throwing in the towel. I had spent the majority of my business just throwing whatever I could at the walls to see what would stick. And that lack of planning and strategy had me living feeble launch to feeble launch. And leaning a lot on "Hope Marketing": just hoping things would work out. No marketing calendar. No quarterly financial goals. No investment in the biz. So after threatening to quit my own biz for the umpteenth time, my mastermind at the time essentially took my ass to school and told me I needed a full reboot. And, so I did. I did all the research and planning that I never did at the beginning when I was flying on the wings of passion and passion alone. I went back and looked at my offerings, my customer avatar, and I got really, really solid on my messaging. And that seriously changed the game. I really think it comes down to the famous marketing concept: a confused buyer doesn't buy. Once I was crystal clear, not only on my messaging but also on my plan for my business, everything shifted.

HOW LONG DID IT TAKE YOU TO REACH 100% DIGITAL FREEDOM?

Like, 14 years. Just kidding. Can you imagine? I value stability like I value oxygen (and whiskey) so I wanted a sound plan if I was going to jump my day-job ship. I started with small goals with the end big goal being total autonomy and working on my digital empire [insert villainous laughter]. While I was in my coaching certification program, I had a requirement to maintain five paying clients as well as hire a mentor coach. My first goal was to make enough money from the certification clients to pay for my mentor coach. In the job I worked at the time, I was fortunate to have the luxury of stepping down in hours. So I gradually leaned out my day job hours and supplemented with my coaching practice. Finally, I got to a point where I could let go of the few days I was working the day job and go 100% self-employed. I think that entire process took me about a year or so. I had a plan and I worked the plan.

WHAT WAS YOUR BIGGEST MISTAKE?

Ew. I'm still bitter about it. No, not really. It actually taught me a *ton* about due diligence in how I invested in my business. My husband and I attended a conference where all the speakers sell from the stage—we all know that drill. We were enraptured with one of the speakers' charisma and bought his marketing program, which you guessed it, came with tickets to another conference. We were pumped. We took time out of our schedules, booked travel arrangements, and when we went to the training it was seriously lacking content. Like, any content. We waited through about halfway through the second day and we both thought, "Where the hell is the content?" We ultimately decided to leave, eloquently requested our money back, only to be brutally rebuffed by the facilitator himself who also threw in some serious shade. The pinnacle of professionalism (she says snidely). After that, I have been extremely choosy about what I invest in, always do my homework, and really watch my urge to buy impulsively. And, I'm also extremely vigilant about how I take care of my own clients and customers.

WHAT IS THE SINGLE MOST EFFECTIVE TACTIC YOU DISCOVERED?

Authenticity. By far. I know, I know, that's such a hippie-light-worker thing to say, but I'm serious. I learned early on that the more I showed up as *me*—the me who is a bleeding heart liberal, me who loves a good scotch (like, often), me who reads each issue of *Psychology Today* mag cover-to-cover, and me who (obviously) cusses like a sailor, the more I find my people. I'm definitely not for everyone, but everyone isn't for me either, so I find it works out nicely. And, the awesome side effect? Those who do dig my message are die-hards.

WHAT ADVICE WOULD YOU GIVE SOMEONE WANTING TO ACHIEVE SIMILAR SUCCESS?

I would say operate within the dichotomy of passion and strategy. When I first started I was 100% passion and zero strategy, and I couldn't figure out why no one was buying. I mean...#WTF!? But, as I've mentioned, my messaging was all over the place, I had no sound plan, and I was confusing the fuck out of my humble audience. I also think that 100% strategy dangerously opens you up to letting go of the human connection. Although it's awesome to see a new funnel work or an email subject line get a great open rate, it's imperative to remember that a human is on the other side of that interaction.

LEARN MORE ABOUT AMY'S BUSINESS:

I welcome all non-creepy stalking at my virtual home, TheJoyJunkie.com and I'm even willing to bribe you. Swing by and I'll give you a free copy of my eWorkbook and audiobook, Stand Up For Yourself Without Being a Dick, which will teach you 9 proven actions to radically influence your self-love and self-confidence.

I also party on Insta daily, so come hang out: Instagram.com/TheJoyJunkie

Oh, and if you dig free shit I release brand-new episodes every Monday on my podcast The Joy Junkie Show: TheJoyJunkie.com/ThePodcast/ My hubs is my sidekick and has a killer "Would You Rather" segment, so yeah... We're a good time.

JASON TREU OF JASONTREU.COM

HOW DID YOU COME UP WITH THE IDEA FOR YOUR BUSINESS?

When I moved to Dallas in 2004, I didn't know a single person except for my mother. And let me tell you, she didn't help me meet people. So I figured out innovative ways to meet a lot of people, and grow my social circle to more than 15,000 people by 2014. People started calling me the "Mayor of Dallas."

In 2010-2011, I had two friends independently ask me to help their friends move. They had friends who were moving to a new city for a job, didn't know a single person in the city, and had to start their lives over from scratch. So I agreed to help these two guys (whom I didn't know at all) make a successful social and professional transition into a new, large and unfamiliar city. Both of the people were men, 28-30 years old, introverts, and socially awkward. They had also lived in the same cities their entire life. So they had no experience of what to do in a brand new city.

I helped both of them focus on the right psychology and mindset, and then put together a social strategy. At the end of 90 days, both of the guys had significantly better social lives than ever before. They were completely crushing it.

If what I was doing worked for two people, then I knew it would work for 1,000. I researched and found there was no one teaching other people how to build a great social life.

I decided to approach someone with an existing coaching business, where I could test out my ideas with zero capital investment. I wouldn't need to grow a customer base, either. I came to agreement with another coach to work on this specific area. I wrote a book,

Jump Start Your Social Life, and came up with product ideas and coaching packages.

Creating this business was challenging because I had a VP of marketing day job as well. So I had to do this in my free time, and work 70-90 hours a week to do both. Ultimately, I wanted to focus on the business market because there is much more money there. And I also had a huge falling out with my business partner (which was a blessing in disguise).

So I went out on my own, and first focused on publishing my book, *Social Wealth*, which I knew would help me get credibility in the marketplace as a business and executive coach. It also allowed me to showcase my ideas. The book did really well in the first month, so I knew I was onto to something.

WHAT WAS YOUR FIRST MAJOR BREAKTHROUGH?

I wanted to see if this business would work so I decided to focus on a couple clients for six months and over-deliver to see what results I could really get. That way I'd know if I was on the right track and be confident in my sales pitch to prospects on what I could accomplish for them.

Through a lot of hard work and outreach, I landed two high profile clients: the chairman of a billion dollar company, and an executive vice president of sales in a technology company.

For the EVP of sales, I helped him vastly improve his leadership and management skill set, and also increase sales by 25% year over year. For the chairman, I helped him get on two very high profile boards and find some very, very lucrative deals.

So by the six month point, I knew I had a great business if I could get more clients.

HOW LONG DID IT TAKE YOU TO REACH 100% DIGITAL FREEDOM?

In my first iteration of my business, I was doing it on the side for three to three and a half years. I then quit my job to focus full time on my current business. I wouldn't recommend people just quit and do what I did. It was a very bumpy road.

WHAT WAS YOUR BIGGEST MISTAKE?

I don't really look at anything as failure. Failure only happens if you stop. I think you learn from everything and then pivot along the way.

I would say I was mistaken in not having enough confidence in myself, and putting myself in a situation to be "Robin" and not "Batman." I did that in my partnership. I learned I needed to take the lead and go my own way...be my own master. I also learned that partnerships with other people often fail so only do them if they are tangential to your core business.

WHAT IS THE SINGLE MOST EFFECTIVE TACTIC YOU DISCOVERED?

Invest in yourself by getting coaching and help. You speed up the learning curve by 10X, meaning what I did in one year would take me 10 ten years to master (at least). Also, someone out there has achieved the success you want, so model what they did and put your specific touch on it. Don't try to figure it all out because it will take way too long, and you will make many more mistakes.

I'd also say that networking is your net worth. It is imperative to build out your network. Go to conferences. Join groups or a mastermind. Get a mentor.

Finally, I'd say you need to come from a place of giving, helping and inspiring other people. If you go around trying to get things from other people to be successful, you will fail. Successful people can see "takers" and they don't want to be around them.

WHAT ADVICE WOULD YOU GIVE SOMEONE WANTING TO ACHIEVE SIMILAR SUCCESS?

I would do three things:

First, "prototype" the business you want. Find at least three people doing what you want to do and speak to them. Really understand their business, what they love, what they dislike, etc. It will help you understand what's involved with the business and if you really want to put years of sweat equity into it.

Second, if your answer was "yes" after speaking to people, then find a person and business you admire and model it. Or find several people and businesses and leverage their ideas, strategies, etc. You will get the business up and running much more quickly and have a much higher chance of success. You can't copy anything completely, but you can take many of the parts and leverage them to design your business.

Third, get help, coaching and a support system (i.e. mastermind group or other groups). You can't go it alone. That's a recipe for failure or very slow growth.

LEARN MORE ABOUT JASON'S BUSINESS:

You can learn more about my business and executive coaching for individual and groups at JasonTreu.com.

I also have a free ebook at BeExtraordinary.leadpages.co/beinfluential on 10 ways to become more influential and persuasive. It's best practices I only share with my clients and you will be able to use the advice to get immediate results.

You can also get my best selling book "Social wealth" on Amazon: Amazon.com/dp/B00N9CA1QY

TEACHING HEALTH AND FITNESS: RIPPED AND READY

BRANDON CARTER OF HIGHLIFE WORKOUT

YouTube.com/HighLifeWorkout

HOW DID YOU COME UP WITH THE IDEA FOR YOUR BUSINESS?

In my 20s I was doing a lot of fitness modeling for brands like Puma, Nike and Adidas and wanted to get an edge by taking fat burners. The only problem was all the thermogenics on the market always gave me stomachaches, head pain and even nausea. When I began doing research on supplements within the industry, I realized the cause of this sickness was so many companies using proprietary blends in their products. Since I couldn't find a company that had an all natural fat burner that I trusted, I decided to make my own, and Bro Laboratories was born.

WHAT WAS YOUR FIRST MAJOR BREAKTHROUGH?

The first major breakthrough was when I began posting YouTube videos of myself playing guitar (music has always been my passion) and the comment section filled with people asking about my arms. While I was hoping they'd love my Trey Songz remix, they just wanted to see workout tutorials to get the impressive physique they saw *holding* the guitar. So I decided to give the people what they wanted and a few years later my YouTube channel hit 100,000 views, my Facebook hit 1.6 million likes and my email list got so big that I've been able to rely on just my social media for promotions with almost zero advertising.

HOW LONG DID IT TAKE YOU TO REACH 100% DIGITAL FREEDOM?

This is a hard question to answer, because I had the good fortune of having a lot of help from my business partner and right hand man, "White Boy" Brian. We were both working at Abercrombie as models and I told him about my budding audience and idea for a supplement company and he provided a good amount of the financial backing we needed to get us started. So it was a few months of planning together before we went balls out and I quit my 9-to-5 job before I actually earned the money to "justify" it. I took a risk and it worked out.

WHAT WAS YOUR BIGGEST MISTAKE?

The biggest mistake I made was actually not trusting myself enough when I first started the company. Everyone kept telling us we needed some big fancy team to run operations (the senior executive for X, the marketing guy for Y, etc.) and we caved. Our new partners tried to reel in my personality and ideas for videos, the very content that got me to where I was in the first place. Our profits stagnated and as soon as we went back on our own, our profits tripled. So I wish I had trusted my own instincts a bit more, but it was a great lesson to learn.

WHAT IS THE SINGLE MOST EFFECTIVE TACTIC YOU DISCOVERED?

Don't hesitate in giving massive value for free. It always comes back to you. 99% of my content is free. In today's day and age it has to be that way. Your true customers will appreciate that and trust that when you do decide to charge for a program or course, that it will be worth it.

WHAT ADVICE WOULD YOU GIVE SOMEONE WANTING TO ACHIEVE SIMILAR SUCCESS?

Upload good content *every day*. No exceptions. This is especially important in the beginning. There was a period of time where I was uploading two videos on YouTube, two on Facebook, and nine social media posts every 24 hours. Your audience is counting on you and with all the competition out there, you've got to give the people what they want or they'll get it from someone else.

LEARN MORE ABOUT BRANDON'S BUSINESS:

For all my latest content, including free workout videos and nutrition advice:

YouTube.com/HighLifeWorkout

Facebook: Facebook.com/BigBrandonCarter

Instagram: @Bcartermusic Instagram.com/BCarterMusic/

Snapchat: @KillerCarter187 Snapchat.com/add/KillerCarter187

SAMANTHA DAVIS OF SAMMYD.TV

HOW DID YOU COME UP WITH THE IDEA FOR YOUR BUSINESS?

I was invited to learn more about an online health and wellness business through a friend. I had heard of the brand before, but didn't realize that there was a business opportunity associated with it. After learning more—specifically about the opportunity to leverage your time and build a business that works for you -–I was hooked. I didn't know how I was going to make it all happen, but I knew I had to take the first leap. I had support from mentors in the business who wanted to see me succeed, so my ideas and vision grew from their experience and mentorship.

WHAT WAS YOUR FIRST MAJOR BREAKTHROUGH?

My first breakthrough was to write a to-do list every night, in a digital document, and keep adding to it throughout the week. I have found that writing to-do lists before I go to sleep is the single most effective tool for my business. I have a team, but I am still a one man show. There is no VA supporting me or a personal assistant who knows my life. We hear this a lot, and I can truly vouch for it: write your to-do list *before* you go to sleep.

HOW LONG DID IT TAKE YOU TO REACH 100% DIGITAL FREEDOM?

I have been working on my own since I was 23 years old. That was when I realized corporate wasn't for me, and if I stayed another few years, I would have wasted my existence on this planet. With all of that being said, I've managed multiple income streams for years that have supported me in living life on my own terms full time. And the freedom—that's what is *most* valuable.

WHAT WAS YOUR BIGGEST MISTAKE?

My biggest failure and time waste is probably scheduling in person meetings when I should focus more on Skype and digital connection. It is actually something I'm working on now. Being in New York City, public transit to places such as New Jersey or Philadelphia is just arduous. I have always had a "do whatever it takes attitude," but when I noticed the commute wasn't necessarily creating results, I knew that I had to take a step back and use digital communication tools first, and follow up in person on the second, third, fourth impression if necessary. This is a delicate topic for me as I want to build a belly to belly business so there is definitely a ratio of in person versus digital connection I am still working on.

WHAT IS THE SINGLE MOST EFFECTIVE TACTIC YOU DISCOVERED?

Make a to-do list before you go to bed and write your MITs - Most Important Things. Make sure these MITs are income generating activities. You have to identify what those IPAs are in your business, and stick to them. Usually, they are the activities we like the least. But the ones that make us the most money. It's a catch-22!

WHAT ADVICE WOULD YOU GIVE SOMEONE WANTING TO ACHIEVE SIMILAR SUCCESS?

Because I work in the health and wellness network marketing industry, I use social media and personal outreach to build my business and serve others. It takes a confident, decided heart to do what I do. Some days, I don't feel like I have a confident, decided heart, and I have to put my cloak of courage on. There will be things that scare you about your business, even when you're a few months or years in. But what scares you is usually what will give you the most results, so if it scares you, good. Doing what you said you would long after the feeling has passed is the fine line that separates winners from losers. Who is willing to do what scares them over and over again?

LEARN MORE ABOUT SAMMY'S BUSINESS:

I help women and men build six figure incomes using the power of Wi-Fi through a business called Arbonne. It is a vegan and European regulated health and wellness business focused on skin care, cosmetics and nutrition. The products ensure that you're as healthy as you can from the bathroom to the kitchen, while the business ensures that you're building wealth that's residual and leaves a legacy.

You can find my business at SammyDavis.arbonne.com, and join hundreds of others in my #healthywealthy Facebook community for inspiration and community surrounding living a healthier, wealthier lifestyle: Facebook.com/groups/1225979254162493/

JEFF MCMAHON OF TBC.FIT

HOW DID YOU COME UP WITH THE IDEA FOR YOUR BUSINESS?

I came up with the idea from my mom. She had a massive stroke when I was 17 and lost the use of the left side of her body. After doing therapy with her for three years, she had the idea of doing exercises at home and getting her other stroke support friends to be able to do them as well when they couldn't make it to physical therapy. The reaction was very positive and the people really loved it. The convenience of being able to work out and not leave their houses was such a new and great concept for them, they were blown away.

WHAT WAS YOUR FIRST MAJOR BREAKTHROUGH?

My first major breakthrough for my success was I heard Pat Flynn on a podcast mention that he wanted to train for a triathlon. At the time I had trained many people to do triathlons and I offered my services to him to train him virtually on his path to his triathlon. After nine months of training he was 110th out of 1,200 male competitors and beat his goal time by over 20 minutes. So needless to say, virtual training for entrepreneurs was born!!

HOW LONG DID IT TAKE YOU TO REACH 100% DIGITAL FREEDOM?

It took me about a year to quit my job and become totally free and independent. I'm not a marketing expert so a lot of trial and error had to occur to make my system more flowing. I watched a lot of videos on YouTube, listened to a lot of podcasts, and wasn't afraid to ask a lot of questions.

WHAT WAS YOUR BIGGEST MISTAKE?

My biggest failure was trying to launch a group training program for people. I did a beta group that went well for three months and had some positive feedback from them, but when I tried to launch it out with a webinar and audience and everything, I only had three people sign up out of 500. So that was proof that the idea was good, but the willingness to buy and hit their pain point was off. I spent about three months getting trainers lined up, lead pages set up, webinar programs organized, and it all was for naught. But that's what happens when you're an entrepreneur. This is what we live for!

WHAT IS THE SINGLE MOST EFFECTIVE TACTIC YOU DISCOVERED?

The single most important tactic I learned to grow my business was networking. Referrals for my service-based industry are so imperative because they allow you to already have broken that barrier to entry. So I constantly love meeting new people and going to conferences and meet my clients friends and associates. That allows great topics to be brought up and a chance for me to offer my free health assessment to people. The free assessment gets people intrigued to know what virtual training is, and then once they see it and enjoy it; it becomes an easy sell.

WHAT ADVICE WOULD YOU GIVE SOMEONE WANTING TO ACHIEVE SIMILAR SUCCESS?

Patience is the key to achieving success. In today's world, many of us want everything now. We want faster internet, faster news, faster cars, faster food service, etc. So waiting and learning and building a business that doesn't take off in one year is a bit hard to deal with. But when you keep your head down and work your butt off, then you get the benefits later and realize that it was all worth it.

LEARN MORE ABOUT JEFF'S BUSINESS:

My website TBC.fit is the best way to learn about my services and sign up for my 1-on-1 free health assessment. I'll go over your cardio levels, your muscle imbalances, your core strength, and your upper body strength, and then chat about your goals and the best path to follow to get you there. My motto is to help those that need it, and in return they will want to help you back!

MERRYMAKER SISTERS—EMMA & CARLA OF GETMERRY.COM

HOW DID YOU COME UP WITH THE IDEA FOR YOUR BUSINESS?

It started back in 2012 when someone at work told Emma about this real food way of living. Then a day later someone at the gym told her about it, and then she got a completely random email about cutting out sugar.

She took this as some kind of magical sign from the Universe that she should investigate. While sitting at her soul sucking desk job she read article after article, and kept sending them all to Carla, who was sitting at the next desk over. We were literally reading them while chucking out our processed crackers and pouring out the Diet Coke.

We started eating this real food… and it was freaking delish… and we felt bloody epic. We'd found a way of living and eating that brought us joy—it just made us more happy. It was like all the negativity from years of yo-yo dieting, disordered eating and guilty feeling was finally fading away.

We started sharing it all on Instagram and people started following us. We shared foodie pics and recipes and loads of positive quotes, we love positive quotes… using #glutenfree #sugarfree #delish… we didn't even know what a hashtag was for! It really started to take off. All of a sudden we had thousands of people following us and we knew we had to turn it into something bigger. We'd found our bliss—we had to follow the heck outta it.

But first we needed a name. It took us an entire five minutes. This new way of living had brought us so much joy, so we googled synonyms—not cinnamon, synonyms—for joy and up popped

Merrymaker... yeah it's like an actual real word. We're real life sisters and so The Merrymaker Sisters was born.

Everyone else was like, ummm what the bleeeep? But we knew it was the right name for us and our vision.

Next step was working out this how to put stuff on the internet thing. So we Googled "what is a blog" followed by "how to start a blog." We wanted to learn as much as we could. We went to conferences, signed up to a zillion newsletters and finally Emma stopped referring to SEO as CEO—yeah, that took her a while.

And we realized people actually do this? Like they make money online and do what they love? We were like, we wanna do that too! So we did.

Fast forward to now. We help over 1.5 million people every year live happier, healthier, more merrier lives. We've travelled the world, self-published two cookbooks, created a #1 best selling mobile app, written thousands of words, taken thousands of photographs, talked a lotta merry on our podcast, eaten A LOT of good food and enjoyed the epic ride.

It may not be the easy road, but it sure is the fun road.

WHAT WAS YOUR FIRST MAJOR BREAKTHROUGH?

Our first breakthrough to success would have been our first ebook that we self-published. We knew our audience loved our recipes, so we packaged up 50 new recipes into a PDF and sold it for $15. In the first day we had over 300 sales and this was only six months into our business. That day, we knew we had something special and we knew we could make this a full time thing.

HOW LONG DID IT TAKE YOU TO REACH 100% DIGITAL FREEDOM?

We started the blog in February 2013 and quit our full time desk jobs July 2014. So just under one and a half years. In saying that, we had no real plan and no real strategy. It took us another year of working on the business full time to really feel "digitally free." And still today, there are times where we have moments of "what the bleep are we actually doing?!" Getting used to the uncomfiness of owning our own business has been another big journey, a continuous one. It takes time to change thought patterns of what "stable" and "secure" looks like. Now, we love the flexibility of our business and the fact that if we want to create something, no one or nothing is stopping us. *Everything* is possible... it's usually only a Google search away!

WHAT WAS YOUR BIGGEST MISTAKE?

Let's get things straight first: we don't believe in failure, we believe in course correction! No matter what happens, the dots will connect and everything makes sense. Our biggest mistake would be turning our successful four-week challenges into a yearly membership model.

We spent a lot of time creating the platform and content for the platform, then quickly realized that we weren't enjoying this very much and it wasn't gaining the traction we'd expected.

As for the dots connecting in the end, this "failure" led us to self-publish our second book as well as learn more about our audience and what they need to live a healthier life. So you see, it all makes sense in the end!

WHAT IS THE SINGLE MOST EFFECTIVE TACTIC YOU DISCOVERED?

Content marketing. It's pretty much free and you control it! Our business started as a blog. We didn't even realize we were content marketing ourselves in the beginning; we just loved blogging and creating so we kept doing it! When we learned that what we were doing could actually market a business, only then did we start thinking about what we could sell. You could say that is a bit backwards but it worked perfectly for us as we now know the power of content marketing.

How can you provide free content to your audience that links to your business that will also solve a problem? Raise awareness? Entertain them? Inspire? Do more of this. Add more value and watch your business and audience trust boom.

WHAT ADVICE WOULD YOU GIVE SOMEONE WANTING TO ACHIEVE SIMILAR SUCCESS?

Focus on three things: quality, consistency and generosity. If you want people to notice you, you've got to produce high-quality stuff, and you have to do it often, or at least consistently, so your audience knows what and when to expect it. Being generous with your knowledge and your time will go a long way. If you add value to someone's life, they'll be way more likely to trust you and invest in your business.

Our other piece of advice is to "follow the fun." What do you love doing so much that time doesn't even exist? Try and weave aspects of this into your business. If you don't enjoy your business, then why are you even doing it? You may as well go get a desk job so at least you have the weekends to enjoy! If something is causing you stress, anger or hate, how can you change things up to bring back the fun? When you're having fun in your business, you create higher quality stuff that you're more proud of. This means you'll be more confident in your promotion. Your audience will also be attracted to this high vibe, fun energy and be intrigued to find out what you're all about!

LEARN MORE ABOUT EMMA AND CARLA'S SERVICES:

You can find everything about Merrymaker Sisters and Get Merry over at GetMerry.com

SAL DI STEFANO, ADAM SCHAFER AND JUSTIN ANDREWS OF MINDPUMPMEDIA.COM

HOW DID YOU COME UP WITH THE IDEA FOR YOUR BUSINESS?

Adam, Justin and myself had been in the fitness industry for a very long time...between 14-20 years. Adam and I had friends in common and we were both individually constantly told we "needed to meet each other." We hooked up on social media one day and scheduled a phone call. Once on the phone we quickly decided we should work together and the idea for a podcast was born.

WHAT WAS YOUR FIRST MAJOR BREAKTHROUGH?

Our first "break" came very early on with a controversial podcast episode. We didn't pull any punches and were extremely raw and unfiltered which seemed to resonate well. Before we knew it people were sharing our episode like crazy which places our podcast in the "New and Notable" section on iTunes. The exposure gave us the foothold we needed.

HOW LONG DID IT TAKE YOU TO REACH 100% DIGITAL FREEDOM?

We decided to not sell a single product until we had built up a solid following. It took us about a year. Once we launched our first program our sales grew relatively rapidly.

WHAT WAS YOUR BIGGEST MISTAKE?

We learned through a few failures that the best way to promote our podcast hand down was through other podcasts. Initially we would pay people with large Instagram followings to post about our podcasts but the results were weak. Platform crossover is a bit of a problem. Then I got interviewed by the host of another popular podcast and the boost in downloads was significant.

WHAT IS THE SINGLE MOST EFFECTIVE TACTIC YOU DISCOVERED?

Cross promoting with other podcasts is the most effective way we grow our show by far.

WHAT ADVICE WOULD YOU GIVE SOMEONE WANTING TO ACHIEVE SIMILAR SUCCESS?

Ideas are great but execution is what's most important. A mediocre idea that is executed fully will do far better than a brilliant idea which is never implemented. Don't be paralyzed by analysis.

LEARN MORE ABOUT MIND PUMP MEDIA:

You can find us at our website MindPumpMedia.com.

Our podcast on iTunes: itunes.apple.com/us/podcast/id954100822.

Our YouTube channel "Mind Pump TV" at:
YouTube.com/c/MindPumpTV

SHERRY THACKER OF SHERRYTHACKER.COM

HOW DID YOU COME UP WITH THE IDEA FOR YOUR BUSINESS?

I fell into it completely by fluke—I had not planned on becoming a personal trainer. About nine years ago I was in between business opportunities and I decided to take on a few personal training clients just to make some spare dough while I was thinking up my next path. A year later I was making more money than I ever had. I was having a ton of fun and was very successful at what I was doing so that's when I started to really take it seriously and build it up and turn it into something great.

WHAT WAS YOUR FIRST MAJOR BREAKTHROUGH?.

I think it was more just building blocks for me from day one. I was always very aggressive about finding clients so I did a lot of cold calling. And I spent significant time reaching out trying to find people to help. And when I opened up my own studio, my income definitely doubled at that point. I started to be able service more clients in the comfort of my own home.

HOW LONG DID IT TAKE YOU TO REACH 100% DIGITAL FREEDOM?

Technically I am not "digitally free." I am still working out of my studio, but I started as a personal trainer and I was doing that full time as of day one.

WHAT WAS YOUR BIGGEST MISTAKE?

I think the biggest failure and waste of time in general is not doing your homework before you invest money in either software, equipment or educational paths and so on. Definitely I've wasted time and money from not doing homework properly enough before just diving in and investing in things.

WHAT IS THE SINGLE MOST EFFECTIVE TACTIC YOU DISCOVERED?

It's all about cold calling. It's all about offering as much free content as you can.

You have to give yourself as much as you can in order to receive. I've done over 400 health assessments in my lifetime and I usually convert about 60-70%, and then of course you have retention after that. So for sure you have to really give in order to receive.

WHAT ADVICE WOULD YOU GIVE SOMEONE WANTING TO ACHIEVE SIMILAR SUCCESS?

Education is very key. You're playing with people's bodies so you've got to really know what you're doing. That takes time and effort and it takes hard work to get up early in the morning and get educated to get at least a couple of hours in a day where you're learning something new.

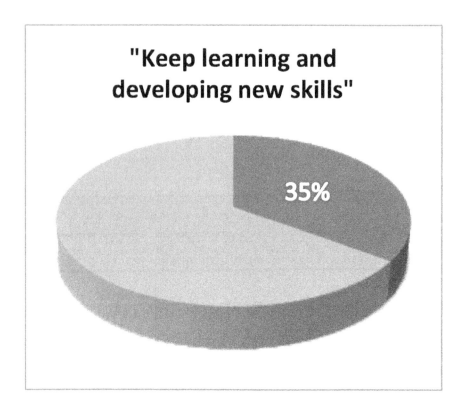

When you're not doing that you're out hustling looking for new clients, and when not doing that you're servicing the clients you already have. So this business is definitely a hustling business. You have to decide if you want to sell your time for money and for how long because it can be long days and you will at some point possibly burn out if you don't properly manage your time.

LEARN MORE ABOUT SHERRY'S BUSINESS:

I have two different spaces online for two purposes. You can go to SherryThacker.com which is my online business where I'm growing my 24 Hour Health kickstart program. I'm in the middle of doing my first launch for this program which I intend on repeating three times a year.

Or you can go to 100PureHealth.com which is a more local website where my direct clients who are in my area know how to book and schedule appointments with me.

TEACHING POKER: UP YOUR GAME

AL SPATH OF ALSPATH.COM

HOW DID YOU COME UP WITH THE IDEA FOR YOUR BUSINESS?

Long before the internet poker boom in 2003, I had combined my passion to teach with my desire to improve poker skills at the only online learning center (PokerSchoolOnline). Helping others advance their game provided me the opportunity to fine tune my teaching strategies and develop useful tools to aid players, and then clients, to succeed at a faster rate than envisioned.

WHAT WAS YOUR FIRST MAJOR BREAKTHROUGH?

I began knocking on publishing doors and finally getting my articles published, first at *Poker Digest* with the assistance of famed owner June Field and contributor Susie Isaacs, then with additional publications as my articles were read across card rooms in America. Once I established myself writing in various print and online sites, I became known within the poker world and called on to present at poker workshops and conventions. Along with Lupe Soto (founder of the Ladies International Poker Series, Woman's Poker Hall of Fame and Poker Senior Tour), we began a poker skin (a mirror of someone else's poker room—in this case Doyle Brunson's room), and developed a following which provided us monthly rake back in excess of our original investment and goals. In later years after Black Friday occurred in the poker world (when internet gaming took a giant hit), we then sold our domain (Victory Poker), to the very popular and well known professional poker player Antonio Esfandiare, who was known for winning the Poker One-Drop Tournament and the most money ever won by a poker player.

HOW LONG DID IT TAKE YOU TO REACH 100% DIGITAL FREEDOM?

I was offered the job as dean at www.pokerschoolonline.com in November 2005 and quit my job as purchasing manager for the San Bernardino County Superintendent of Schools in December, assuming my full time duties as dean in January 2006. As a result of this full time position change, additional doors swung open to me, and I created an online presence to supplement my income stream, doing webinars, private lessons, group sessions for clients around the world. I've since taught poker in Australia, Europe, Africa, Southeast Asia, South America, Canada and recently in China. Currently I am developing a poker school in India (GoPoker.In), which will be available on an app for billions in that country alone. I continue to be contacted by most poker writers and I am often asked to edit or review their books prior to publication. The latest review was for a book by Mike Sexton (World Poker Tour host and champion), *Life's A Gamble*. Although this is a departure from the poker coaching books on the market, Mike provides the reader with the history of poker in a way that entertains, informs and brings smiles to your face. It's a bona-fide best seller!

WHAT WAS YOUR BIGGEST MISTAKE?

Relying on others who didn't have the motivation or drive that I maintain in doing my best everyday, thus producing outstanding results. Case in point, my published book, *The Poker Journal*. I did not receive good pricing, marketing strategy or distribution, hence the low sales numbers. However, I didn't let that deter me. I used the book as another means to enhance my resume and provided free distribution of said books at poker workshops, thus advertising my coaching availability. This paid dividends over the past 10 years.

WHAT IS THE SINGLE MOST EFFECTIVE TACTIC YOU DISCOVERED?

Network, meet everyone, ask questions, and offer to assist, contribute, learn from and share information. Grow your foundation—you don't know everything; others have plenty to impart and allow you to better understand your ultimate goals. Do podcasts, interview others, and allow others to delve into your career and life, share your experiences and grow. I presently host a TwitchTV show where I interview the shakers and movers in the poker world and publish them on my own YouTube Channel (see below for details).

WHAT ADVICE WOULD YOU GIVE SOMEONE WANTING TO ACHIEVE SIMILAR SUCCESS?

Love what you do first and foremost, then put the required and necessary effort into building whatever it is you are attempting, into the finest product or service available. Customer service is #1, make sure your audience, client, user, are *more* than fully satisfied. Provide "knock your socks off" service! Go the extra step, anticipate their needs, over provide, never leave them feeling they didn't get their hard earned money's worth from you product or you. Motivate education and convert them into your best marketing tool (word of mouth, or better yet, social media sharing).

LEARN MORE ABOUT AL'S BUSINESS

Folks can contact me on Facebook: http://bit.ly/2sTcqwk

TwitchTV: Twitch.tv/PositivePokerInsiders

View over 250+ of my free poker instructional videos on YouTube: http://bit.ly/2rVeZRv

Or you can contact me directly at alspath@alspath.com as well.

BRAD WILSON OF ENHANCEYOUREDGE.COM

HOW DID YOU COME UP WITH THE IDEA FOR YOUR BUSINESS?

I don't know if most people have a "eureka"-type moment whenever they create their "thing" to share with the world, but I most certainly did not.

I've always loved discussing complicated poker theories (I mean, who doesn't?) with fellows pros, so on a whim I decided to download a trial version of Camtasia, record myself playing a session, and voice-over narrate the thing. I was so excited about my first 45 minute training video (my first real piece of content) that I uploaded it onto the "automotive" section on YouTube and promptly forgot about it.

About a month later my wife and I were out shopping and my phone sent a little notification saying someone had left this comment on my little video: "Really solid video. I enjoy being able to see all hands vs. just the interesting spots. Gives more insight to a typical session and your commentary was very good. I've watched a lot of poker videos, but rarely do I make it through one that is 46 min long. I know that if you continue doing the work you're doing you will get a following. I'll be hoping you post more. Thanks."

Talk about an awesome feeling! I put something out in the world and (despite my fear that it was the most awful piece of content that has ever existed) another fellow human being found it to be valuable. As someone who had lived a pretty isolated professional existence up to that point, I decided that perhaps I should create more things. And the rest, as they say, is history.

WHAT WAS YOUR FIRST MAJOR BREAKTHROUGH?

Success is really hard to define. I assume most people want to hear about financial windfalls but, for me, it was the realization that my time and knowledge is absolutely worth the cost of the lessons that I give. Most people feel as if they charge $100, $500, or even $1,000 per hour for coaching that they are being greedy but that's just not true. Life is about adding value to fellow humans so, whatever your gift is, start sharing it with the world and money will be created as a side effect.

HOW LONG DID IT TAKE YOU TO REACH 100% DIGITAL FREEDOM?

I've been a professional poker player pretty much my whole adult life (not counting being a server at Applebee's when I was 18) so in that sense I have always had a good level of autonomy when it comes to having control of my time, which is of course our most valuable resource.

Creating my website, for me, wasn't about "quitting my job"– it was about creating a balance in my own life and giving me the opportunity to serve other people in the poker community. Poker can be very isolating and predatory (after all, isn't the goal to take everyone else's money?), so being able to give back filled a huge void in my professional life.

WHAT WAS YOUR BIGGEST MISTAKE?

At the end of the day, the most important project that any of us can work on is ourselves. The absolute biggest mistake that I have made was waiting so long to get started. In the online world content is king and the biggest goal is to provide value to your audience and get your "thing" in front of them.

Simply put: Ignore the bells, whistles, and random tactics people will try to sell you in order for you to "get rich." There is no substitution for pouring your heart and soul into a piece of content and sharing it with the world. And believe me if your content is awesome and you are diligent about creating it every single day, the masses will show up.

WHAT IS THE SINGLE MOST EFFECTIVE TACTIC YOU DISCOVERED?

If you do not put your time, energy, and soul into creating awesome content that will impact lives, then you better just close up shop. Everybody and their mom has their own website or blog but what are you going to do that can really change lives? I can't remember who said it but the quote, "The easiest way to becoming a millionaire is to help a million people" has always rung true to me. But don't start with the goal of a million; start with trying to change a couple of people's lives and let them be your ambassadors to the world. Brand ambassadors are a uniquely powerful tool.

If you suck at creating content then take a creative writing class. Scared of creating videos? Join Toastmasters and learn how to be a pubic speaking powerhouse for your YouTube videos. These fears are the barrier to entry and they keep most people from truly realizing their fullest potential. Do what the others are unwilling to do and bust through that barrier.

WHAT ADVICE WOULD YOU GIVE SOMEONE WANTING TO ACHIEVE SIMILAR SUCCESS?

Set appointments with yourself to create your "thing" that will impact other people and show up every single day. Most people severely overestimate what they can do in a year and severely underestimate what they can do in 10 years. If you keep showing up day after day then, in however sense you define it, you will become a success.

Most people focus on tactics like SEO or website design. To be frank, who really gives a shit about having the prettiest website? If your content is remarkable then nothing can stop you.

LEARN MORE ABOUT BRAD'S BUSINESS:

My website is EnhanceYourEdge.com and I am also a training/ instructor for the membership site CardRunners.com.

TEACHING ANIMAL BEHAVIOR: TRAINING THE HUMAN

DR. IAN DUNBAR OF DUNBARACADEMY.COM

HOW DID YOU COME UP WITH THE IDEA FOR YOUR BUSINESS?

My wife had an "intervention." She told me to sit on a rock in Bodega Bay, smoke a cigar and have a good think about how I was going to inject some money into the relationship. I made a mental checklist: whatever I did had to be a passion, worthwhile, enjoyable and reproducible, i.e., so that I could employ others to do the same thing. Since I was a veterinarian and had just spent 10 years researching dog behavior at UC-Berkeley, I thought it would be nice to do something with dogs. The notion of teaching off-leash puppy socialization and training classes just popped into my head within five minutes.

WHAT WAS YOUR FIRST MAJOR BREAKTHROUGH?

A healthy success was immediate, since I knew many local veterinarians and told them that I was starting classes to teach puppies to be easy-to-handle adult dogs. They referred so many puppies that I had to hire my first trainers after just one month and had five branches by the end of the year.

However, real success didn't come until recently. It took a long time for technology to allow me to do what I wanted to do. Trainers and veterinarians were fascinated by what I was doing and came to observe the classes from all around the world. (Before I started SIRIUS® Puppy Training to teach young puppies off-leash with an emphasis on preventing predictable behavior and temperament problems, people could not attend classes until their dog was six months to a year old and even then, the classes were restricted to repetitive on-leash obedience drills.) I wanted to disseminate the format to others. I wrote a book but was royally ripped off by the publisher. I made a video but there were distribution problems. I gave over 1,500 one-day seminars but had to be on the road all the time and barely made 12% of gross. And so, I started a publishing company to publish my own (and others') books, produce my own videos (and later DVDs) and schedule and host my own seminar tours around the world. But it all took so much time.

Then it became possible to post books, videos and seminars online for download or streaming and everything changed. Now, it is quicker, easier and more effective to disseminate information around the world. People may buy anytime, anywhere—even when I sleep, or while I sit in the sunshine smoking a cigar.

HOW LONG DID IT TAKE YOU TO REACH 100% DIGITAL FREEDOM?

At the time, I didn't have a money-earning job. I was a house-husband. But I was absolutely happy with my earnings after just a couple of months in business.

WHAT WAS YOUR BIGGEST MISTAKE?

It's difficult to pick the "biggest" because there were too many to mention, but trying to do everything myself inhibited progress more than anything. I used to typeset my own books, edit my own videos, give my own seminars, and run the company. Only recently have I learned to delegate time-consuming work and employ talent to make up for my shortcomings. My former wife and son now run the company, and my son is beyond efficient at digitizing his dad's brain, i.e., filming and editing what I do and say and zapping it into the cloud for sale.

Additionally, I was very happy with the company and never really hungry for expansion. Now though, we've decided it's time to grow the business exponentially. Rather than a money-making goal, our decision to expand is because the three of us enjoy working together and feel that our information is unique and important. I still love what I do; dog behavior and training is my passion.

Of course, all of this would be moot, if I had been born later and started now with today's technology. What a wonderful time to start a business!

WHAT IS THE SINGLE MOST EFFECTIVE TACTIC YOU DISCOVERED?

Selling digitally local to international selling worldwide, anytime, anywhere. A business needs customers, yet conventional advertising is prohibitively expensive, so we created a free, multimedia, educational website to capture emails. People love the site (DogStarDaily. com) because it's useful, free and fun. Now, for us, advertising is free.

WHAT ADVICE WOULD YOU GIVE SOMEONE WANTING TO ACHIEVE SIMILAR SUCCESS?

Choose a business that *can* grow, do it now! In the service industry, reproduce your services, e.g., if you're a hairdresser, think several employees and then, several salons. Better yet, embrace technology; learn to program (to run an efficient website) and make oodles of short, punchy videos to make the website sparkle and for social media, and then, sell *any* product online. And of course, the best products to sell are ones you don't have to ship, i.e., information. It's all just so easy these days.

"The best time to plant a tree was 20 years ago. The second best time is now."

LEARN MORE ABOUT IAN'S BUSINESS:

The company has a bunch of websites but my favorite is DunbarAcademy.com. I just love doing business this way. Instead of printing books and duplicating videos and shipping them to all parts of the world, they are available for download—anytime, everywhere, with no manufacturing costs and no shipping expenses. Instead of me spending nine months in hotels a year giving the same seminars in different parts of the globe, we film each seminar and make it available for dog owners and pet professionals to stream online. It's truly amazing how much easier, cheaper and more efficient running a business has become over the past few years.

TEACHING PEOPLE ABOUT MONEY: FINANCIAL ADVISORS

JESS LARSEN OF MYELINADVISORS.COM

HOW DID YOU COME UP WITH THE IDEA FOR YOUR BUSINESS?

I used to be a CEO of a private equity fund and realized that I liked what my management consulting firm did better than what I did, so I switched industries to do this. It was a way to become profitable by helping other people make their businesses more profitable and their personal lives happier, and that just seemed more valuable to society and personally gratifying than buying and selling energy companies.

I saw that inbound marketing was what got the other consulting company their millions a year in clients and realized it was going to be the most efficient way to scale so I started the podcast to be my first inbound marketing arm.

I had been very focused on how much money I could make, thinking that would prove how important I was. Instead I felt like it helped me get so dialed in to other humans and what was going on for them that is was like learning how to do what they do in that movie, *Inception*. Except when people are awake—and for their benefit, not just mine, and not with cool movies stars (OK, so not *that* much like *Inception)*, but really it was an incredibly powerful methodology for helping people make decisions about things they have been having a hard time making a decision about. And once I helped them do that, they loved me and were happy to help me out by buying my stuff or making a referral for me etc.

WHAT WAS YOUR FIRST MAJOR BREAKTHROUGH?

It was when I realized digital was going to work for me because I got an email from an executive at a $4 billion/year organization that said: "I found your podcast in a desperate search for insights...We have the ability to make direct impact at scale—but it is an enormous challenge... We have funding for coaching and so I'd like to see how we can best work together... Thank you for all you're doing—finding your podcasts this weekend was such a relief for me."

This is company number 12 for me, so I have had other successes. Those were based on observing the patterns of others' success, listening to 400+ business books on Audible, and taking executive education classes at Harvard and Stanford. Top of the list was having good mentors and paid advisors to guide me through my attempts to duplicate others' proven patterns. Most of my other 11 companies were total failures—a couple made very large amounts of money which I then proceeded to lose on bad investments both times on my ownership roller coaster. Hence my current obsession with Warren Buffett's philosophy from Ben Graham about investments that provide safety of capital and adequate (compoundable) return.

HOW LONG DID IT TAKE YOU TO REACH 100% DIGITAL FREEDOM?

I did it in the reverse order and quit my job at the other consulting firm, which I considered my "apprenticeship," and sold off my stuff, plus I did side project work for the first two years before my current company really hit its stride and I could quit the other things.

WHAT WAS YOUR BIGGEST MISTAKE?

I tried to split my focus for the first 18 months by starting this company plus another private equity fund in New York buying energy investments. Neither really got anywhere so I ditched that one and focused on this one and it finally worked.

WHAT IS THE SINGLE MOST EFFECTIVE TACTIC YOU DISCOVERED?

Moving from the goal of trying to sell something to the goal of trying to become a valuable advisor. Getting super dialed into the client's world and problem, being willing to adapt and invest in them first even when it wasn't a guarantee to land them, and just care about them more than the completion. One client in the Army changed their mind from a $60,000 one time order to a $2.8 million multi year order because of it. I had a different client grow from a $100,000 start to eventually doing $8 million with us.

My second tactic is hiring staff that have way more credibility then me to bring up the level of the whole company. (Currently we have former NFL, NHL, FBI hostage negotiator, entertainment CEO, intelligence officer, investment banker and an operator from the most classified unit of U.S. Special Operations.)

WHAT ADVICE WOULD YOU GIVE SOMEONE WANTING TO ACHIEVE SIMILAR SUCCESS?

Search for "Smartcuts," but be willing to pay the price where you have to. Look for the patterns of how the highest achievers of what you want to do accomplished what they did and copy them. Buy the books that teach those patterns and be willing to pay for good advice from those who have "been there and done that"—the lawyers, mentors and advisors. And as author Steven Pressfield would say in *The War of Art*, figure out how to overcome resistance and "become a professional." Become a student who never stops learning higher efficiency, higher reliability patterns.

Then figure how to contract or hire people with tons of credibility in the space. Typically you can get a contract and just ask them how much per hour they would charge if you can get some work for them through your company, and they will be happy to let you use their name if you're landing them business.

Then read *The Trusted Advisor* by David Maister. Quit selling and start helping.

LEARN MORE ABOUT JESS'S BUSINESS:

MyelinAdvisors.com or just email me J.Larsen@MyelinAdvisors.com

WHITNEY NICELY OF WHITNEYNICELY.COM

HOW DID YOU COME UP WITH THE IDEA FOR YOUR BUSINESS?

Not to boast, but some say I'm the queen of real estate investing in east Tennessee. After graduating from the University of Tennessee in Knoxville, like most 2007 college graduates I found myself without a job. If you know anything about a Communications degree, you probably know those aren't always the most sought after new grads for major employers. Luckily, I come from a family of entrepreneurs. In fact, I was the fourth generation to join the ranks at her family's dump truck company that was founded in 1939. The Great Recession was in full swing while I was trying to learn the ropes of owning, operating and sustaining a small business of 100+ employees. Unfortunately, 75 year old companies weren't immune to the repercussions of a slow economy.

If someone were to say I cut my teeth amongst many obstacles and came out a stronger negotiator and business woman, that would be a great compliment. I pride myself on keeping a level head and using what my mama gave me to win over bids, deals and contracts that other people wouldn't be awarded.

As the economy improved, I started to chase my passions and fine tune my skills in the real estate market. I flipped my first house in 2009. In 2015, I flipped six houses while planning my October wedding. My real estate portfolio has grown from zero, zilch, nada to 17 residential houses, 19 apartment units and 7 chunks of vacant land across east Tennessee. I don't plan on stopping until I reach $100,000 in *monthly* income from my real estate portfolio.

I believe every woman should control her own destiny by investing in real estate as soon and as much as possible. It doesn't take a trust fund or $100k in the bank to get started in real estate. In fact, I teach women how they can use no money, no credit and no banks to finance real estate deals across the country.

WHAT WAS YOUR FIRST MAJOR BREAKTHROUGH?

There are more houses available in America than I can buy, so I've started teaching other women how to catapult their cash flow and retirement into the stratosphere. Fun fact: There are enough empty houses that every homeless person could have their own house. Once you figure that out, you can buy as many houses as possible!

HOW LONG DID IT TAKE YOU TO REACH 100% DIGITAL FREEDOM?

Two years.

WHAT WAS YOUR BIGGEST MISTAKE?

I don't believe in failure or competition. Failure is quitting and I won't quit. Don't dwell on events that didn't pan out for you. Don't worry about who else is doing the same thing you're doing. Iron sharpens iron. Lessons prepare us for the next battle. Do the best job you can do and the rest will work out.

WHAT IS THE SINGLE MOST EFFECTIVE TACTIC YOU DISCOVERED?

Facebook. Your Facebook friends have houses they don't want. They also have money if you need a private money lender. You don't need paid ads or anything fancy to collect more house leads than you can handle from free Facebook posts. I have a 7-Day Lead Challenge to show you how easy it is to get started buying houses with no money, no credit and no banks.

WHAT ADVICE WOULD YOU GIVE SOMEONE WANTING TO ACHIEVE SIMILAR SUCCESS?

Proverbs 31:16 says that every woman should be a real estate investor: "She goes to inspect a field and she buys it." She also helps other ladies climb to the top and that's my goal.

LEARN MORE ABOUT WHITNEY'S BUSINESS:

Instagram @WhitneyNicely: Instagram.com/WhitneyNicely

To get started or find out more information, go to: QuickStart.WhitneyNicely.com

JOHN POLLOCK OF LOWERTAXHIGHERPROFIT.COM

HOW DID YOU COME UP WITH THE IDEA FOR YOUR BUSINESS?

It wasn't an idea as much as it was an evolution. I lost a job and jumped into insurance sales to make ends meet. I did not like the transactional nature of the business model so I migrated to a wealth management firm. The success I had led to taxes. I quickly noticed that taxes grew at a much faster rate than my income. So when my income doubled, my taxes actually went up more than triple. At that time Barack Obama was running for his first term and I kept hearing "rich people don't pay their fair share." I saw what I was paying and I wanted to figure out how to not pay my fair share, because what I was paying seemed way beyond fair to me.

WHAT WAS YOUR FIRST MAJOR BREAKTHROUGH?

The realization that an entire industry does not do the thing that everyone thinks that industry does. I am talking about tax planning as the thing and the industry is the Certified Public Accountant industry, or CPA as they are most commonly referred to in the U.S. The problem got worse when virtually every tax plan I did was either blocked completely or highly discouraged by CPAs. This was despite the fact that I delivered the plan with direct references to the exact Internal Revenue Code that we were using, so the plans were explicitly legal. My attempts to solve a problem they did not solve but still include them in the solution started to break down. So instead of joining the CPA industry, I instead decided to disrupt it. I then figured out that there really are no national firms that do tax planning. That is what we began to build and led to us going public on the Over The Counter market. OTCQB: FGCO.

HOW LONG DID IT TAKE YOU TO REACH 100% DIGITAL FREEDOM?

As I mentioned above my job left me. We have been working hard to digitize every aspect of our business. The financial services and accounting industry are not known for being progressive in their adoption of technology, but if they don't they will become like the cab driver, a dead industry that is clinging on to a model that is being wiped out by ride sharing, and eventually autonomous cars.

WHAT WAS YOUR BIGGEST MISTAKE?

My failure was a flawed assumption. I assumed if I designed a tax plan, which we call a Tax Blueprint®, that the "architectural" plan would be implemented by our clients' CPA. I assumed that when the CPA saw the legal, moral and ethical plan that saved their client tens of thousands of dollars in taxes every year and added complexity that would get them paid more they would eagerly join us. We would be the "architect" they would be the "home builder" who implemented the plan and then we would "furnish" the plan with the tax efficient products and services that best served the client's needs. It seemed to me that we would end up with CPA partners all over the U.S. That did not happen. We couldn't join them, so we decided to beat them.

WHAT IS THE SINGLE MOST EFFECTIVE TACTIC YOU DISCOVERED?

Going digital. Traditionally our industry has used direct mail to get clients. We have shifted everything to online marketing. Facebook ads have been surprisingly effective. So has being a guest and starting our own Financial Gravity Podcast.

WHAT ADVICE WOULD YOU GIVE SOMEONE WANTING TO ACHIEVE SIMILAR SUCCESS?

Look for what Dan Sullivan of Strategic Coach calls an "unfair advantage." They are everywhere; you just need to have your eyes open and then once you have identified it, exploit it! Our unfair advantage is that we understand tax planning better than an entire industry that is considered an expert in it. The shocking truth is the CPA exam does not cover tax planning and largely covers Generally Accepted Accounting Principles (GAAP), which is mostly unhelpful to the small business owner and entrepreneur.

LEARN MORE ABOUT JOHN'S BUSINESS:

If you are a financial advisor or accountant that would be interested in adopting our business model into your practice, go to: FinancialGravitySystem.com

If you are interested in a free ebook called Bust the 10 Tax Myths that are Sabotaging Your Small Business Growth, go to: JohnPollockInc.com/taxbook

If you are an entrepreneur or small business owner and are interested in a free course on tax planning go to: LowerTaxHigherProfit.com

Finally, if you would like to invest, our ticker is OTCQB: FGCO OTCMarkets.com/stock/FGCO/quote

TEACHING SMALL BUSINESS SUCCESS: OFFLINE AND BEYOND

GRANT CARDONE OF GRANTCARDONE.COM

HOW DID YOU COME UP WITH THE IDEA FOR YOUR BUSINESS?

I have several businesses. One of my companies, Cardone Training Technologies—a training company I created to increase people's revenue—came from the idea that people need sales training. I learned the art of sales in my 20s and I knew sales is the path to riches for countless people who are struggling financially.

WHAT WAS YOUR FIRST MAJOR BREAKTHROUGH?

I recently wrote a book called *Be Obsessed or Be Average* and that's because it wasn't until I got obsessed that my life turned around. I was a drug addict, and when I got out of rehab, I gave myself permission to become obsessed with my career. Becoming obsessed is the breakthrough many people need before they will ever see big results.

HOW LONG DID IT TAKE YOU TO REACH 100% DIGITAL FREEDOM?

I was a car salesman until the age of 28 when I finally went out on my own. My income dropped immediately and it was almost three years until I was earning as much as I was back when I was working for somebody else.

WHAT WAS YOUR BIGGEST MISTAKE?

I regret the fact that I didn't go bigger sooner. My thinking was too small from the beginning, like the idea that I would just have a small number of clients and somehow service them better. Bigger is always better.

WHAT IS THE SINGLE MOST EFFECTIVE TACTIC YOU DISCOVERED?

Things like prospecting and closing are important, but one thing you must have is follow up skills. It's the greatest sales secret of all time. Most people are not sold on the first, second, or even third contact. You must be persistent. Follow up is where the money is —and I created an entire module in Cardone University specifically for this.

WHAT ADVICE WOULD YOU GIVE SOMEONE WANTING TO ACHIEVE SIMILAR SUCCESS?

Invest in yourself first. If you won't invest in you, why should anyone else? I'm always looking for ways to improve, reading new things, and finding ways to become better.

LEARN MORE ABOUT GRANT'S BUSINESS:

You can go to GrantCardone.com where I have lots of material that will benefit people. From the novice entrepreneur to the seasoned sales professional, I can increase your revenue.

LISE CARTWRIGHT OF HUSTLEANDGROOVE.COM

HOW DID YOU COME UP WITH THE IDEA FOR YOUR BUSINESS?

Hustle and Groove started as a blog to help others looking to start a side hustle—figuring out what skill or idea they should start with. When I got started as a freelance writer, I was lucky enough to be part of an online community where I could get feedback and help. I wanted to provide that same community feel to new people discovering another way of living their lives. It's evolved into a business that not only helps people choose an idea, but also provides them with strategies to grow their business, as well as how to transition out of their day job by crafting an exit strategy. All of this is done through sharing ways to use self-publishing to build their brand, and email marketing strategies to find their raving fans.

WHAT WAS YOUR FIRST MAJOR BREAKTHROUGH?

For me, there have been two major breakthroughs. The first was quitting my job in June 2012 to go full time as a freelance writer working with clients on Upwork (I know that's a dirty word to some, but it was a treasure for me in finding awesome clients!).

Doing this allowed me to replace my full-time income of $65,000 AUD within eight months of going full time and really pursue things I was passionate about.

The second was deciding to self-publish in September 2014. I had just finished three months of intense training at self-publishing-school.com and had launched my very first book. Within three short months, that book was bringing in over $1,000 per month without much effort on my part.

These two things combined showed me that through side hustles you can build the dream career you want. You just have to be willing to put in the effort to get there.

HOW LONG DID IT TAKE YOU TO REACH 100% DIGITAL FREEDOM?

From the time I started getting freelance writing clients on Upwork, it took me 10 months to earn enough to be able to quit my job and go full time. This was while balancing my full time job. I would work a normal day, come home from work and then put in another 2-3 hours in my side hustle.

My goal was to be earning enough in my side hustle that I could replace half of my full time job income. And I did that in 10 months.

WHAT WAS YOUR BIGGEST MISTAKE?

My biggest mistake was not creating a buffer in savings with the extra income I was making while I was working my full time job. Four weeks after I quit my job, my husband was laid off from his full time job and we had less than a month's worth of savings.

I almost went back to work with my previous employer, but I felt sick to my stomach at that prospect, so instead I vowed to make the freelance writing work. And it did! I was able to support myself and my husband for the next 18 months while he retrained.

I've been very cautious with how I spend money and because I reside outside of North America, everything always cost more, spending NZ dollars. So I've never wasted money because I always did my due diligence before investing money into a program.

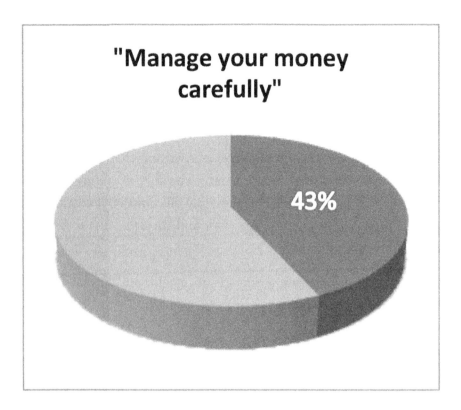

"Manage your money carefully"

43%

Where I have wasted time though, is in procrastinating and thinking I have to know *everything* before I could do anything. This kept me in a constant loop of taking no action. I spent close to six months like this before taking the plunge and joining Self-Publishing School. And once I did, I had amazing success. I wish I'd done it sooner!

WHAT IS THE SINGLE MOST EFFECTIVE TACTIC YOU DISCOVERED?

For me, it's been promoting my blog posts on Pinterest. This alone brings in more than 80% of my traffic and consequently my subscribers and eventual customers.

The other is writing books. I have new people joining my email list daily from links inside my books.

These two tactics alone bring in 100% of my business.

I'm also seeing a growth from doing live videos and videos in general. But the videos are about my personal life, not always business related, but people respond to these more. I guess they like to see that you're a real person, with a real life and that it's not all sunshine and rainbows (which it isn't!).

WHAT ADVICE WOULD YOU GIVE SOMEONE WANTING TO ACHIEVE SIMILAR SUCCESS?

Be consistent in building your business. Choose no more than two or three tactics to build your business and consistently, daily, do those things over and over again until you reach success. Then and only then, switch up your tactics and repeat the process.

Protect your dreams and goals from those who try to dissuade you. They don't know you and what you can do, but that won't stop them from giving you their unsolicited advice. Simply smile, thank them and then move on.

You got this!

LEARN MORE ABOUT LISE'S BUSINESS:

You can learn more about me at HustleAndGroove.com and if you are struggling with figuring out what your side hustle idea is going to be or how to get started, take the free 7-Day Side Hustle Challenge now: HustleAndGroove.com/Side-Hustle-7-Day-Challenge

You can also live vicariously through me on Instagram: Instagram.com/lisecnz/

Connect with me on Twitter: Twitter.com/LiseCnz

And learn more on Pinterest: Pinterest.com/lisecnz/

BEATE CHELETTE OF BEATECHELETTE.COM

HOW DID YOU COME UP WITH THE IDEA FOR YOUR BUSINESS?

After I sold my company to Bill Gates, I was offered the position of senior director for the Global Entertainment Division at a Gates company, Corbis. Although I lasted twice as long as most entrepreneurs do after they sell, I always felt I had a much bigger mission to accomplish.

My daughter Gina tells the story by saying I retired for a day before I got bored. The business idea of The Women's Code was born out of my desire to mentor women on how to be successful in their careers and their lives. Many women struggle to remain feminine and vulnerable while balancing the demands of a career and family. It's much, much harder for women and we are up against a lot of bias. Plus, we have very few role models and a lack of honest how-to information. Without these, each of us has to figure it out on our own.

Those of us who have made it have an obligation to share with others how we did it and what we learned. If successful entrepreneurs don't share the how-to information, we are all in trouble.

WHAT WAS YOUR FIRST MAJOR BREAKTHROUGH?

My first major breakthrough was when I avoided bankruptcy. This was after an employee betrayed me and then I lost my production business in 9/11. Just when I thought it couldn't get any worse, my father passed away due to pancreatic cancer. In desperation, a few months before that I had written to the White House. It worked! I was put in touch with the Small Business Administration, which helped me secure a loan based on my business plan.

Within a few months I went from being $135K in debt to being able to restructure my debt and free up my line of credit. In three months my stock photography syndication business was breaking even. After 18 months, I sold it to Bill Gates.

Let's be clear—there are three B's. First, there must be a Breakdown that forces us to push through our breaking points. Sorry to share this piece of news, but it will happen over and over. This step repeats every time we want to break through a barrier or make a quantum leap. It is important to feel that intensity of struggle because it pressures you to take a hard look at what you want and detach yourself from the outcome. This is the point where your idea becomes a business. You have to decide if you want to put it all in or let it all go. To be clear, this happens to all entrepreneurs and it is extremely uncomfortable.

After the Breakdown comes the Breakthrough. That's when our clarity begins and energy shifts into creation mode. Now we can identify what it is that we want to achieve and start to create it.

Finally, there is our Breakout because we stayed the course and went all the way through the tunnel and come out on the other side. That's when things really start to come together.

HOW LONG DID IT TAKE YOU TO REACH 100% DIGITAL FREEDOM?

I was laid off so there was no decision to quit. I felt I had no choice but to set up my own business. It only took me 13 years to become an overnight success!

WHAT WAS YOUR BIGGEST MISTAKE?

There are simply too many to count. One of the bigger ones was when I tried to create an app with a development team in India. It was a pretty expensive disaster. We cannot look at our mistakes as mistakes, though. As entrepreneurs we must view them as learning experiences, as signs that say "Not This Way." You'll sleep better if you internalize your mistakes as learning experiences and stepping stones along the path to clarity.

WHAT IS THE SINGLE MOST EFFECTIVE TACTIC YOU DISCOVERED?

Know how you roll. For example, the world is made up of extroverts and introverts. There are people who love to geek out behind a screen, and there are people who must be out networking or else they'll explode. Personally, I have learned that my strength is to be in front of people. When people hear and see me, they get inspired and start to shift into gear. I understand now that it is imperative for me to get out of my office, meet people, and have them hear me speak.

When I work with my private clients, we do a Myers-Briggs personality assessment which helps me identify their strengths. I do not believe in exploring and improving upon weaknesses. Rather, I teach how entrepreneurs can hire to our weaknesses. If we can focus on what we do best by playing to our strengths, we can be much more successful and get there faster.

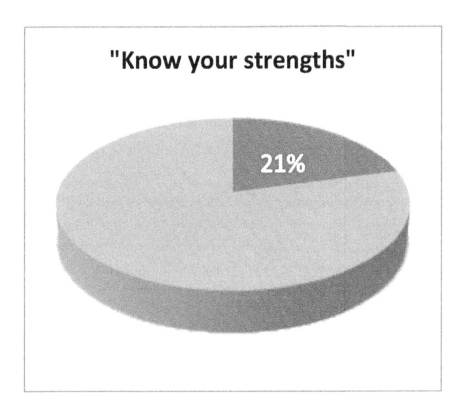

WHAT ADVICE WOULD YOU GIVE SOMEONE WANTING TO ACHIEVE SIMILAR SUCCESS?

Well, I have a few pieces of advice to share...

Perfectionism doesn't work, but getting stuff done does. Consistent execution and a strong belief in our own success will get you to the goal. Learn to move on from mistakes as quickly as you can.

As a Shark Tank addict, I want to remind you that the business philosophies we hear on the show are only partially right. These guys have a formula that works for *them*. They look for a business at a particular tipping point that follows *their* model and what they know works. Just because you don't fulfill certain criteria or someone else's blueprint doesn't mean you will be a failure. It just means it won't fit *that* mold.

I built a creative business. It was a stock syndication for architecture and interior photography of celebrity homes. There was little hope that I would be able to sell a business when I didn't own the content (I only owned the licensing rights). And yet I did sell. Big time. The most important thing is to understand that there is no chance of extraordinary success without an equal chance of extraordinary failure.

Finally, know your number. What I mean by that is it would behoove you to have a price in your head that you would be willing to sell your business for. Always, always set up your business so that you could sell it if you want to. And if someone hits your magic number, all you have to say is yes. It's liberating to be ready.

LEARN MORE ABOUT BEATE'S BUSINESS:

If this resonates with you, please go to BeateChelette.com/ce-free-gifts and check out the $888 in free gifts I created for you. For example, the Uncovery Session that will help you to discover what is unconsciously sabotaging you from taking your business to the next level.

Please also join our communities on LinkedIn: CreativesWhoShare.com.

And Facebook: Facebook.com/GrowthArchitecture/

NICOLE DEAN OF NICOLEONTHENET.COM

HOW DID YOU COME UP WITH THE IDEA FOR YOUR BUSINESS?

I've been earning a full time income online for over a decade, so my origin story is a bit older than some, but not as old as others. I'll take you on a little journey to get the big picture of the start—although it certainly isn't the big money part yet.

Back in September 2001 I had it pretty darned good. My husband and I had bought our dream house a year earlier. He had an amazing job. At this point, our sweet, funny son was four years old and we were pregnant and due with a healthy baby girl any day.

September 11th changed a lot of things for a lot of people. Some tragically. Others, like me, it affected but in a different way. My daughter was born a few days afterward, and my husband's entire department at work was closed in a knee-jerk reaction by the company that he worked. They feared that the Christmas season would tank and decided to downsize that department of nearly 300 people. So, practically overnight, I went from one child and a very nice family income to two children and no income—and a home we could no longer pay for.

We did what people do in these situations. We came together and figured it out, but during the transition I watched my husband go through 50 shades of emotion. Fear, guilt, stress, panic, anger, blame, and so much more. He had the world (his entire world) on his shoulders and it was unbearable to watch him go through that.

I decided then that I would find a way to make money. I started looking online seriously and found nothing but scams. So I decided to create a little website at the time to help moms like me to find real ways to earn money part time from their homes. It took off and launched everything that I've done since then.

WHAT WAS YOUR FIRST MAJOR BREAKTHROUGH?

My greatest breakthrough was to watch what people were responding to in order to give them more of what they wanted. I pored over my stats like crazy and created more websites and content and ebooks around those topics. It was so easy to just let my audience tell me what they wanted by letting my stats tell me rather than guessing. And it was much much more profitable.

HOW LONG DID IT TAKE YOU TO REACH 100% DIGITAL FREEDOM?

I didn't have a job when I started, but it took me about three years to earn more money than I had been making working in purchasing and operations before I became a stay at home mom. Now I earn a very nice multi-six figure income and have financial freedom.

WHAT WAS YOUR BIGGEST MISTAKE?

My biggest waste of time was probably trying to be like everyone else. I thought I had to be all professional and perfect and edited. Frankly, I'm not at all like that. I never want to be. So, instead, I decided to embrace my imperfection and show my audience by example that it's not necessary. My podcast episodes were never edited with a fancy intro and outro. There are goof-ups and giggles and even a snort here and there. Big deal. I decided to lead my tribe by example and show that they don't have to be perfect to profit, because I sure as hell am not. In my not-so-humble opinion, perfection is just a nice word for procrastination. It gives a lot of people the excuse to not move ahead on projects because "t's not perfect yet." "That book, well, sorry coach, it's not ready yet. We'll have to put it off." Yeah. That doesn't fly for very long. The truth is that nothing is ever perfect. But done is better than perfect and done makes money and helps people. So done is the path to profits.

WHAT IS THE SINGLE MOST EFFECTIVE TACTIC YOU DISCOVERED?

The single most effective tactic is not really a tactic, but a strategy. It's leverage. I love to leverage other people's audiences. I love to leverage what's already working for me to work even better.

Leverage is like magic pixie dust. It makes your traffic numbers go up, your lists grow faster, your conversion spike, and your overall profits soar. And there's no end to how much you can tweak for better results, so it's something that's always super exciting for me when working with my clients. One tweak can affect their bottom line for years. That's fun!

WHAT ADVICE WOULD YOU GIVE SOMEONE WANTING TO ACHIEVE SIMILAR SUCCESS?

Baby steps in the right direction is still progress. As long as you're building your audience, offering them something that will help them that they can buy (and they're buying it), and you've got a way to get more, you're set. Just work on finding more people to help, and come up with more things for them to buy that they'll love.

And when it all feels overwhelming and you think of quitting, I encourage you to look back in order to see just how far you've come. I don't know about you but this has happened to me a few times. I've been paddleboarding or canoeing and I get into the groove and keep paddling and paddling. All of a sudden, I go to turn around and I'm so much further from the shore than I even realized. I had *no* idea. I was too busy paddling to take the time to look back to appreciate my own hard work. It's the same with you and your business. Take a break to look back and give yourself a big hug and a high five for all that you've accomplished. Because you are awesome! And then get back to work.

LEARN MORE ABOUT NICOLE'S BUSINESS:

The best way to learn more about me would be to go to NicoleOntheNet.com. That's my blog. I also co-own two other businesses that are pretty awesome, as well. CoachGlue.com (we make your clients stick to you) is where I provide done-for-you training for business coaches, service providers, authors, speakers, and other experts to use to create their own e-courses and workshops. And Beachpreneurs.com is my fun project where I host mastermind retreats for female entrepreneurs and we have bold breakthroughs at the beach.

KATE ERICKSON OF EOFIRE.COM

HOW DID YOU COME UP WITH THE IDEA FOR YOUR BUSINESS?

I didn't—it was John Lee Dumas's idea, and I joined the team six months post launch.

WHAT WAS YOUR FIRST MAJOR BREAKTHROUGH?

Realizing that no one else was going to give me what I wanted to see in my life—I had to create it. This happened back in 2011 when I lost out on a promotion at my 9-to-5 job. I had been in the same position, at the same desk, with the same title and salary for three and a half years. I had *finally* jumped at an opportunity to stretch out of my comfort zone and move into a position that would challenge and motivate me—one that my boss told me I had in the bag.

When the call came that I thought was going to be my "congratulations—you got the promotion!" call, it was instead a "sorry, we've chosen to hire a candidate outside of the company" call.

That day I promised myself I wasn't going to wait for someone else to give me what I wanted. I realized that nothing was going to be handed to me—no matter how hard I worked, or how good I was at following the rules. That day I realized that what I wanted to see in my life was up to me to create.

I quit that job 6 months later, after a lot of brainstorming about what I could create a business around, and of course, after saving up some money.

HOW LONG DID IT TAKE YOU TO REACH 100% DIGITAL FREEDOM?

The first time I took my entrepreneurial leap, from corporate to running my own business, was six months.

WHAT WAS YOUR BIGGEST MISTAKE?

Not taking responsibility from the very beginning when it came to managing our payment system; I was delegating something that I should have been taking full responsibility for, and it cost us thousands of dollars and dozens of hours to fix.

WHAT IS THE SINGLE MOST EFFECTIVE TACTIC YOU DISCOVERED?

Creating a platform—a community—for our audience to come together around. Everything we've created at EOFire is a result of the questions, pain points and struggles that Fire Nation (our community) has shared with us. Without their feedback, guidance and engagement, we'd likely be creating things that either no one actually wants or needs, or no one is going to pay money for.

Fire Nation was able to form because we provided a platform for them to come together around—through our website, our social media channels, and through making them a part of what it is we're creating. We don't create the podcast, our blog, or our free courses for ourselves—we create it for them, and therefore they play a major role in what we're creating.

As humans, we all want to be a part of something. So give your audience something to be a part of. When you have a community to go to—that you can ask, "what is your biggest struggle right now?" or "how can I help support you on your journey?" or "what are your biggest aspirations in life?"—then you have actual feedback to work with, versus assumptions.

When you have a community to go to—that you've been providing free, valuable and consistent content to and that has grown to know, like and trust you as a result—you're able to share opportunities with them, like products, services, or resources that can help them on their journey.

When you have a community to go to, you start to understand who they are, and how you can serve them best.

WHAT ADVICE WOULD YOU GIVE SOMEONE WANTING TO ACHIEVE SIMILAR SUCCESS?

Take one small step forward every single day. You can't get from point A to point Z with one huge leap—there are several steps you must take in between in order to continue moving yourself forward. Stop thinking about it and just *take action*.

LEARN MORE ABOUT KATE'S BUSINESS:

Everything we do is over at EOFire.com!

DAVE FULLER OF PROFITYOURSELFHEALTHY.COM

HOW DID YOU COME UP WITH THE IDEA FOR YOUR BUSINESS?

My name is Dave Fuller and I live in Northern British Columbia Canada, where the moose and deer play in my backyard, and the black bears are dangerous, but that is another story. A few years ago, after 25 years in business, I decided I wanted to go back to school and get my MBA. That process started me on a change in my thought processes. No longer was I satisfied in doing the same old thing anymore. I felt that I was called to do something different, but I didn't know quite what. At a business conference one year, I encountered a business coach giving a talk and decided to use some of the information he shared and incorporate it in my business practice. You see, I have a multi million dollar health food business that employs dozens of people. The techniques I learned at the seminar changed how I interacted with my management team and how we made decisions. I thought that I would like to make a difference for other small business owners just like that speaker did for me.

After I finished my MBA and considered my options, I joined the Professional Business Coach Alliance out of Syracuse, NJ. Jon Denny has a great training and certification program for business coaches. I became certified as a professional business coach and joined a wonderful group of coaches who are making a difference in the lives of business owners in North America and around the world. But how successful could I be in the middle of nowhere? While I was immediately successful in finding some clients in my local community, my goal was to do something bigger. I wanted to help business owners in other communities learn how to run their businesses differently so they could actually make money and have less stress.

WHAT WAS YOUR FIRST MAJOR BREAKTHROUGH?

My first breakthrough was the realization that it doesn't matter where you live—running a small business with employees is tough going. I have had businesses that have lost hundreds of thousands of dollars in a single year, had the bank manager and partners calling me on a daily basis, and faced bankruptcy before turning the business around. I have also been very very successful in my businesses and enjoyed healthy profits and the feeling of making a difference in the lives of my customers, my employees, and my community. According to the National Federation of Independent Business, 30% of businesses never make money and 29% of businesses are only marginally profitable. Once I realized that my market was not limited to my local geographic area, and that with technology I could reach the world and maximize my efficiencies in communication, I was on the road to success.

HOW LONG DID IT TAKE YOU TO REACH 100% DIGITAL FREEDOM?

The truth is that I still own my multi-million dollar brick and mortar business. Currently I am in the process of negotiations with my partners about who will own that business. We have a shotgun clause and while I am making an offer to buy the business outright, my partners might have other ideas. For the past couple years, I have been running my coaching business online 2-3 days a week and going into my other business on Mondays and Fridays. This is a balance that I love. Working online full time takes a different kind of energy, and a lot of brain processes. I love going into the physical business, moving boxes, pricing product and interacting with real live people. Yes I could have quit after about a year and continued to grow my online coaching business and become 100% digitally free; however, some things are too good to give up! My life is about balance and I need that balance of online and brick and mortar.

WHAT WAS YOUR BIGGEST MISTAKE?

I have a number of online businesses besides my coaching business. Online retailing can be tough. My biggest mistake was to assume in both businesses that I would have immediate success, that I would put my shingle out and that people would come to me. Marketing online takes different skills, knowledge and know-how than simply marketing in your local newspaper. While the basics are the same, you need to capture the attention of your prospects, give them a reason to believe in you and call them to action. Finding the right prospects and getting them to take action is different.

WHAT IS THE SINGLE MOST EFFECTIVE TACTIC YOU DISCOVERED?

In 2016, I wrote a book called *Profit Yourself Healthy*. It is aimed at helping small business owners earn more money, and have less stress. Once I had the book finished, I had more confidence to go out and engage with larger audiences. I did podcasts, built an online school, and grew my mailing lists, all as a result of the exposure that the book gave me. Yes it was a lot of work writing the book. I started with an idea, a framework for the book, and then spent 10-20 hours each week dedicated to writing. I had the support of my business coach Dennis Bonagaura from NJ who pushed me each and every week and kept me accountable. But writing a book is only part of the equation. Marketing a book takes almost as much energy, if not more, to be successful, and I hired some assistants to help me. I have learned that you can't do everything yourself and that there are people who do things a lot better than I ever can. When you find these people, you need to bring them into your camp and maximize their potential and your time. Do what you love and what you are good at and hire the rest!

WHAT ADVICE WOULD YOU GIVE SOMEONE WANTING TO ACHIEVE SIMILAR SUCCESS?

In business we need to figure out a market that we can become the expert in. We need to find ways to stand out from the crowd, and understand how we can monetize profitably what we have to offer. The truth is you are good at some things and not so good at others. To be successful you need to build on your strengths and go out on a limb at times and take chances. Stepping out of your comfort zone with little things on a daily basis helps prepare you for those situations where you are going to really have to be uncomfortable on the road to success.

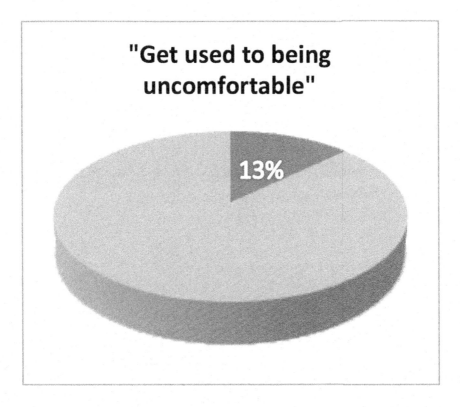

My final tip is to be patient. Success doesn't happen overnight and if you take the time you can learn from your failures. Taking time each day to meditate or pray and reflect on what is happening around you and to you can be huge in this regard. It allows you a different perspective and helps you understand that you are not the center of the universe, that you are achieving something and that when you follow your heart, you can make a difference in the lives of so many other people, and make a living doing it!

LEARN MORE ABOUT DAVE'S BUSINESS:

My passion is to help business owners who are stuck in some aspect of their business move forward. I coach business owners who are doing between $500k-5M in business and want to get those businesses more profitable and take them to the next level with less stress. If this is you and you would like to know how to get your business working, I encourage you to head over to my website ProfitYourselfHealthy.com/free and download a copy of my book. It will get you on the path to less stress and more money. Alternatively you can buy the book from Amazon for $24.99. That works better for me, but hey this is about you. If you are really stuck in your business or know someone that is, and need a business coach that cares about getting you results, and has the experience to back it up, fire me off an email at dave@profityourselfhealty.com, I would love to hear from you!

GAIL GARDNER OF GROWMAP.COM

HOW DID YOU COME UP WITH THE IDEA FOR YOUR BUSINESS?

When I first resigned from IBM in 2000 after 23 years as a field engineer (managing and repairing computer equipment), I had no idea what I was going to do. I only knew I needed a change. So I actually quit my career before I started making any money. Having built the largest horse site on the internet starting in 1994, my first thought was to build websites for local businesses. I knew that the key was to specialize in a particular niche—horse businesses—so that work would come to me instead of me chasing it.

WHAT WAS YOUR FIRST MAJOR BREAKTHROUGH?

But then I fell into learning and then teaching pay-per-click (PPC) advertising management because of a neighbor. Every time I went into town, I would see him with another horse hot walker loaded on a trailer. I'd ask where he was headed, and it was always many states away. "How many hot walkers do you sell a month," I asked him, "and how far away are you delivering?" But the main question I asked was how was he selling them?

He wasn't even sure, himself. He said, "a friend is advertising them online somewhere". So I went home, got online and started looking for his ads. He had the most horrendous freebie website. But the ads were PPC ads. I called him up and asked, "how much are you spending a month to advertise"? "Oh $20 or $30 dollars a month," he replied.

He was spending $20-$30 a month to sell thousands of dollars of product! What an idea! So I read up on it and went to another neighbor—a Mennonite family business manufacturing buildings and playhouses. I offered to create a website for them and manage the ads for free to test out the idea if they would pay for the advertising—just to find out if it worked.

They weren't willing to try it out, but he happened to mention my offer to his brother-in-law, another Mennonite family business that built gazebos. So I built a site for them and started selling gazebos. This was in the early golden days of pay-per-click when Yahoo! ads had been around a while and AdWords first got started.

When it worked for them, next I built a site and ran ads for the buildings and playhouses, too. I went to SearchEngineForums.com (long gone now) looking for answers to my questions. Because no one answered, I would figure it out and then come back and post the answers to my own questions. I ended up being the moderator of the PPC section where I taught and answered question for others.

Because I would work with very small businesses—some with only $100/month to spend on ads—and made sure every ad was profitable, I quickly had all the PPC managing work I was willing to take. I offered $100 evaluations of existing accounts and provided three pages of recommendations for what to change. Almost every evaluation turned into a paying customer.

I charged $100 per hour cash in advance via PayPal, but then I would spend as many unpaid hours as needed to make every ad profitable. Soon learning that many shopping carts did not work properly, I focused on Yahoo! ecommerce stores because the shopping carts worked, and they provided graphs and past sales information which allowed me to advertise the right products the right time of year.

But I saw storm clouds on the horizon. Yahoo! trashed their ad platform trying to copy Google. And Google broad match would repeatedly take away our most profitable keywords. The best way to understand that is this example. My gazebo builders sold oval gazebos. I never found a single other source for this shape of gazebo. So early on, we could buy "oval gazebos" for 5 cents a click. But then Google started showing every "gazebo" broad match for that phrase. We would have to bid $2-$3 a click to have the oval gazebo ad show up for that specific search. Even though no other seller even had oval gazebos, their ads filled multiple pages. The buyers couldn't find an actual oval gazebo and my neighbor would not increase his price to cover the increased ad cost even though his prices were far lower than his competitors. He felt that would be taking advantage of his buyers even when I explained it was a reasonable way to make sure they could find him.

I decided to stop managing PPC accounts and figure out how small businesses could survive when they were priced out of AdWords or lost their organic rankings during their most important selling seasons. I saw that happen repeatedly for multiple clients and Problogger wrote about it three different years. That is when I launched my GrowMap.com blog—to share what I learned.

Sad to say, there is no one strategy that can convert like search because people search when they're already ready to buy. Converting traffic from every other source is a very complicated, longer-term project. The answer to what to do when you can't get to the top of the search results is that you must do many, many things exceptionally well.

HOW LONG DID IT TAKE YOU TO REACH 100% DIGITAL FREEDOM?

I was already earning $400+ a month from AdSense and had been paid to build a few websites before I chose to leave my career. I left for other reasons, but I planned to make a living online somehow. I had other income to rely on the first few years. But as soon as I found a way to make money for other people and came up with a way to get leads to convert, it only took a few months to make as much money as I had time to work.

WHAT WAS YOUR BIGGEST MISTAKE?

Ironically, my biggest failure is also my biggest success. GrowMap does not directly make money and my list there is pitifully small. I am also just really not into Facebook, so my reach there is pitiful. I know the reasons for this, but made a conscious choice not to change it, yet.

The reason my list is small is that my topic is too broad. The narrower and more targeted your niche, the stronger your list and relationships will be. I'm not influential on Facebook because I just don't use it enough and never really got into interacting with people there. There is only so much time, and Facebook works better for people who love to do live video. Slow upload speeds, which make live video impossible, are the trade-off of living a quiet, rural life in the middle of nowhere.

WHAT IS THE SINGLE MOST EFFECTIVE TACTIC YOU DISCOVERED?

For me, the single most effective strategy I used to grow my GrowMap brand is a combination of long-form content and social media, but particularly Twitter. Early on, I discovered Twitterfeed and was able to convince over a dozen other serious bloggers that we should share one another's content. When Cornell University and Yahoo! Research did a study, they named 32 bloggers and 12 of them were in my group sharing for each other.

When Twitterfeed recently shut down, I moved 125 of my feeds to Dlvr.it. Most of the original bloggers still share content for each of us today. That, combined with many other tools I use, is the reason I have 104k+ followers on Twitter, and Klear ranks me in the top 0.5%

of Twitter users. Twitter is a major source of my traffic and all my tips are compiled in this article: Growmap.com/twitter-best-practices/

WHAT ADVICE WOULD YOU GIVE SOMEONE WANTING TO ACHIEVE SIMILAR SUCCESS?

Focus on what is new or most complex. In the early days of any new platform—just as in the early days of AdWords, and later Facebook—there is much more profit to be made. Jump in the deep end and learn the latest network, skill, or talent that others who are already established have less motivation to learn. For example, you could become an expert at social selling on Instagram. Or you could be the most valuable member of any business team by learning how to analyze data and analytics to increase conversions through conversion optimization.

The best way to learn advanced skills is to combine training and experience. Take courses, but only the very best. I recommend the Simplilearn Digital Marketing Masters Course I'm currently taking; you can take individual sections instead of the full stack. Or find the most talented person doing what you want to do and become their intern. And whatever you do, always have mentors to make your learning curve as short as possible. Join a mastermind group and collaborate with others. Anyone going it alone is bound to miss out on a lot and have trouble staying on top of the continuous changes.

You must both learn how and actually use what you are studying in order to retain it and become exceptional at it. Average is simply *not good enough*. If you have a head for strategy, that is where your success will lie. Even though I set out to become the Neil Patel of small business, I'm still not there yet. I got sidetracked by the huge demand for content marketing. Today, I field requests for ghost writers, blog managers, media creation and social media managers and funnel them to 25+ top writers, plus video creators, and two teams of virtual assistants (VAs).

LEARN MORE ABOUT GAIL'S BUSINESS:

If you could use a connection to talent, would like to access our Blogger Mastermind group or dozens of Trello boards full of resources, or want more advice or an answer to a particular question, drop by GrowMap.com or tweet @GrowMap: Twitter.com/GrowMap

Alternatively send me a connection request on Skype (username growmap)

Or LinkedIn: Linkedin.com/in/growmap/

I am "GrowMap" on every major platform and active on Inbound.org and GrowthHackers.com.

JAMES HELLER OF WRAPIFY.COM

How did you come up with the idea for your business?

I actually needed the service and thought it already existed. I spent my own time effort and money to see if there could be a viable business and then I quit my cushy Fortune 100 job to start Wrapify. A handful of people tried to do similar things in the past, but we are the first technology platform that leverages the sharing economy to pay regular people to advertise on their car.

WHAT WAS YOUR FIRST MAJOR BREAKTHROUGH?

Getting into Jason Calacanis' LAUNCH Incubator was HUGE for us. It opened doors that would have been otherwise out of reach. His approach to product development and presenting helped us focus on what is important and it gave me the tools to win almost every pitch event we ever did. Life changing to say the least.

HOW LONG DID IT TAKE YOU TO REACH 100% DIGITAL FREEDOM?

It was about 6 months into moonlighting before I quit my job, cashed out the 401k, savings and sold the race car.

WHAT WAS YOUR BIGGEST MISTAKE?

That's a tuffy. Lots of mistakes and failures along the way. We've learned from each one of them. We wasted a ton of time pitching to VC's that ultimately would have been horrible partners. We also started Wrapify with the notion that it would be consumed programatically. We learned that wasn't the case and pivoted quickly. If we didn't, we would have gone the way of the dodo bird.

WHAT IS THE SINGLE MOST EFFECTIVE TACTIC YOU DISCOVERED?

Leveraging retargeting throughout has made an incredible difference and has proven to be one of the cheapest, most effective places to spend money online as a marketer.

WHAT ADVICE WOULD YOU GIVE SOMEONE WANTING TO ACHIEVE SIMILAR SUCCESS?

Be relentless, be persistent and don't take "no" for an answer from anybody. If you are worried about hurting somebodies feelings or if you think you might piss off a potential competition by being too aggressive, don't hold back. I have regretted being too nice on way too many occasions. Winning as a startup is a zero-sum game. There are plenty of other companies that will take your spot, your cash, your employees. Don't lose sight of that.

LEARN MORE ABOUT JAMES'S BUSINESS:

Download the Wrapify app or go to Wrapify.com to learn about becoming a driver or a brand on our platform

JASON LITTLE OF LEANCHANGE.ORG

HOW DID YOU COME UP WITH THE IDEA FOR YOUR BUSINESS?

Completely by accident! I spoke at an Agile conference in 2011 about how to get started with Agile practices when you didn't know where to start, and I was approached by Pearson Education to write a book about it. A year later that turned into a video series that launched InformIT's Live Lesson series. Over the years the ideas shoved their way into a new book that was funded by my publisher, Happy Melly Express, through Indiegogo. We had a variety of levels that people could pay to support the launch of the book. The highest level would give someone the chance to help create the first workshop based on the book. We had no idea if that would work, but someone bought that package and arranged the first two workshops in Munich in 2014.

The book led to the workshops, which led to recurring revenue through a global network of facilitators, which led to virtual workshops, which has now led to a global professional association of people looking for better ways to facilitate meaningful change in their organizations. I suppose the technical term for that is have a diversified suite of services!

WHAT WAS YOUR FIRST MAJOR BREAKTHROUGH?

It was definitely the demand for the workshops and the association I had with Happy Melly, who owns the Management 3.0 brand. That whole ecosystem gave me people to bounce ideas off of, and a support network to help spread the ideas.

HOW LONG DID IT TAKE YOU TO REACH 100% DIGITAL FREEDOM?

I had been working for myself for a number of years already, but I was spending about 80% of my time doing consulting and doing my book, workshops, etc., part time since there wasn't enough income. I'm more or less finished with consulting work now and have enough stable income to flip those percentages around. So in total, it took about three years from the time the book was released to where I'm at right now.

WHAT WAS YOUR BIGGEST MISTAKE?

Missing out on a revenue stream by putting too much emphasis on spreading the idea through my network of facilitators. After people attend my workshop, they can buy an annual license to run their own workshops. That annual fee gets them other perks as well. I decided to keep this fee low to grow the network and also offered help to market their workshops, design their courses and more for no extra cost. Funny thing is, this entire business was built on purpose, not profit so it wasn't a big deal to me, but people who are all about the money tell me I'm dumb for doing this.

My biggest waste of time and money was not jumping into doing this full-time sooner. We're a single income family and it's worse when that single income is from self employment. People think that entrepreneurship is about designing a product, building an audience, getting funding and selling it off. Not true. Find something you love, and find people who are willing to pay for it. I have little overhead and my sandbox is the entire planet, so people will say I'm unfocused, but that's how my business grew—by casting a wide net.

WHAT IS THE SINGLE MOST EFFECTIVE TACTIC YOU DISCOVERED?

Treat people fairly and keep your eyes and ears open. My last personal coach told me that there are these invisible threads of silver hanging out in front of your face. All you need to do is know which one to pull on.

I know entrepreneurs who fall into the trap of being too close-minded about their idea. My virtual workshops happened because someone asked if I offered one. I said "not yet," but then I did an experiment to see if there was demand, and I sold out the first one in an hour after sending the newsletter. Of course, the problem was I had to build the course, but that was a good problem to have! Today's world is different, the market directs your products and as long a new idea aligns with my purpose, I'll give it a shot.

WHAT ADVICE WOULD YOU GIVE SOMEONE WANTING TO ACHIEVE SIMILAR SUCCESS?

Find what you love, and find out how to get paid for it. That is, find a problem that companies have, or societies have, and fix it. What bugs me about entrepreneurship is the overemphasis on success being about the million dollar valuation. If you value profit, good for you. I value the purpose of what I'm doing and I've found enough people to make it a sustainable business. The book was never the real idea; it was a way to figure out what the business could be. Now it's evolved to a global ecosystem of people who want to figure out better ways to change their organizations for the better.

My advice: chase your purpose, not dollars.

LEARN MORE ABOUT JASON'S BUSINESS:

LeanChange.org is the best place to find out about the book, workshop and network. I speak frequently at conferences all over the world and people can connect with me on Twitter @jasonlittle: Twitter.com/JasonLittle

PATRICK MCGINNIS OF PATRICKMCGINNIS.COM

HOW DID YOU COME UP WITH THE IDEA FOR YOUR BUSINESS?

My business is investing, advising, and founding companies while holding down a steady "job." This is also the subject of my recent book, *The 10% Entrepreneur*. I wrote the book as a direct result of living through the 2008 financial crisis at a private equity firm housed within a division of AIG. When AIG blew up, it was chaos. That's when I decided that I would never put all my hopes in one company again. That's also when I realized that pursuing entrepreneurship while holding down a day job could serve as an insurance policy.

Once I started telling people about my 10%, lots of friends asked me how they could do the same for themselves. This made me ask myself if I should just write everything down and share my experiences that way. Once I did, I wondered if perhaps this could be the basis for a book. I also started to notice that lots of people were taking a similar path so I searched high and low for great stories from all over the world.

WHAT WAS YOUR FIRST MAJOR BREAKTHROUGH?

My first 10% investment was working with my friend named Marcelo Camberos on a business that matched YouTube celebrities with commerce. While Marcelo had experience working in startups, I had never sold or pitched anything before in my life. All of a sudden I was pitching something new, different, and way beyond traditional companies. I was outside of my comfort zone and I faced rejection on a daily basis, but having a partner who understood how to sell something new allowed me to learn how to overcome those challenges Then one day I got a major consumer goods company to put $25,000 into testing our product and that turned into hundreds of thousands of dollars in businesses within months. The key to making this happen was having confidence in our ability to execute, pitching to people whom I knew previously and who knew they could trust me, and not giving up—with each rejection I learned something that could allow me to better pitch the next potential client.

Although the company did fine, it was difficult to scale. Still, I had learned a lot and set myself up for another project in the future. When Marcelo and some partners started another company called Ipsy, I invested and it has become one of the best investments to date. I felt confidence investing because I had worked on this previous project with him, so it made it far easier to write that check and invest in an early stage company.

HOW LONG DID IT TAKE YOU TO REACH 100% DIGITAL FREEDOM?

I follow a different philosophy. Although many people dream of becoming entrepreneurs, depending on your particular skills, your interests, and your stage in life, you may find that taking an entrepreneurial course is not practical or that you aren't willing to give up the stability of your current career. The good news is that you don't have to become a full-time entrepreneur in order to be *entrepreneurial*. Instead, you can become a 10% Entrepreneur, setting aside at least 10% of your time and, if possible, 10% of your capital, to invest in, advise, or launch new ventures, all without leaving your day job.

To date I have made over twenty 10% investments in everything from tech companies, to real estate, to a play in London's West End. I have done so while maintaining employment.

WHAT WAS YOUR BIGGEST MISTAKE?

I have learned—from trial and error—never to follow other people just because they are well-known or "successful." I only engage in projects where I personally have the knowledge and connections to make a smart decision. I also only engage in projects where I can personally make the project more successful—if I cannot, I shouldn't be there.

WHAT IS THE SINGLE MOST EFFECTIVE TACTIC YOU DISCOVERED?

All of my businesses—whether looking for investments or promoting the book—are predicated on my ability to set a clear objective and then convince people that I can deliver on that objective in order to make them or their companies more successful. I have invested significant time and energy into create digital assets—whether they be videos, blog posts, or PR hits, that provide context and credibility for what I'm building.

WHAT ADVICE WOULD YOU GIVE SOMEONE WANTING TO ACHIEVE SIMILAR SUCCESS?

Today, the new barrier to entrepreneurship is mindset. The cost of starting new ventures and the barriers to entry have fallen so much that you don't need millions in the bank and you don't need to go full-time. So it's mindset that can hold you back. That's what makes 10% Entrepreneurship so great. If things don't work out, you don't have to feel bad or feel like a failure. In fact, you learned something in the process. So you can consider it an experiment and not a failure—and you can count your blessings that you didn't go all in on this one.

LEARN MORE ABOUT PATRICK'S BUSINESS:

You can find more at PatrickMcGinnis.com, where you can download a free chapter of the book, and link to my YouTube page and my blog. You can also find the book at most bookstores and at Amazon (physical, e-book, and audio book) or on Audible.

You can also find me on:

Facebook: Facebook.com/The10PercentEntrepreneur

Twitter: Twitter.com/PJMcGinnis

CHRISTINA NICHOLSON OF MEDIAMAVENANDMORE.COM

HOW DID YOU COME UP WITH THE IDEA FOR YOUR BUSINESS?

When I was working to get my first clients after starting my public relations business, I learned many of them did not have a budget to pay the monthly retainer that is associated with media relations. They've tried to handle earning media exposure on their own, but it wasn't working. After a few months of hear the same "no budget" story, I decided I'd create a course to teach them everything I know so they can save money and earn media exposure.

WHAT WAS YOUR FIRST MAJOR BREAKTHROUGH?

A variety of breakthroughs happen—and a variety of lows, too, but I think my biggest breakthrough was when I started using LinkedIn to promote myself more. At first, I looked at the platform like an online resume to apply for jobs, because that's what I used to use it for. Now, I look at it as a way to network and promote my expertise. It's helped me grow my following of potential clients and paying clients.

HOW LONG DID IT TAKE YOU TO REACH 100% DIGITAL FREEDOM?

I quit my job before I had enough money to really be free, but I was into what I called my "side hustle" for 6 months at that point. I knew I was working toward being my own boss and knew I'd never admit to being ready, so I quit my job when I just couldn't handle my boss anymore.

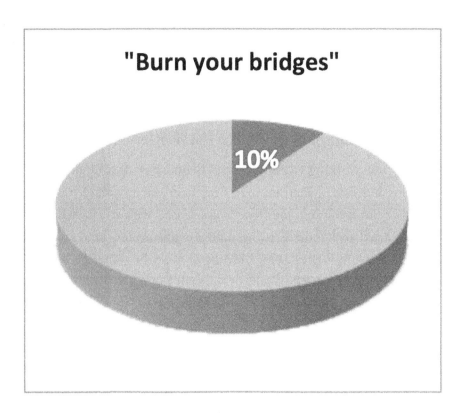

"Burn your bridges"

10%

WHAT WAS YOUR BIGGEST MISTAKE?

I think my biggest failure was putting all of my eggs in one basket. When I worked with one client for six months, I stopped networking and putting myself out there to get more clients. When that client left, I was in trouble.

WHAT IS THE SINGLE MOST EFFECTIVE TACTIC YOU DISCOVERED?

Promoting myself. Never be afraid to share what you do with as many people as you can. It's how to get referrals and grow your business. I am the queen of self promotion! It's basically what I teach clients— pitch yourself and put yourself out there. By practicing what I preach and treating myself as a client, I'm showing people the work I do and using myself as a success story.

WHAT ADVICE WOULD YOU GIVE SOMEONE WANTING TO ACHIEVE SIMILAR SUCCESS?

Don't worry about failure. You will fail, because everyone does. It's not only the best way to learn, but the best way to move forward and succeed. Do what you need to do to achieve what you want to do. Know that you will work more than you ever have in your life, but you can do it from your home in between loads of laundry at 11 p.m.

LEARN MORE ABOUT CHRISTINA'S BUSINESS:

Please visit my website MediaMavenAndMore.com. I have lots of free resources and information in my blog that is updated weekly, as well as information about a course that teaches you how to handle your own public relations if you do not have a budget to hire someone.

BARBARA FINDLAY SCHENK OF BIZSTRONG.COM

HOW DID YOU COME UP WITH THE IDEA FOR YOUR BUSINESS?

Like many business ideas, launching Bizstrong was a responsive move. After selling the ad agency my husband and I had founded and owned for 15 years, I began writing books for those in small business. First I wrote *Small Business Marketing Kit For Dummies*, then I co-authored *Branding For Dummies* and *Business Plans Kit For Dummies*, and after that I wrote *Selling Your Business for Dummies* and the BizBuySell *Guide to Selling Your Business*. Along the way, I saw need for a single place where people could access the full range of advice—from planning to branding to marketing to selling a business. That's when I opened Bizstrong.com as a free online small business resource center and hub for my digital communications.

WHAT WAS YOUR FIRST MAJOR BREAKTHROUGH?

Shortly after launching Bizstrong.com I had the chance to leverage the content of my books into online training for Microsoft Small Business, which led to a role producing advice columns and videos for several MSN small business programs. That opened opportunities with other major brands and opportunities, and the chance to present video training internationally through CreativeLive. I can't point to a single breakthrough so much as a series of good breaks.

HOW LONG DID IT TAKE YOU TO REACH 100% DIGITAL FREEDOM?

Thanks to the sale of our ad agency and the chance to write For Dummies books, I don't look to my digital presence for revenue so much as to support my publishing and presentation efforts, provide an online home base, and serve as a resource for those who buy my books or training programs. I tell people that whether they're aiming to support themselves by building a brick-and-mortar or a digital business, build a business you can someday sell. That way in addition to however much money you make through your business, you can also reap another payoff on the day you turn it over to a new owner. In other words, don't just build a business that makes money. Instead, build a business that becomes a salable asset that can provide funds for your next chapter.

WHAT WAS YOUR BIGGEST MISTAKE?

I've proposed books that never got published and projects that never panned out, but I think the only real mistake is a misstep you learn nothing from. So long as I don't make the same mistake twice, I consider it a lesson.

Once I sent a proposal for a multi-part program, along with an explanation that each part would cost $2,500. I didn't provide a bottom-line total since I didn't know how many parts the client would want to authorize. I did, however, include a lineup of subsections so the client could see an outline of each part. The client thought fees applied not just to the major parts, but also to the subsections—and approved the whole works, basically quadrupling my fee for the project. The lesson: Like many service providers I was underestimating the client's perceived value and, as a result, my fee structure. It's a lesson I share with others who sell service. Emphasize, explain and deliver value and don't sell yourself short.

WHAT IS THE SINGLE MOST EFFECTIVE TACTIC YOU DISCOVERED?

Find a way to set yourself apart from others with similar offerings and then develop your business or personal name into a brand that people believe is different, better, more trustworthy and of higher value than competitive alternatives. People—whether they're selecting people, businesses, products or services—have a huge range of choices. They narrow the possibilities only to those they consider safe bets. Usually that means a name—a brand—they know of and respect or, if the name is new to them, a first impression, in person or online, that stops them and makes them think, "this is what I'm looking for." Authors win distinction by the quality of their book titles. Bloggers earn it through the reach and authority of their voice and online presence. Those selling products or services gain credibility through distinctive offerings, testimonials, reviews, and ratings. And everyone relies on the quality of search results for their personal or business name.

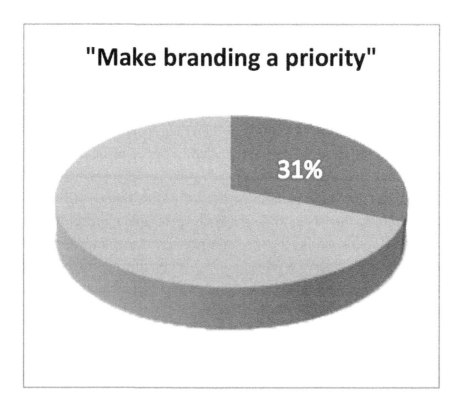

If you can think of even one way your offer is meaningfully different and better than competing options, you have at least one reason to build a brand people can know and trust. Thousands of books and blogs tell how. My recommendation, for obvious reasons, is *Branding For Dummies*.

WHAT ADVICE WOULD YOU GIVE SOMEONE WANTING TO ACHIEVE SIMILAR SUCCESS?

Three things. First, develop a name and reputation—a brand—people respect and trust. Second, develop multiple streams of revenue; multiple ways people can buy the solutions you offer so you can get away from simply selling time by the hour, which is what limits the income potential of too many service providers. In my case that means revenue from book sales, presentations, and affiliate product sales through my site. An attorney friend offers hourly and retainer services, a weekly ad-sponsored podcast, seminars, and a book.

Third, make it easy for people to buy. One of my friends put it well when he said, "just give them something to pick or click to buy." Don't bury the offer deep in the proposal, below the fold on the web page, or well into your sales pitch. Offer a great product, make it easily available, then get out of the way and let people buy.

LEARN MORE ABOUT BARBARA'S BUSINESS:

The home page of my site, BizStrong.com, has links to webinars, video presentations, and free sections of my books. There's also a resources page with links to many of my MSN, *Entrepreneur*, and *Forbes* columns and other works, as well as links to my @ Bizstrong Twitter feed and the Bizstrong Facebook page. My books are available at most bookstores and on Amazon: Amazon.com/Barbara-Findlay-Schenck/e/B002BM9BSW

LISETTE SUTHERLAND OF COLLABORATIONSUPERPOWERS.COM

HOW DID YOU COME UP WITH THE IDEA FOR YOUR BUSINESS?

I was working for a famous author (Jurgen Appelo) who created a workshop to teach the methods that he'd written about in his book (Management 3.0). His workshop was extremely successful and he created a licensing program so that other people could teach his workshop all over the world.

Around the time we started working together, out of my own curiosity, I started interviewing companies about how they successfully worked remotely. Jurgen encouraged me to copy his business model and create a workshop out of the information I was collecting.

I started by creating short segments and then tested them out at every opportunity. Eventually, I took the most useful and most popular topics and put them together to form the Work Together Anywhere workshop. The workshop is now offered in several languages, all over the world, and of course, online.

WHAT WAS YOUR FIRST MAJOR BREAKTHROUGH?

I knew my workshop material was useful because I had spent years testing the material, but I was still having trouble selling it. I hired a business coach to help me and she taught me how to package and market the workshop. I am now a big fan of reaching out to others when I'm not sure of how to do something. I don't spend time trying to figure things out by myself anymore.

HOW LONG DID IT TAKE YOU TO REACH 100% DIGITAL FREEDOM?

It took 3 years of daily promotion and saying yes to every opportunity that came my way. I spoke at conferences for free, gave away workshops, started a podcast, participated in online communities, and posted on social media daily.

WHAT WAS YOUR BIGGEST MISTAKE?

When I was first putting my business together, I was contacted by a woman (let's call her Ellen) who said that she liked what I was doing and wanted to help out. Shortly after we met, one of my clients offered me a large project to work on. I could have done it on my own, but it seemed more fun to share the experience with someone else. I wanted Ellen to feel that I had confidence in her abilities so I offered her a generous salary. After three months, I noticed she was increasingly unreliable, and the quality of her work was becoming inconsistent. After one event, the client complained about Ellen's performance and that was the last straw for me. I fired her immediately. I learned to be much pickier about the people I worked with, and to fire people faster. Keeping people on board for too long wastes money and drains the energy of the rest of the team.

WHAT IS THE SINGLE MOST EFFECTIVE TACTIC YOU DISCOVERED?

Speak in results oriented language. Tell people what they get when they use your product or service. For example, instead of promoting my webinar with, "Join my webinar about remote working," I say, "Run problem free online meetings where everyone contributes," or "Work online like you're in an office together." No one wants to join a webinar. Focus on how you are solving people's problems.

WHAT ADVICE WOULD YOU GIVE SOMEONE WANTING TO ACHIEVE SIMILAR SUCCESS?

Find a topic that you love and start interviewing people about that topic. Do something with the information: create a workshop, start a podcast, write a book, start speaking, etc.

Be focused about your subject matter and deliver as much value as you can. For example, I help teams create a roadmap for successful remote working through the Work Together Anywhere workshop. I don't help people become digital nomads. I don't do consulting to help teams transition from collocated to remote. I focused on one thing, and one thing only.

Start small and iterate. Don't waste time perfecting things. Get something small up and running and then improve on it as you go. Don't try to figure it all out by yourself. Surround yourself with people who are better than you. Reach out to people in your business network and ask for help.

LEARN MORE ABOUT LISETTE'S BUSINESS:

Visit CollaborationSuperpowers.com where you can get the secrets to successful remote working. Collaboration Superpowers helps people work together from anywhere through online and in person workshops. I also produce a weekly podcast highlighting the challenges and successes of working with remote teams.

TEACHING MAKE MONEY ONLINE: THE GOLD RUSH IS STILL ON

DENNIS BECKER OF EARN1KADAY.NET

HOW DID YOU COME UP WITH THE IDEA FOR YOUR BUSINESS?

I owned a retail store at the time, but I had a background in computer programming, consulting, etc. When I learned about eBay, I started selling there in pretty huge volume, so much so that the eBay fees were over $2000/month, and I investigated the idea of setting up a website of my own with a shopping cart, to avoid the fees.

This was back in 1998, and the technology wasn't what it is today, but I stumbled through the steps—while still selling on eBay and trying to divert repeat orders to my own site.

I started to notice people advertising that you could "make money in your pajamas from the kitchen table," etc. I started following all the gurus of the time and became consumed with the idea of making money online. It took three years of pretty consistent failure to turn the corner.

WHAT WAS YOUR FIRST MAJOR BREAKTHROUGH?

In 2005 I was so far in debt that I knew something had to give. My back was against the wall, and I sat down and imagined a strategy where I could focus on one project per week, with a goal to make $5 per day, setting up a recurring income stream.

That strategy worked very well, and I continued to build on those $5 per day income streams until I was making over $500 and more per day, some days much more.

HOW LONG DID IT TAKE YOU TO REACH 100% DIGITAL FREEDOM?

Well, I was self employed, so I technically didn't have a job, but it took about two to three years for me to decide to close my retail store and devote full time to my online activities.

WHAT WAS YOUR BIGGEST MISTAKE?

My most embarrassing and frustrating mistake was failing to build an email list back in 2005-2006 when I was using Google AdWords to send traffic to external sites. During that period, I purchased more than 3.5 million clicks from AdWords. If only I had included a squeeze page on my pages, and even if I only captured 2% of those visitors, it would have been something special.

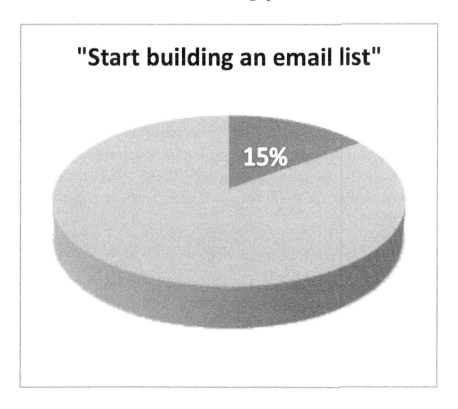

WHAT IS THE SINGLE MOST EFFECTIVE TACTIC YOU DISCOVERED?

Don't be afraid to do things you've never done before. After my initial success, I wrote an eBook about my strategy, designed and wrote the sales copy for the sales page, set up a free forum for buyers, and then ended up creating a paid membership site. The book took me about two weeks to write, and the other tasks took around a day each, even though I had absolutely no clue when I sat down to do them.

So I guess the effective tactic could be summed up as "just do it." Then you can refine and improve from there.

WHAT ADVICE WOULD YOU GIVE SOMEONE WANTING TO ACHIEVE SIMILAR SUCCESS?

Don't be afraid to fail. You can just pick yourself up, dust yourself off, and learn from your mistakes. As I say often: Failure is your friend.

LEARN MORE ABOUT DENNIS'S BUSINESS:

I have been an author and creator of membership sites since 2006. You can get free access to all of my books, and a whole lot more, by joining the famous Earn1KaDay Insiders Club, which has been responsible for more success stories than you could count: Earn1kADay.net

Or if you just want an intro to my writing style and strategy, you can pick up "5 Bucks a Day: Revisited" for less than $10: 5BucksADay.net/revisited

JIMMY D. BROWN OF EARNCOME.COM

HOW DID YOU COME UP WITH THE IDEA FOR YOUR BUSINESS?

Back in the late 90's I owned a bricks-and-mortar sports cards shop and came online to find specific items for my customers. Back then, spam was unregulated and a standard part of doing business online for many people. Somehow my email address landed on a list and I started receiving emails about "making money on the Internet."

I've always fancied myself as a writer and have entrepreneurial blood in my veins, so after visiting a few of the sites from the emails I was receiving, I decided that I could write and sell ebooks like they were doing.

WHAT WAS YOUR FIRST MAJOR BREAKTHROUGH?

I learned about a banking institution at X.com that that would pay anyone $25 to open up an account with them. They would also pay whoever referred the new account holder $25 as a referral fee. I wrote a little ebook that taught, "How To Get $25 Deposited To Your Account Over And Over Again."

I sold the ebook for $12.95 and, of course, earned $25.00 additional for every customer who ordered the ebook and then opened up an account with X.com. Back then, there was little automation. I had to hand-key in credit card orders on my retail machine! But it was a great start to my business!

HOW LONG DID IT TAKE YOU TO REACH 100% DIGITAL FREEDOM?

X.com was bought out by PayPal a few months after I started selling my ebook. They decided they would *not* pay $25 for each new account or referral, but rather would pay $5. This essentially put me out of business.

But I had seen enough success to know that this was a viable business opportunity to pursue. So I wrote some original materials, licensed some content from other people and assembled them into a package that I sold for $39.95 at ProfitsVault.com. My first order for this was in August 2000. I was full-time a month later in September 2000 and never looked back.

My first 12 months saw me earn a six-figure income. I'm now in year 17 as a full-time Internet marketer and have made multiple millions of dollars with the business.

WHAT WAS YOUR BIGGEST MISTAKE?

There really haven't been many, and none really come to mind enough to merit discussion. Every mistake led to a discovery that propelled my business forward. I've never viewed "failures" as ultimate negatives. Learning what doesn't work helps you to eliminate them and devote your time toward things that do work.

Failures are only failures when you call it quits. If you learn and improve, these stumbling blocks become stepping stones.

Example: I don't think money spent on a "loser" ad is wasted if it helps you find a "winner" ad that you can really profit from. I don't think time spent on a "bad" product is wasted if it produces a light-bulb moment for future successful offers.

WHAT IS THE SINGLE MOST EFFECTIVE TACTIC YOU DISCOVERED?

Focus. I'm a big, big believer in taking as few steps as possible to get the result. Probably the biggest barrier that people cannot move past is a lack of focus. Rather than dabbling in dozens of different options for creating products, generating traffic, building lists and so forth, it's better to master a few strategies.

If you can't sum up your business model in one sentence, you're probably working with too many moving parts. And that almost always ends badly. People get so distracted by all the shiny objects that they lose sight of the fundamentals. The fundamentals are like Novocaine: give them enough time and they always work.

There are three things—and only three things—that you need for Internet business success. They are: something to sell, a list of prospects, and a source of traffic. List, traffic, products. Or as I say it at Earncome.com: Database, Acquisition, Revenue. Or, if it's easier to remember: Prospects, Promotion, Products.

To make money you need to connect an offer with a buyer. Don't make it any more complicated than that. Just repeat that process over and over again.

WHAT ADVICE WOULD YOU GIVE SOMEONE WANTING TO ACHIEVE SIMILAR SUCCESS?

Learn the power and profitability of this word: "ONE." One product. One list. One source of traffic. When you are generating significant income from this setup, start adding more products, more lists, and more sources of traffic … one. at. a. time.

Start with the absolute minimum things you need in order to make money. Here is a bare bones approach to Internet business that will work…

1. Create a lead magnet to set up your list.
2. Offer a low-cost product to convert prospects into paying customers.
3. Use one source of traffic to drive visitors to the list page.

From there, add in a core product to increase income from the paying customers. Add in a recurring income offer (e.g., a membership site) to the back end to get stable monthly revenue coming in. Create additional lead magnets to start new lists. Find a secondary source of traffic. Prepare your next tripwire. Prepare your next core product. Everything should cross promote each other in follow-up emails, product files, download pages, etc.

All of this should be done—say it with me—one. step. at. a. time.

You don't need to have a funnel in place up front. You don't need to have a perfect process. You don't need to have a blog and a social media presence and a webinar and whatever else is being pitched at you as a "must-have." All of that can be added later, one piece at a time.

I've used the same blueprint for 17 years. I've taught it for 17 years. Whenever someone uses it, it works. t's simple by design. Overcomplicated means getting stuck!

LEARN MORE ABOUT JIMMY'S BUSINESS:

Everything I do is at Earncome.com. Anyone who is interested in learning how to master the fundamentals should check out Traffictivity, Emailtivity and Ebooktivity at the site. In these uber low-cost products, I share my own "operations checklists" for how I run my business. There is also free weekly group coaching available at the site.

If you want shiny objects and lots of hyped up empty promises, I'm not your guy. But if a simple, workable plan sounds like a breath of fresh air, I can help you like I've helped thousands of others: Earncome.com

BILL BURNIECE OF HIGHPAYINGAFFILIATEPROGRAMS.COM

HOW DID YOU COME UP WITH THE IDEA FOR YOUR BUSINESS?

I've always been a believer of selling high-end products even before the internet was born. And I know by admitting that observation I just tipped my hat about my age. Yes, I'm in my 50s. I was in outside direct sales right out of college and learned that selling big ticket items took no more energy than selling small ticket ones. The same principle applies in online sales.

So when I got into affiliate marketing, I was searching Google for a good resource website on big ticket items to sell and was surprised that I couldn't find any good sites that had what I was looking for in *one place*. So I decided to create my own website on that topic to fill that marketing segment. I settled on the long, but aptly titled, domain name HighPayingAffiliatePrograms.com.

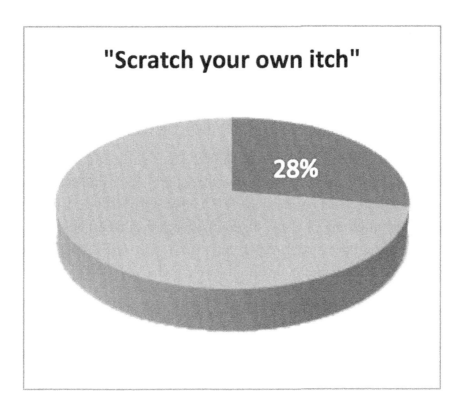

I had no vision or plan for what the site would become. In fact, when I started building out the site, I had no idea what I was going to do with it, but I somehow knew I was on the right track. I created the site organically, by building at least a page a day, and it began to grow and get noticed very quickly. By the end of its first year it was included in the Affiliate Summit's list of Top Affiliate Marketing Blogs of 2013.

WHAT WAS YOUR FIRST MAJOR BREAKTHROUGH?

The day I checked my SEO rankings and found my site on the first page of Google for several of my targeted keywords. In fact, a few of them were in the *#1 position* on the front page of Google. I was stunned. That's when my site traffic and income really took off. I no longer needed to spend as much time reaching out to others because

I now had both affiliate marketers and affiliate networks coming to me first. That's the moment I knew that I had become the authority in my market segment.

HOW LONG DID IT TAKE YOU TO REACH 100% DIGITAL FREEDOM?

It was actually the other way around. I was a successful mortgage loan broker for a decade when I was laid off by my company when the real estate crash occurred in 2007. If that wasn't bad enough, my employer stole my final five-figure paycheck and filed bankruptcy before I could get it back. After that catastrophic series of events, I vowed to never work for anyone else ever again.

I stumbled into affiliate marketing by pure luck and found it to be exactly the kind of business I wanted to do. Since I mentally burned my bridge back to the corporate world, I had no other choice but to make it work. I only lost money one month and that was my first month online. Now, I'm financially independent and have never been happier. The freedom that comes from working *when* you want to work, *where* you want to work, and *never worry about money again* is amazing!

WHAT WAS YOUR BIGGEST MISTAKE?

Failing to build my own email list when I first got started. I waited until almost a year in and that mistake cost me a lot of money in the beginning and it also lengthened my learning curve by months. I think you should start building your email list from day one even if you have no clue what you're doing yet.

WHAT IS THE SINGLE MOST EFFECTIVE TACTIC YOU DISCOVERED?

List building and email marketing by far. Email marketing delivers a huge return on investment and is more cost effective than any other single form of marketing. When you set it up right, it allows you to literally make money on demand. Send out an email...get paid. It's really that simple. I believe if you're not incorporating email marketing into your online business strategy you're making a big mistake and leaving a ton of easy money on the table.

WHAT ADVICE WOULD YOU GIVE SOMEONE WANTING TO ACHIEVE SIMILAR SUCCESS?

If you want to follow my path, simply find a need in you marketplace and fill it. There is a common misconception that the internet is already too crowded and all of the great ideas have been fulfilled. That's BS. Even in popular online markets such as health or relationships you can find a small segment of passionate people who are looking for a product or service that nobody has provided yet. Or maybe just a better platform for finding those products or services. Probe, research, and survey possibilities until you find such a segment and make sure its part of a larger market where money is already being spent. Become the go-to person in that market segment, the authority, and eventually branch out into the primary market to scale your business out.

You need to have a unique approach or voice to cut through all of the clutter in your marketplace. If you do what everyone else is doing you'll never have a big enough audience to build wealth online. Set yourself apart and always give a ton of value away for free up front before you ask your customers to buy anything from you.

Trust is the only thing that matters online and if you lose it you may never get it back. Keep things real and treat every site visitor and customer as if they were a million-dollar client.

LEARN MORE ABOUT BILL'S BUSINESS:

My flagship website is HighPayingAffiliatePrograms.com. I can also be found on Facebook at Facebook.com/HighPayingAffiliatePrograms.

Come on by and say hello. I still answer all of my emails and phone calls myself because I think it's important to be reachable no matter how successful you get.

DEBBIE DRUM OF DEBBIEDRUM.COM

HOW DID YOU COME UP WITH THE IDEA FOR YOUR BUSINESS?

In March 2010 I was doing outside sales. I was traveling about 80% of the time so I was away from home from Sunday to Thursday, and I was on the road. I was driving, I was taking trains, I was taking planes and I was just traveling so much. I was only 30 years old and I felt my body breaking down, and I'm like "You know, this isn't the life that I want to live anymore." Even though I was very successful and making a good living, it was a big trade-off and I wanted my life back—one without hotels and takeout food all the time.

I saw all these people with income and they didn't have to go out to Pennsylvania and Washington D.C. and leave home like I was. They were just making money from the comfort of their own home and I thought, "if they can do it, why can't I do it?" I was intrigued and I Googled terms like "how to make money online" or "how to make money from home." So I started to explore, because there are so many different ways that you can actually make an income from home. That's one of the reasons a lot of people get tripped up—because they get distracted and go in too many directions.

It wasn't initially obvious, but one of the ways I found that was perfect for me was book publishing—self-publishing on the Kindle and other self-publishing platforms. It was perfect for me because I was able to just be in my own world and while I was making a full-time income with my real job, I was producing a book a week. I was writing a book a week and I had some tricks that made it go a lot faster to get it done in one week and that's where I actually made my first money online.

At this point, I wasn't doing any marketing or anything because at that time Kindle wasn't very competitive and you could put out a book on the paleo diet and make some passive income on it, but these days it's a little bit different. So naturally when I started to find success I went ahead and started teaching other people how to do what I was doing and that just grew and grew. The more I started making products to help people, the more I saw that there were a lot of people who actually needed help. So it was a great space for me to help people and also grow my own business.

WHAT WAS YOUR FIRST MAJOR BREAKTHROUGH?

I got lucky and found somebody to work with and partner with who was very like-minded and had the same kind of work ethic as I had. We were able to partner up with a lot of projects and split up the work. A lot of times when you're first starting out and you have to do everything, that can be very overwhelming, so if you have somebody that has complementary talents, that's a perfect dream team because while you're over here doing one set of tasks they're over there doing another set of tasks. Then you bring it together and something very magical happens.

I was lucky enough to find somebody that I was able to do multiple projects with, have a great working relationship, and in the very beginning it's a great way to catapult your success. It's important that they have the same work ethic as you do. You're not getting a paycheck so you've got to have that self-drive and you have to find somebody else that has that same self-drive. Otherwise, if you're working to push them then you're not getting things done.

HOW LONG DID IT TAKE YOU TO REACH 100% DIGITAL FREEDOM?

I Googled "How to make money online" in 2010, and by January 2013 it was smart for me to actually go out on my own and run the business full-time without having the backbone of the steady paycheck coming in every single month. So I was really working and gearing myself up to that point. I'm very thankful that I wasn't relying and desperate for that online income because I already had an income. So I was able to try a little bit and put some money in different places to see what worked for me. I wasn't held at gunpoint to make money, as much money, as I do today online as I did when I first started.

Because that success usually doesn't happen very very quickly. It takes a lot of work, a lot of time, a lot of effort, a lot of energy. The first time I made a book royalty from selling a $3.99 book, that was a good time for me. It wasn't a lot of money—it was the fact that I had accomplished something and I actually made money online. I had made my first couple dollars online and that was more important to me than the actual amount I got paid because of the situation I was in. So I think that night I actually went out to celebrate and have a steak dinner for making a small royalty.

If you can do both in the beginning, that's kind of a perfect scenario for starting your business because you're not so desperate for money. Sometimes the opposite works too. If you are desperate enough, then you will find a way, and I know people who have. So it kind of works both ways.

WHAT WAS YOUR BIGGEST MISTAKE?

Nobody likes to really talk about that, but there are always failures along the way with anything that you do. Not everything is going to be a home run. The one thing that comes to mind is the mindset.

There are times when you don't have that confidence and you think you cannot do something without somebody else's help or without some outside influence that will help you make what you want happen. A lot of times you don't have that confidence of, "yeah, you can do it yourself." But you don't need that third-party entity, or second-party entity, that will make or break whatever it is you're trying to do.

I think hesitation and not thinking that I can do something without that other "force" was probably something that has held me back quite a bit at times. You just have to make a decision and that decision is sometimes not the best decision, but ultimately when you do make a decision you reflect back and you kind of see, you try to pick out the great parts of the direction you ultimately took. You can always think about the direction you didn't take and think of the potential outcome, but don't harp on it and just move on.

Having confidence is something that I've always struggled with and it's something that I'm always working on, and something I definitely encourage other people to constantly work on. Especially women. Women tend to put themselves down or they think they can't do something or they apologize too much and there are all these underlying confidence issues that women tend to have. You just have to push through that and try to build that confidence over time and just stop apologizing!

WHAT IS THE SINGLE MOST EFFECTIVE TACTIC YOU DISCOVERED?

The single most effective tactic to grow your business is having assets that you own and that you sell. There are two types of ways (mostly) that I make money with my business: with my own assets, meaning my own products that I sell, and with other people's assets, with affiliate marketing. Affiliate marketing is great because you don't have to do all the work to put together whatever it is you're selling.

However, at the end of the day, when you don't own something and you're relying a lot on other people's work, that could be a little bit risky.

I tend not to be pessimistic, but you can't trust everybody, right? You can't trust that if you're selling a product that you're getting paid for that product every single time. You'll never really know, because you don't see the back end. You don't see the settings that are on the back end of that product. It's a little bit risky if you're only selling other people's stuff. Now if you're working, obviously, for an established company and you get credit for sales, that's different, but sometimes with online affiliate linking stuff it can be a little bit tricky and you put a lot of trust in the "unknown" and I don't like running a business that way.

The best thing to combat that is to have your own product where you're selling those products and affiliates are selling those products for you, they're helping you grow your business. At the end of the day, having your own stuff to sell, having your own assets, your own products that you control is very important and that takes a long time to build up. The more you can strive to get that done, the better off you will be for sure.

WHAT ADVICE WOULD YOU GIVE SOMEONE WANTING TO ACHIEVE SIMILAR SUCCESS?

The advice I would give somebody wanting to achieve similar success is to strive for that go-getter work ethic mindset. Because if you don't have it, especially in the beginning where you're rolling up your sleeves and doing everything you possibly can to get things done—to get things out the door to sell and make money—if you're not doing everything you possibly can, it's not going to happen for you. Don't think there are certain things and tasks that are beneath you. When you're running your own business, there is nothing that is beneath you.

As small as a task is, you need to get it done and figure out a way for the work to get done. You need to have that go-getter mindset because no one else is going to pick up the pieces for you when you're in a business and you're trying to grow your business. It starts and ends with you and you only. There's nobody, there's no assistant walking around helping you or getting those little annoying things done for you. If you have that, that is amazing if you can get that help, but most people can't afford to pay themselves enough and they can't necessarily hire somebody right out of the gate.

For instance, when I was working a full-time job, I told you I was traveling a lot, but I would wake up at 5 a.m. and work on my business from 5 till 8 in the morning, then work a whole day for my day job. I'm not really a night person, but about 7 to 9 p.. I was back working on my business. I was relentless like that, and that's, I think, what it takes to really make it, by being relentless and not giving up and experiencing that failure and picking yourself back up and just keep doing and doing and doing and doing. That is the attitude that is going to get you very far, especially when you are in business and working for yourself.

LEARN MORE ABOUT DEBBIE'S BUSINESS:

The best way to contact me is to visit my website at DebbieDrum.com. I'm also a big YouTuber. I have a lot of video tutorials on YouTube, I have a lot of playlists catered to different topics like productivity, book marketing, and getting more exposure for your business and brand. You can find me on Facebook, I hang out there as well.

BUCK FLOGGING OF QUITN6.COM

HOW DID YOU COME UP WITH THE IDEA FOR YOUR BUSINESS?

My very first business was a blog that led to some great book sales and a pretty high level of success by my standards at the time. The only reason I started it was for sheer pleasure and curiosity. To get paid anything for that is the ultimate dream as far as I'm concerned.

I was pleased, but I also got burned out and curious about what I could do next. I decided to leverage all the experience I had accumulated from having a successful online business from 2011-2014, and applied that to a career in the self-publishing industry.

It all started when I realized that my assistant (at the time) was providing a great service to me by taking my messy manuscripts and turning them into real, actual books on Kindle, Createspace, and Audible. So I threw the idea out to him about us teaming up to start a service for authors, making the process of publishing easier.

That led to a whirlwind of ideas and experiments after that, which has now led to the creation of a book promotion site (www.BuckBooks.net), a book cover design site (www.100Covers.com), an advertising service for authors (www.BookAds.co), and more. It's been a wild ride.

Ideas are important, but following that first idea and letting new ideas continuously flow in as your skills and expertise grow is how you progress across the major levels of success:

» Struggling

» Scraping by

» Making a Living

» Making Stupid Money

WHAT WAS YOUR FIRST MAJOR BREAKTHROUGH?

It may sound stupid, but the first major breakthrough I had was after I lost *all* of my money and was faced with about 30 days' worth of money in my bank account. Desperation struck, and I was faced with the real possibility of having to go back to w*ork (gasp!) if I didn't figure it out.

Luckily, I had a breakthrough, just at the right time.

Someone left a comment on a busy website and linked back to one of my articles. My traffic surged from a few hundred hits per day to 1,600.

It was no big deal, but I saw how much power that had. So I dutifully went about refreshing 100 or so popular blogs all day every day and leaving the first comment on every new post, for all to see—linking back to a relevant article of mine when possible, and being contentious when possible as well (I didn't hide or subdue my opinions, I just let 'em fly).

The results were insane. I was pounded with vicious posts about me, podcast invites, and much interest and controversy. I became a mini internet celebrity almost overnight. Within 30 days I went from making just $300 a month to almost $3,000, enough to cover my living expenses.

That first breakthrough that got me to the point of being able to really *believe* that I could be successful—like really successful—completely changed my life. I haven't looked back since.

HOW LONG DID IT TAKE YOU TO REACH 100% DIGITAL FREEDOM?

Just four years! Don't panic when you hear that, though. I became successful more or less in 30 days from doing something that actually got results. Before that I was just blah-blahblahgging waiting for the world to discover me and tell me how great I was. If I had kept up with that tactic I still wouldn't be successful.

I'm a firm believer in the power of having quick success and even have an entire website dedicated to helping people get to the point of earning a completely internet-based survival income in six months or less (QuitN6.com). It need not take longer, and if it does take longer it's probably because you're doing something that doesn't work—and it may *never* work.

WHAT WAS YOUR BIGGEST MISTAKE?

I've made *huge* mistakes. I tried to start a paid podcasting platform that pretty much bombed (you know, because people are sick of getting their podcasts for free!), tried my hand at network marketing and published a book that got 2.1 stars, paid $20,000 for a website and a bunch of SEO ninja shenanigans that produced more or less $0, blogged for *two years* before I realized you could put images in posts...

Although I consider myself to be by far the smartest person that ever lived in the history of the world, I didn't get to the pinnacle of human existence without scars and bruises.

WHAT IS THE SINGLE MOST EFFECTIVE TACTIC YOU DISCOVERED?

It's really hard to single things down to one tactic. As silly as it may sound, I think the most important thing is creating a great product or service and a great process to sell that product or service.

Let's say you create a truly life-changing product or service that, because it's so awesome, it can fetch $500 and still blow the socks off of the people who purchase it. And let's say you can get 1% of site visitors to buy it (I know several people with even better numbers than this). That means that you're making $5 per site visitor on average. That's a tremendous budget for hiring someone to drive traffic, advertising at various places, and so forth. Almost everything you try would get a positive return. That's what determines scalability. And you can scale it without being dependent on becoming an internet celebrity (which depends as much on luck as it does skill).

In short, the tactic is to be awesome and swing for the fences with quality. One great product or service that sells well can change your financial future forever. Don't forget to get the product right before you run out there and try to market something that's crappy. That's a tough hill to climb, and that's what almost everyone is doing.

Let's not forget also how hard it is to go out there and try to market a product that isn't selling well that you're not very confident in. Create something awesome and you won't be able to resist telling the world about it. People that complain about not liking "marketing" are usually those that created products and services not worth telling people about.

WHAT ADVICE WOULD YOU GIVE SOMEONE WANTING TO ACHIEVE SIMILAR SUCCESS?

Well if my number one secret tactic to grow your business is making a great product or service, then that means you'll have to become really knowledgeable or good at something to be able to do that.

The real secret to my success is my die-hard belief in the power of self-guided education. When we actively want to learn about something, our minds are in peak form. We learn faster and retain the information longer. Our brains literally work several hundred percent better when we pursue information, skills, and expertise by our own volition instead of having it forced upon us (as happens in traditional education). It's not a chore. I even find it to be addictive.

The internet is an unprecedented playground for self-guided learners. You don't need a teacher. No teacher ever learned anything for their students. Learning is something that only *you* can do. And you can get started immediately, building specialized knowledge, skill, and talent that can be turned into a product or service that is highly valuable to others. All you need is an internet connection. If you think you need a teacher, Google and YouTube have thousands of teachers waiting to show you an infinite amount of things.

That's what it's all about, and those that try to skip that step end up either failing completely or making some money unethically for a while until they fail.

So my advice is to get out there and become someone worthy of success.

LEARN MORE ABOUT BUCK'S BUSINESS:

There's no question that the best thing I've created to date—the sum of all my knowledge, skills, experience, and self-guided exploration—is my signature course, Quit Your Job in 6 Months (QuitN6 for short).

I answer every course comment personally, and take great pride in helping my students get over the many obstacles that keep people from finding online success—from books, courses, coaching, freelancing, blogging, podcasting, and more.

And it comes at the low, low price of WTF you want to pay and not a penny more.

Check it out at: QuitN6.com

QUINTON HAMP OF CUBICLEHOUDINI.COM

HOW DID YOU COME UP WITH THE IDEA FOR YOUR BUSINESS?

In 2008 I completed a copywriting training course from American Writers & Artists Inc. I suddenly realized that even the best writer has no value without clients.

I began researching how to get free traffic from Google. In the fall of 2010, I stumbled onto Pat Flynn's Security Guard Niche Site Case Study. Pat was ranking a website in Google for security job search terms and then monetizing that traffic with AdSense.

This case study excited me. Here was a guy with a little site who was making more than I made at my call center job.

WHAT WAS YOUR FIRST BREAKTHROUGH ON YOUR PATH TO SUCCESS?

There have been three major breakthroughs in my journey.

The first one occurred in 2011 when I started making consistent income from a solar panel blog that I had put together. At our highest point, we were generating over $600 per month! This was exciting as the money was enough to pay rent with and made a noticeable impact on our lifestyle.

Unfortunately, we lost all of that income in April of 2012 when Google began using the Penguin Algorithm updates to weed out spammy SEO practices. It was a depressing time for me. I walked away from the computer for several months.

The second breakthrough happened around that September. I met a lady online who was making money building Squidoo lenses and referring people to Amazon. I wrote over 100 lenses (Squidoo's term for "articles") over the next few months and began realizing consistent income of over $1,000 per month. This breakthrough was key in that it taught me a lot about keyword research and how to position an affiliate offer in a way that Google's customers would appreciate.

The final breakthrough happened in August of 2013. I had created a small niche site, and it started ranking well and consistently delivering affiliate revenue. For me, this demonstrated that I could get back up from the hits the entrepreneurial journey doles out, and keep moving forward.

HOW LONG DID IT TAKE YOU TO REACH 100% DIGITAL FREEDOM?

I jumped a little sooner than I should have into full-time digital marketing. The boss had just passed me over for a promotion, and I came home and told my wife I was going to quit. For a stay-at-home mom, those declarations are anything but easy to hear.

We had $10,000 in retirement, and the Squidoo lenses were making $1,000 per month. I calculated that we could make it until December. On April 1, 2013, I turned in my two week notice.

In an amazing twist of fate, within ten days of me announcing to her my planned resignation (and without telling anyone else,) we were both offered part-time jobs to work that summer.

We lived cheaply and worked hard. Sixty-hour workweeks were standard for me.

That December, just as our runway was ending, we had our first $10,000 month of affiliate income.

WHAT WAS YOUR BIGGEST MISTAKE?

After my success, I decided to live the passive income lifestyle. We packed up, moved to the beach, and became permanent tourists.

What I didn't realize is that the world is full of hungry entrepreneurs willing to work harder than you.

The hardest working (and most persistent) guy always wins.

While I was sitting on the beach, young, hungry kids from India (and Denmark!) were putting up better sites with better content and biting into my income.

The lie of passive online income is just that, a lie. And I had bought into it hook, line and sinker.

I realize now that a better strategy is to build massive wealth and to use that money as an investment tool in offline investments that offer less volatility.

WHAT IS THE SINGLE MOST EFFECTIVE TACTIC YOU DISCOVERED?

Focus. Focus and simplification.

Pat Flynn has the slogan "be everywhere." And while it is nice to "be everywhere," it is more important to measure ROI and focus on those channels that are creating the most profit.

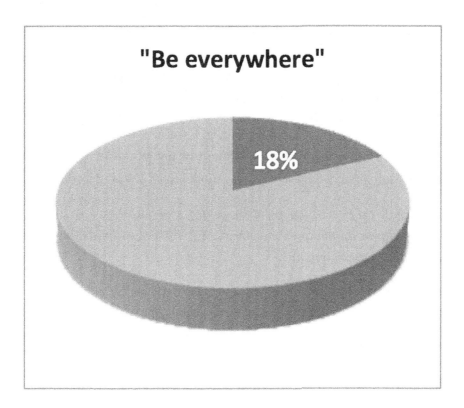

Today, I am aggressive about saying "no" to new opportunities. I am 100% focused on building a team who pushes our two key performance indicators (KPI) forward every single day.

In my experience, simplification is the key to growth.

WHAT ADVICE WOULD YOU GIVE SOMEONE WANTING TO ACHIEVE SIMILAR SUCCESS?

The first thing is to ask better questions. Your goal is to identify and name the problem that is holding you back so that you can find a solution.

In my case, I had to identify how to get more traffic. While that never led me to copywriting clients, the questioning process did lead me to a profitable business model that I love.

My second piece of advice is to choose the path that meshes with you the best. Could I have made more money by getting copywriting clients or by offering SEO services to companies? Absolutely!

However, I quickly discovered I did not enjoy the daily client interaction. By pivoting to affiliate marketing, I was able to build a business I like working on. And that enjoyment of my job ultimately means that I could stick with the business model until I was successful.

If I could give one final piece of advice, it would be to stick with your business model until proven wrong. Most of us switch between opportunities too quickly.

You need to stay in an industry long enough to be able to troubleshoot the problems with your business idea. In most cases, this means that you will overcome those problems and continue to move forward.

The entrepreneurs who jump from opportunity to opportunity never learn the skillset of overcoming obstacles, and this leaves them stuck in a frustrating rut.

LEARN MORE ABOUT QUINTON'S BUSINESS:

I occasionally blog at CubicleHoudini.com, sharing insights from my journey and interviewing other successful entrepreneurs. You can stay in touch by following our Facebook page Facebook.com/CubicleHoudini

DAVE HUCKABAY OF GRABAPPLE.COM

HOW DID YOU COME UP WITH THE IDEA FOR YOUR BUSINESS?

The best answer to this is kind of hard to believe, but this is how it went down:

Today we run a successful, multi-site ecommerce company. But it wasn't always that way...

Way back in the late 1980s I got out of the Navy, and landed a job in industrial equipment sales. I spent the next decade busting my butt—driving the wheels off of a series of cars up and down the east coast.

It was hard work, but I had a dream. I was going to own my own company. It took years, but I got what I wanted.

There was just one problem: My customers were disappearing, and fast. Factories were closing down left and right. Manufacturing was moving to Mexico, and then to China. I had my company, but it was starting to look more like a nightmare than a dream.

Help from an unexpected place...

I was sitting in my home office, grinding away when my oldest son came in with my laptop - a Zenith with a "massive" 4GB hard drive.

"Dad, look at this."

He had a browser open and it showed a picture of a microscope, with a price and a phone number underneath. This was long before online shopping carts.

"I bet you could sell your stuff this way too."

He was right.

I found out that one of my suppliers had a web page. I called him and he hooked me up with his designer, and we were off to the races.

Now it's nearly 20 years later, and we're still going strong. I've managed to weather all of the booms and busts, the birth of the search engines (and their subsequent destruction by Google), and much, much more.

WHAT WAS YOUR FIRST MAJOR BREAKTHROUGH?

When I realized that the internet could actually create enough revenue to live off of. I ditched my rep business and went full time, and it exploded. This didn't happen overnight though (see below), and you have to remember that this was the early days of the net.

HOW LONG DID IT TAKE YOU TO REACH 100% DIGITAL FREEDOM?

Two years to get enough money to buy the company I worked for, then another year and a half to shut down the non-internet part of it.

WHAT WAS YOUR BIGGEST MISTAKE?

Not jumping on SEO when it was easy. Looking back it's easy to see that I could have made a fortune.

WHAT IS THE SINGLE MOST EFFECTIVE TACTIC YOU DISCOVERED?

Picking a market and drilling down—then expanding websites/ product selection to serve it. We started out just selling one type of equipment on one site, then expanded to other gear for a specific industry, then finally an entire website for that industry.

WHAT ADVICE WOULD YOU GIVE SOMEONE WANTING TO ACHIEVE SIMILAR SUCCESS?

Learn as you go. Spend as little as possible while your company is a small and build up reserves.

LEARN MORE ABOUT DAVE'S BUSINESS:

Visit Grabapple.com where you can grab my free ecommerce training.

ZAC JOHNSON OF BLOGGING.ORG

HOW DID YOU COME UP WITH THE IDEA FOR YOUR BUSINESS?

I always had an entrepreneurial mindset, even from a very early age. I first started making money online in the mid 1990s when I was in high school. At first, I knew there was a way to make money with the Internet; I just had to figure it out. After trying a few different methods and failing, I started making a few websites of my own. The first "real" dollar I made online was actually from designing graphic banners for site owners in the AOL Web Diner chat room. This was way before online payment systems like PayPal were around, so I would actually get physical dollar bills in the mail.

That was the beginning, but things start to get serious when I discovered the world of affiliate marketing and being able to earn a commission without actually selling something or needing to hold inventory. The concept of affiliate marketing is simply getting paid a commission for a referral or lead to a website or business. This is when things really started to come together and get exciting.

WHAT WAS YOUR FIRST MAJOR BREAKTHROUGH?

Things really started to get serious and show potential when I discovered Amazon.com had an affiliate program. I would earn a commission (5-15%) on all referred book, movie or music sales to their site. This was back in the day when they just were selling books, movies, and music. At this time I was already pretty decent at creating sites, so I made a celebrity directory with all of the products from Amazon.com and made individual pages for basically every celebrity out there. The site did really well and ranked organically in Google for many celebrity names. The end result was six figures in sales through the site, and a decent amount of commissions from Amazon.

This was great, but then I came across the world of affiliate marketing in the form of CPA offers. Now I could earn a commission from having visitors complete a survey, requesting a new credit card or filling out sweepstakes and contest forms. Not only did I no longer need a customer to use a credit card to earn a commission, I was also earning higher commissions in the process.

Now, instead of focusing on Amazon sales, I was placing these CPA offers throughout my site. I started to see the numbers really start to scale, and that's when I focused my efforts more on the CPA side and would start launching free stuff and sweepstakes sites, while also growing what would soon become a 2 million person email list in the process.

HOW LONG DID IT TAKE YOU TO REACH 100% DIGITAL FREEDOM?

Since I started making money online when I was in high school and I didn't have a previous job (and never had a boss), I didn't have the opportunity to "quit my job." However, at the time I was making more than any other kids in the school and likely more than most of the teacher and education staff at the time as well. By graduation, I was earning mid-to-high five figures.

However, with all of that said, I was also reinvesting money back into the business. I knew this is what I wanted to do for the long run, so I had to keep growing it and make the most out of it.

WHAT WAS YOUR BIGGEST MISTAKE?

Looking back at the past 20+ years, it's easy to mention all of the success stories and highlights, but there have been even more failures along the way. Without these failures, you simply wouldn't be able to keep learning the industry, improving your own skill sets and becoming better at running your own business.

One disaster that happened many years ago was when I had a mailing list with around a million subscribers on it. This was back when all mailing lists were sent out and billed on a CPM basis (cost per 1,000 emails sent). This was on a more clunky Lyris based email platform as well. In short, every day a mailing would go out to this list with the latest free stuff offers for the day, and it was set as a "promotional" one-way email. This means I would send out the email and all replies to it would be sent back to me. Well, one day the mailing went out and somehow it was changed to a "discussion list," which meant each reply would then be re-sent to everyone on the mailing list!

Needless to say, when one person replies and it goes to every person on a million-size mailing list, you know it's not good. Long story short, I was freaking out and told my dad he would need to come up from work and help me figure out what to do. At the time it was a horrible disaster and I wanted to close up shop and never do anything online again. We ended up paying $5,000 in email hosting costs for all the emails bouncing around that day, and it was a lesson learned. I still have no idea how it got changed to a discussion list, but it definitely makes for a memorable story.

WHAT IS THE SINGLE MOST EFFECTIVE TACTIC YOU DISCOVERED?

You need to eat, sleep and breathe this stuff. I've been doing this for over 20 years now and I still enjoy what I do. Along with having 20 years of my own experience, I also have 20 years of seeing and hearing people say things like, "I want to do that," or "You are so lucky," but at the end of the day, 99.9% of people will never put in the same amount of time, work and effort I have.

At the same time, I've also always kept my business and brand squeaky clean, which isn't something you commonly see in this space. In 2007, I decided to launch my own blog at ZacJohnson.com to share my story and help others learn how to do the same. I provide amazing content and answer all of my emails. The opportunities from the blog and growing my personal brand have been amazing. I put myself out there and personally answer all of my emails—no matter who or where they are from.

WHAT ADVICE WOULD YOU GIVE SOMEONE WANTING TO ACHIEVE SIMILAR SUCCESS?

Everything thinks it's easy to start an online business, website or blog. Sure, it's easy to get started—but it's not easy to find success or make really good money. There are over a billion active websites on the internet today. That means it's you against the whole world, and creating "great content" simply isn't enough. If you want to find success with an online business, you need to treat it like a real business.

LEARN MORE ABOUT ZAC'S BUSINESS:

You can read my personal blog at ZacJohnson.com and my complete guide to blogging at Blogging.org. You can also reach me on Twitter at @ZacJohnson: Twitter.com/ZacJohnson

As mentioned earlier, feel free to contact me at any time, and I will definitely get back to you.

JOHN LAGOUDAKIS OF JOHNLAGOUDAKIS.COM

HOW DID YOU COME UP WITH THE IDEA FOR YOUR BUSINESS?

My online business has changed a lot over the years. When I first started out online in 2006, all I was interested in was trying to build my MLM downline. I had exhausted speaking with everyone I knew, so I needed more people to approach, but I didn't want to approach strangers face to face. The Internet was the best place to pitch my network marketing opportunity. I was having success with that and signed up several people to my business. This was through using safelists, traffic exchanges and even Skype.

While I was doing all that, I kept seeing ads about making gazillions with affiliate marketing. I didn't know what it was so I ignored it for a while, but it was so incessant that I finally gave up and bought some ebooks. Most of the info I read was rubbish, but I did finally get my hands on a book by a successful and helpful affiliate marketer (Alok Jain) and he showed me a simple strategy on how to make money promoting CPA offers with Google AdWords. I gave it a go, and was so happy—no, I was ecstatic, when I made my first sale. It was only a $2 commission. What was exciting, though, was that I had only spent $1. That meant I had doubled my money!

As it was the first campaign I had set up, and I had instant success with it, I knew that I could make this work. I created some more campaigns and they worked too. I was a man on fire! At that point, I set a goal for myself to work my butt off for five months and retire by my 33rd birthday in October 2007.

I didn't reach that goal in October, but in January 2008 I did. That was the day I called my clients and told them I wouldn't be coming around to fix their computers anymore. It was the best day ever. I was finally free to work from home, build up my online business and live the Internet lifestyle.

I kept promoting CPA offers but then moved to promoting Clickbank products with Google AdWords, Yahoo and Bing. By 2009 I had become one of the top 100 Clickbank affiliates worldwide. But it wasn't always smooth sailing. Not by a long shot. In July 2009 my world came crashing down around me when Google suspended my AdWords account—indefinitely. It was a crushing blow. 90% of my income was gone. Literally overnight.

Having seen the writing on the wall, I had already started phase two of my online business: building an email list. For the next five years that's what I did: email marketing. And I was no longer selling other people's products on Clickbank. I had by then created my own product and was promoting it to my list via webinars and autoresponder sequences.

Today I still sell my own coaching programs, but I also have a service for business owners who want someone to build their website, social media presence, and their online sales funnels. The reason I started offering this service to business owners is because I've seen so many of my friends get scammed by SEO companies and get fleeced by Internet marketing agencies for services that are way overpriced and that underdeliver.

WHAT WAS YOUR FIRST MAJOR BREAKTHROUGH?

It was understanding the power of having a recurring billing product as the foundation for your business. It's so much harder when you're always chasing the sale and looking for new customers to make money. Whatever business you're in, incorporate a recurring billing product into it. Knowing exactly how much money you've got coming in each month gives you a lot of peace of mind and the financial strength to grow your business. It also makes your business four times more valuable when you decide it's time to sell it.

There's a common saying that is so true: "It's much easier to sell to an existing customer, than to try to find a new one."

HOW LONG DID IT TAKE YOU TO REACH 100% DIGITAL FREEDOM?

Reading Robert Kiyosaki's *Rich Dad, Poor Dad* in 2005 was when the seed was planted to stop working for money, and to set up a business that would allow me to not have to trade my time for money, and eventually to be financially free. It took me two and half years to reach the goal of being 100% digitally free. I'm still working on the financially free part!

WHAT WAS YOUR BIGGEST MISTAKE?

Getting into a partnership unprepared. If you are going to go into a business partnership with anyone, make sure you both agree to a contract that specifically states what the objective of the partnership is, what your ownership and payment terms are, what your respective roles and responsibilities will be in the business, and what your exit strategy will be. The partnership worked well in the beginning, but when things changed and it didn't work well, a lot of time was lost and money was wasted.

WHAT IS THE SINGLE MOST EFFECTIVE TACTIC YOU DISCOVERED?

Making paid traffic profitable. There's no more important skill in any business that knowing how to get targeted traffic on demand that doesn't cost you anything because the value of the new customer is greater than the cost to acquire that customer. When you can do that, you can literally print money on demand. I still use free traffic strategies such as video marketing, blogging, podcasting and interviews, but those strategies take a lot of effort and don't bring you in results immediately.

Another traffic option is to get JV partners on board, but if you can't drive paid traffic to your funnel and make it profitable, it will be because your funnel doesn't convert very well, and if that's the case, JV partners won't want to promote your offer either.

WHAT ADVICE WOULD YOU GIVE SOMEONE WANTING TO ACHIEVE SIMILAR SUCCESS?

Don't rush success. Creating a successful online business, like any business, takes time. There are no real get rich quick schemes. When people learn that I make money online, many of them ask for advice on how to make money online quickly. I tell them up front that there isn't a way to do it. Because there isn't! There's no way to make money fast. Not if you want to build a growing, enduring business.

Yes, you can make money fast online if you're willing to be a freelancer or do gigs on Fiverr. But that's trading time for money, so it's just a job and not a business. If you want to have a successful online business you need to decide what product or service you are going to offer to the world that is of value. That's the hardest part. Once you've decided, the rest is easy. Simply find someone that has a successful online business in that niche and model your business after theirs.

Get yourself a mentor and follow their program. Follow it to a "T." Don't deviate and cut corners and reinvent the wheel. Do exactly as they say until you achieve the same success.

LEARN MORE ABOUT JOHN'S BUSINESS:

I have a lot of great free training on my website: JohnLagoudakis.com. You can also go to that website if you'd like me to help you set up your online business.

If you enjoy listening to podcasts, make sure you check out my weekly show on:

ITunes: itunes.apple.com/podcast/id790758889

or Stitcher: http://bit.ly/2sTusPk

It's called "John Lagoudakis dot com Podcast."

STEPHANIE LOCSEI OF HOMEMADE-GIFTS-MADE-EASY.COM

HOW DID YOU COME UP WITH THE IDEA FOR YOUR BUSINESS?

My husband and I had always been intrigued by the idea of running a business but really had no idea where to start. Back in 2008 we came across an article by personal development blogger Steve Pavlina reviewing a product called Site Build It (SBI) that would teach you how to build an online business. We signed up to SBI and that was the beginning for us.

We wanted to build our business around an existing interest so that (a) it would be fun and (b) we'd have some credibility, rather than building a business around something completely foreign to us. So we explored three different niches: health and fitness (my husband was on a health kick!), science for kids (we're both scientists by training), and gifts and crafts (both of us love making things with our hands). For each of these niches we looked at how much demand there was (i.e. how many people were googling for those topics), how much competition, and how much opportunity there was for monetization. When we did our research, gifts and crafts came out as the clear winner, so we ran with it.

Looking back it was great that we chose a topic that both of us felt excited about. Building a business is so much work, and we benefited a lot from supporting each other. If we'd picked something that only one of us felt excited about then I think our chances of success would have been smaller.

WHAT WAS YOUR FIRST MAJOR BREAKTHROUGH?

Honestly I don't know if there was any single breakthrough that I could point to. There were some early exciting moments, though. A few months in, after focusing purely on creating content pages to generate traffic, we put AdSense on our site. We immediately earned $1 on our first day. We were enormously excited, hugely out of proportion to the amount of money, because it meant that it really was possible to make money through our website.

I remember the day we made about $10, and I excitedly told one of my sisters. She laughed and made a joke along the lines of, "You could afford a happy meal at McDonalds." For me, though, I could see that if we could make $10 per day, then we could make $100 per day, and then we could eventually earn enough to live on.

Another thing that happened was during our business's first Christmas, we started getting messages from people around the world about how much they appreciated our website, and that gave me confidence that we were providing content of real value. One lady wrote to say that she'd lost her job and that her family didn't have enough money to buy presents for each other, but thanks to our website they'd been able to make and give presents to each other and that it meant the world to them. I felt so touched and it made me want to continue growing our site and reaching more people.

HOW LONG DID IT TAKE YOU TO REACH 100% DIGITAL FREEDOM?

When we started our business, we expected that it would take three to five years for it to enable us to quit our jobs. We based that prediction on stories we'd read about other people and their online businesses. In reality, it took just under four years. Our website went live in May 2009, and by February 2013 my husband and I had both quit our day jobs and were living from the website.

The transition from day job to online business was gradual. We earned our freedom bit by bit. First I went part time at work, and then about six months later I left to have a baby and didn't return to my day job after my maternity leave. During my maternity leave my husband went part time, and then a year later he quit his job. Going part time on our day jobs gave us the extra time and energy to accelerate the growth of our business.

WHAT WAS YOUR BIGGEST MISTAKE?

One mistake we made was to spend a lot of time and money on conversion rate optimization that in retrospect could have been better spent on developing new products and areas of our business.

Conversion rate optimization is so tempting because you think, "If I can just increase my conversion rate 10%, then I could make so many thousands more dollars each year." The trouble is that in the time you spend optimizing your conversion rate by 10%, maybe you could have developed a new product line that would grow your business by 20%.

I think that conversion rate optimization is worthwhile up to a point. It's important to understand how visitors interact with your site and whether there are simple improvements you can make to encourage sales, but there are diminishing returns beyond a certain point. I think you also have to consider the whole user experience and some of the current strategies to increase sales conversions (e.g. intrusive pop-ups) that might be detrimental to your business in the longer term as they are quite annoying to the user.

WHAT IS THE SINGLE MOST EFFECTIVE TACTIC YOU DISCOVERED?

Content marketing. We write free content that's genuinely useful to our visitors, and that attracts people to our website without us spending any money on advertising. Sometimes we spend a week or more writing a really great article, which is a huge investment of energy, but then we reap the benefits of that effort with visitors coming to read that article for years afterwards, and some of those visitors earn us money through advertising or product purchases.

The trick with content marketing is understanding that the value of information is governed by the laws of supply and demand, just like anything else. So, for your content to be perceived as valuable, you need to write about topics that (a) a lot of people are searching for and (b) there isn't already great content about. If there's already a lot written about a particular topic that you want to write about, then you need to either pick a subset of people to market to (e.g., "girls hair styling tips for dads with daughters" instead of just "girls hair styling tips"), or find a new spin on the topic.

WHAT ADVICE WOULD YOU GIVE SOMEONE WANTING TO ACHIEVE SIMILAR SUCCESS?

For the first several years of our business, I believed that there was "one true way" to succeed online, using the particular content marketing strategy that we used. But I've come to realize that there are many ways to succeed, and many tactics that work. So, I'd encourage budding entrepreneurs to think about they own particular strengths and interests, and build a business that plays to their strengths.

Some people hate social media, and some people love it. Some people like working alone, some people love working with others. Some people thrive on analytical challenges, some people like to wing it and run with their intuition. There are ways of running businesses that fit any of these styles.

When you're first starting out, it's hard to know what to do, so my advice is to find someone who's running a successful business and whose working style matches your own, and then see what you can learn from them. If they offer a course, then buy it and learn from it.

Personally, I'm very comfortable with analytical thinking, and the training I took (a business building program called "Site Build It") played to that strength, because it offers a very methodical approach to planning and building a business.

So, how do you find an approach that suits you? I'd recommend subscribing to some web business newsletters, blogs, and podcasts, and see what appeals to you. Spend three months or so listening and reading. After that, pick one particular course or system, and just do it. Don't get stuck in analysis paralysis trying to pick what business idea to go with, or what system to follow, or which guru's course to purchase. Just pick one and go with it. Most of your learning will come from doing, rather than reading or listening. Just get started and adjust course as you learn and grow.

LEARN MORE ABOUT STEPHANIE'S BUSINESS:

See my website at Homemade-Gifts-Made-Easy.com and read my story at Homemade-Gifts-Made-Easy.com/About-Me.html

BRITT MALKA OF GETMONEYMAKINGIDEAS.COM

HOW DID YOU COME UP WITH THE IDEA FOR YOUR BUSINESS?

Back in 1995, I was bored at work and woke up one Monday morning wishing it was Friday. I decided that I would not waste my life waiting for time to pass, so I quit my job.

My first business idea was to do bookkeeping for small companies, but I also wanted to teach adults how to use computers, so I didn't do bookkeeping for long. The teaching led to writing tutorials, which again led to writing books for Danish publishing houses. After that, writing became my business, and that's where I am today.

WHAT WAS YOUR FIRST MAJOR BREAKTHROUGH?

One of my first teaching assignments led to writing a tutorial for me and another teacher to use. That was what got me started writing nonfiction books, even though my dream had always been to write fiction.

HOW LONG DID IT TAKE YOU TO REACH 100% DIGITAL FREEDOM?

I quit my job first, which made it necessary to make enough money, so that's what I did. When I moved to France in 2000, I had to earn my living full time online, because it was hard, even for the French people, to get a job, so I didn't even want to try.

WHAT WAS YOUR BIGGEST MISTAKE?

Whenever I didn't trust my intuition and did something against my gut feeling, I lost money. After a few of those incidents, I learned to trust my intuition, so even if a deal looked good, but I had a bad feeling about it, I didn't accept it.

WHAT IS THE SINGLE MOST EFFECTIVE TACTIC YOU DISCOVERED?

If you have a security net, you'll often fall back on it and not work enough on your business. So get out there, go all-in, and put all your efforts into your business.

WHAT ADVICE WOULD YOU GIVE SOMEONE WANTING TO ACHIEVE SIMILAR SUCCESS?

If you want something to happen, only you can make it happen. Don't wait, until the stars are aligned, the children have moved out, or for other ideal conditions. Make it happen now.

Failure wasn't an option for me. I had no job or other support to rely on. I had to make it. I've seen the same thing happen for a friend. He "tried" to make money online for ten years, while he had a job. The moment he got laid off, he had to succeed, and guess what happened? Today he can support himself, his wife and kids, with the money he makes online.

LEARN MORE ABOUT BRITT'S BUSINESS:

If you're interested in writing fiction or nonfiction, you can sign up for my emails on WriterByChoice.com

If Internet marketing is your stuff, then join my list at GetMoneyMakingIdeas.com

I aim to entertain with my emails, so give them a try.

MATT MCWILLIAMS OF MATTMCWILLIAMS.COM

HOW DID YOU COME UP WITH THE IDEA FOR YOUR BUSINESS?

The idea for my business was born in January 2004 when I started in affiliate management.

I had started a business with a couple of friends of mine, and we sold leads to insurance agents. One day I heard about these people called affiliates. This was attractive to me because in the previous few months we had spent half of our $10,000 seed money. It was all the money we had: we were either going to succeed or fail with this $10,000. We spend half of that on banner ads. Now don't laugh! This was late 2003, early 2004. We didn't know any better, and that $5,000 returned exactly zero.

We didn't have a lot of money left, we had to hire a developer, and quite frankly we were looking for a way to make money without paying anyone, at least initially. Then we discovered this thing called affiliates. The great thing about affiliates is that you pay them after you make the money, whereas the banner ads were paid up front. Same with Facebook ads, same with most anything—with most marketing you're paying before you make money. Affiliates were super attractive to us.

We started this journey that I've been on the last 13+ years, of finding affiliates, managing them, motivating them, and getting them really excited to promote our product. At first it was leads for insurance agents. Today I'm excited to work with great entrepreneurs such as Mike Hyatt, Ray Edwards, Ziglar, the list goes on and on. I'm super excited to work with those people, but it all started with that necessity of meeting affiliates for our business.

WHAT WAS YOUR FIRST MAJOR BREAKTHROUGH?

I think I'm on that path. I don't know that I've ever really had this monumental breakthrough, other than the time I heard about affiliates in early 2004. But one of the moments that stands out for me was I went through a period from 2011 to 2015 where I was running affiliate programs for people, companies like Shutterfly, Adidas, Reebok—big brands. But I was also doing online platform building, and I didn't really know how to "marry" the two. Quite truthfully I was unhappy. I was doing this blog about personal growth and productivity, and I was just not happy while trying to figure out what I'm doing, making all this money working with these clients.

The breakthrough was when Jeff Goins interviewed me for his book, *The Art of Work*. It was about to come out, and about six weeks before his launch, he emailed me. When we spoke he basically said, "Hey, you run affiliate programs, right? Would you like to do it for this book?"

I thought about it. I'd never done anything that small before, but that was kind of the introduction that opened my eyes, and it also opened me up to a new audience, working with people I like: "my people," so to speak. Ray Edwards, Michael Hyatt, Jeff Goins, those are my people, these are the people I work with, and that was a big breakthrough for me.

HOW LONG DID IT TAKE YOU TO REACH 100% DIGITAL FREEDOM?

I'm a born entrepreneur. I started my first company in 2001; I was 22 at the time. In the 15-16 years since I've had exactly one job. It lasted about 18 months. I was very fortunate, I was able to leave that on my own terms, which is the first time that had ever happened. Prior to that, the first four jobs I ever had I was fired from. It didn't take me long to get to 100% because I just kind of decided to do it.

I think the question is flawed: "How long did it take to earn enough money to quit my job?" I don't know that's necessarily what needs to happen. Were I employed by somebody today in the situation I'm in with a wife and two kids, yes, that would certainly change things. But I think if you believe in what you're doing, and you know that you can make enough money to survive, then make the leap, because otherwise you're probably going to be thinking about it and dreaming about it for the next five years and not making that move. That's close to being a wasted five years, in my book.

WHAT WAS YOUR BIGGEST MISTAKE?

Definitely the biggest mistake we made happened in early 2008. The company I mentioned earlier that kind of got me into affiliate stuff was growing rapidly. We had 52 employees, a big office, and we were doing about $18 million a year in revenue. The year before, we actually had an offer to sell for quite a bit of money. I would instantly have been close to a deca-millionaire. We turned them down, kind of laughed at their offer: "Well, if you're going to offer us that much money we're bigger than we thought! What are you talking about? We're not selling. We're big and we're growing, we're coming for you! We're going to be buying *you* in five years!"

In early 2008, despite making close to $18 million that year, despite the growth, we didn't have a lot of cash on hand. We really didn't even have probably a three-week emergency fund. We probably had about two to three weeks of cash on hand. We wanted to buy another company. This was a game-changing thing, this was a game-changing move, an industry-changing move, quite frankly, but we didn't have the money. It was about a $1.25, $1.3 million buy, and we had about $4 million.

So we said let's borrow the money, let's work out a deal with them, we worked out a deal, and then 2008 hit, you know, the economic collapse.

Long story short is, from 2007 to 2011 we went from a company that had offers well into the tens of millions of dollars to buy us, to a company that sold for debt. The lesson I learned is that you cannot borrow money and be successful in business. It does happen from time to time, and there are certainly exceptions to the rule, but it is really challenging. We introduced an element that we had never had in our business before, and that was massive amounts of risk. We introduced an element of owing somebody something. We introduced an element of, "if we have a bad month we're out of business. If we have a bad month, we have to lay off people"—not, "If we have a bad month, no big deal, we'll get through this." It completely changed the game, and I would never, ever do that again.

WHAT IS THE SINGLE MOST EFFECTIVE TACTIC YOU DISCOVERED?

For me it's working with affiliates. You're very limited when you're relying on an ad network such as Facebook or Google—the pie is very limited in the number of people who are looking for your product or service on a daily basis. It may be big, but it's limited in terms of whether they're out there really looking. You can only target so many people on Facebook before you are casting too wide of a net.

The great thing about affiliates is you're introducing your product or services to new potential customers, to new audiences. I love that, especially when you're starting out, because you don't have millions (or hundreds) of dollars to throw around on ads that might not make you any money. When you work with affiliates, you don't have to pay until after a sale is made. So if that affiliate turns out to be a dud and doesn't make you a dime, no big deal: it didn't cost you anything.

If that Facebook ad turns out to be a dud and you spent $374 and made zero dollars, that's a problem, especially for people starting out.

I believe that working with affiliates is the key. Here's the thing: not only are small businesses, solopreneurs, small companies, companies making less than $100,000 a year working with affiliates; so are the top companies in the online space: Jeff Walker, Michael Hyatt, Ziglar, Ray Edwards, Jeff Goins, Russel Brunson, they're all working with affiliates. And if you want to go to the next level, so are Walmart, Reebok, Adidas, Target—they're all working with affiliates. If everyone all over the spectrum is working with affiliates, why wouldn't you? It makes sense.

WHAT ADVICE WOULD YOU GIVE SOMEONE WANTING TO ACHIEVE SIMILAR SUCCESS?

I always recommend two things very early on, especially if you're building an online platform:

- Start promoting affiliate stuff right away. It's a great way to get some income in without creating your own product. It's a great way to learn what your audience wants. For example, you promote product A and product B, and you sell more of product A than B, that tells you something about your audience over time. I know that's a small example, but over time you begin to learn what your audience is interested in and what they're not interested in, all from those affiliate promotions.

- I recommend bringing on affiliates to promote your stuff. Early on you're going to work with small affiliates. You're not going to be working with the big names unless they happen to be close, personal friends. You're going to be working with small ones early on. That's how you build up over time.

LEARN MORE ABOUT MATT'S BUSINESS:

Go to MattMcWilliams.com. I've got tons of free resources there. If you want to learn how to run an affiliate program and work with affiliates, find them, recruit them, manage them, motivate them and get them making you a lot of money, I can help. Or if you're looking for how to make money as an affiliate, especially if you're starting out and looking to make that first thousand, two thousand online, I've got tons of free resources on my website at MattMcWilliams.com.

DAVID PERDEW OF MYNAMS.COM

HOW DID YOU COME UP WITH THE IDEA FOR YOUR BUSINESS?

I've had several businesses in my life, some successful and some not. But I've always been an entrepreneur at heart, even when I was working in the corporate world.

In 2003 I took a year off from my consulting business with one of the largest corporations in the world to build a house on 100 acres of land in North Alabama. It was a log house and it had always been a dream of mine to build it using my own two hands. From a hole in the ground to finishing the roof, over that year long period I had a lot of time to think as well. And because I worked in technology as a consultant, I understood the way the world was moving with digital technology and the Internet business world. So, I really wanted to participate from a business perspective.

What I brought to the consulting business was powerful belief in solving problems. Any business that I created online would need to solve specific problems as well. And of course, we know that good businesses—all good businesses—solve problems. Otherwise, there's no business there.

But I knew nothing at that time about doing business online. So I found the best online business training program that I could, and it did happen to be produced by Corey Rudl. He was the godfather of Internet marketing until his death in an auto racing accident in 2005.

I studied that course at night while building my house during the day to understand niche marketing, and that meant understanding desperate problems with simple solutions. Since I was in the consulting world and the newspaper business for 25 years prior to building my house, I realized I could use my content creation skills with my business training skills to create a solid business. And that's always been my focus.

WHAT WAS YOUR FIRST MAJOR BREAKTHROUGH?

The most important thing I ever did was get honest about my skill level.

In the beginning, I was at the beginning. But I wanted to use my writing skills to create my first business. So, I decided I would write a book about parenting, *Bad Dad: 10 Keys to Regaining Trust*. It was about building relationships with your kids after you have pretty much destroyed those relationships. It sounds like I was creating a niche book, but in reality, I was creating my first training program for business owners.

I had no list, no product, no following, and no idea how to accomplish any of this, but I thought I could not be alone with my dream of building an online business from my experience. I ran an ad in *Writer's Digest* for $600 saying I was a former newspaper editor who was going to create an ebook and a business around that ebook but I was starting from scratch and with little knowledge. If that described them too, they could follow me and my progress if they opted into my autoresponder system to watch me succeed or make the mistakes. Before the ad, I had zero people on my list. Within a week, I had 750 people following me through my year-long process of building this business.

My first training business was called The 60 Day Experiment. It has since been retired but the result of the book is still available at Bad-Dad.com. The proof was in the process of learning, doing, and telling other people about it. Basically, my business model has always been, "If you look over my shoulder, I'll show you how to do something, and how not to do it." And it still works for me today.

HOW LONG DID IT TAKE YOU TO REACH 100% DIGITAL FREEDOM?

Within five years of doing niche marketing and affiliate marketing, while consulting full-time and maintaining three offices in Atlanta, Dallas and Seattle, I finally quit my job to stop traveling and focus 100% on my business. And I gave up nearly $250,000 in annual contracts. I was not making nearly that much money at the time in my business, but I was doing well enough that I was committed to working in my own business at home versus traveling all the time. Before quitting the consulting work though, I had started the NAMS Workshop and the MyNAMS membership site, and was consistently working to maintain those during the evening hours and while at airports.

Entrepreneurship is not for the faint of heart.

WHAT WAS YOUR BIGGEST MISTAKE?

I think failure is an ugly negative word for awesome opportunities to learn positive steps in negative situations. I like to say that I have never had a problem in my life. Every problem I've ever had was the stepping stone to the next big win. Too many people see a challenge, and quit. That's the only failure that anyone can make that counts because it's permanent.

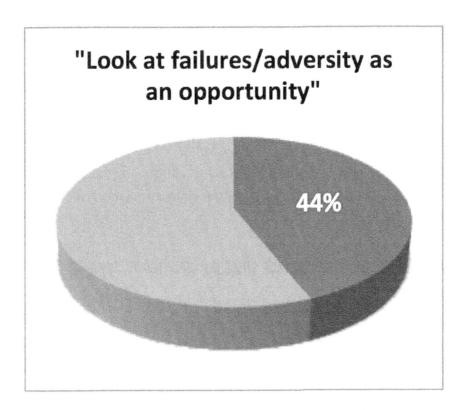

"Look at failures/adversity as an opportunity"

44%

For example, during one of our workshops, our website was hacked and taken over by a Jordanian criminal. At first, I was desperate and scared. But once we stopped the bleeding, I saw my mistake in that whole mess was I was not running a secure enough website. The lesson from that mistake (and it cost us about $75,000), was to create a much more secure operation. I enlisted the help of some very smart people, another big lesson.

Was it a failure? By financial standards, yes. Was it embarrassing? Absolutely. The result, though, has been much greater than the $75,000 I lost during that episode because I don't make the same mistake twice (if I can help it).

WHAT IS THE SINGLE MOST EFFECTIVE TACTIC YOU DISCOVERED?

You can't run a business successfully without two things:

» Dumping everything that doesn't work, and dumping it quickly. That's the only way you can get clear on success paths, without cluttering up your life with distractions.

» Mastering sales funnels that convert. You can get all the traffic in the world, but if your sales funnel doesn't convert, its wasted money.

WHAT ADVICE WOULD YOU GIVE SOMEONE WANTING TO ACHIEVE SIMILAR SUCCESS?

Don't handcuff your success by limiting the investment you put into your business, health, relationships, money, and your spiritual well-being. I spent $22,000 on $27 products before I made a nickel online. I thought I could get the answers and the skills that I needed without investing in real solutions. That was a huge mistake. I needed a coach and mentor to guide me along the way, and when I discovered that, I never looked back. I've had a coach every day since 2007.

LEARN MORE ABOUT DAVID'S BUSINESS:

The best way to connect with me is to come to our blog at MyNAMS.com and subscribe to our email list. It's not the usual fare that you find on other business sites. And from there, you can learn how to take advantage of our free training, as well as many of our free groups and downloadable checklists.

To learn more about me on Facebook, go to Nams.ws/fb.

CONNIE RAGEN GREEN OF HUGEPROFITSTINYLIST.COM

HOW DID YOU COME UP WITH THE IDEA FOR YOUR BUSINESS?

I was looking for a business I could run from home and found out about online marketing. It seemed like the perfect way to change my life at the time. I was working six or seven days a week as a classroom teacher and also as a real estate broker and residential appraiser. After 20 years of that and also having some serious health issues, I was ready for a change. I didn't have a clue what the business would look like, but I embraced the concept and got to work learning and implementing every single day. I started with niche sites and affiliate marketing, then moved into the ebook writing and marketing space. Within two years I was known as an online marketer.

WHAT WAS YOUR FIRST MAJOR BREAKTHROUGH?

I wrote an ebook on real estate farming, which was a topic I had lots of experience with. It began to sell and that gave me confidence. Then I sold an affiliate product by writing articles and blog posts about the topic of dog training, and I was ready to conquer the world of online marketing. If I hadn't taken these early steps, I never could have moved forward with my entrepreneurial dreams.

HOW LONG DID IT TAKE YOU TO REACH 100% DIGITAL FREEDOM?

I had already quit working when I came online and was living on my savings. I replaced the income I had earned as a teacher and in real estate within about 18 months of coming online. It wasn't easy, but I learned the importance of perseverance, discipline, persistence, and goal setting in my life.

WHAT WAS YOUR BIGGEST MISTAKE?

During my first year online I paid a big name marketer $5,000 to teach me how to build a profitable online business. As soon as my check cleared the bank he forgot my name and was slow to respond. But I tried to make the best of it and learned what I could. He's still around, but almost no one mentions his name any longer, so I know I wasn't alone in this experience. I would have to say my next biggest mistake was to not attend live events sooner. I would have been able to grow my business so much more quickly if I had borrowed the money to go to those events from the very beginning. When I finally did this, everything changed for me almost overnight.

WHAT IS THE SINGLE MOST EFFECTIVE TACTIC YOU DISCOVERED?

I would have to say it was affiliate marketing at first. I had no products or courses of my own, so this was definitely an "earn while you learn" approach to making money online. I was able to watch how experienced marketers and entrepreneurs ran their businesses, and this was an education in itself. There was no way for me to create as many products and courses as I would have needed, so having an almost unlimited inventory from other respected and experienced marketers was perfect for my business. I also built some relationships I still value to this day.

WHAT ADVICE WOULD YOU GIVE SOMEONE WANTING TO ACHIEVE SIMILAR SUCCESS?

Make the decision to become a successful online entrepreneur, learn as much as possible about the business model you want to begin with, and then spend time every single day in implementing what you have learned. Once you take action you will have completely different questions, so get to that point as quickly as possible. Also, do something every day that takes you out of your comfort zone. For me that was writing and public speaking. This business is definitely a worthwhile endeavor, so do the work and make it happen.

LEARN MORE ABOUT CONNIE'S BUSINESS:

Visit my main site at HugeProfitsTinyList.com to become a part of my community. Hit "reply" to any of my email messages and I will respond to you personally.

Also, take a look at my books on online entrepreneurship at ConnieRagenGreenBooks.com.

And you may want to connect with me on Twitter @ConnieGreen: Twitter.com/ConnieGreen

YARO STARAK OF ENTREPRENEURS-JOURNEY.COM

HOW DID YOU COME UP WITH THE IDEA FOR YOUR BUSINESS?

My main business is teaching people the art and science of making a living from two essential tools: a blog, and an email list. I focus on teaching people who are knowledge experts: people who have something to share and who want to help other people, whether it's losing weight or trading stocks or traveling around the world on a budget or fixing a bad back. Whatever a person is good at, I help them translate that knowledge into an online audience through blogging and then sell digital products like ebooks, membership sites, and online courses using the power of email marketing along with the blog.

When I started my business, it wasn't intended to be a business. I wish I could say I had this idea that I was going to be a professional blogger and I'd make money selling my own courses and my own products. But the fact is, the first half of my career actually had nothing to do with blogging whatsoever. I was an online entrepreneur. I had an online editing business focusing on university students and I was connecting them with editors who were helping with their essays and their thesis documents at university. And that was my main bread and butter income for a number of years.

I also had a little e-commerce store selling Magic the Gathering collectible cards, and I had another site, a content site making money from advertising. I had a few failures along the way, like an English school and some other websites, but basically from the years 1998 to 2005 those were my business projects and those were how I made money.

In 2005 I started a blog, Entrepreneurs Journey, where I was going to enjoy the process of being an entrepreneur and writing about it. So I actually started my blog not intending for it to be a business. I thought it could make some money because I was very much aware that blogs could make a bit of money from advertising. But it wasn't like today where people set out to become a known blogger and there's a clear pathway and a clear format and a clear process like I teach today. For me it was just a case of let's blog—let's write shares and ideas. I was 25 years old; I didn't have a lot of confidence as an entrepreneur. I was making a living from it but I certainly didn't see myself becoming a leader and a person who would do an interview like this for example way back then. But as a result of starting a blog, it actually grew and became my full time income. My biggest earning business, my blogging business, came about because I simply wanted to share stories from being an entrepreneur and blogging was new, it was exciting. I was discovering the fact that I enjoyed writing so I was going to just see what happened and blog and eventually podcast as well about this subject. It became a real business in about 2007.

WHAT WAS YOUR FIRST MAJOR BREAKTHROUGH?

My first major breakthrough was actually my editing company because it became a full time income at its peak. It made over $100,000 a year and I deliberately built to runs without me. This was before Tim Ferriss popularized the four hour work week. It was in the era where the most popular book was *The E-Myth* and it talked about how you could create a business that you didn't operate inside of; you sort of ran it from above. That was my goal with my editing business, to set it up so that other people would run it. It took a few years to get there but eventually I did. Around 2003 was the first year where I made a full time income, and around about that time I also hired my first assistant to take over the e-mail and the customer service. Today I teach a short course called Services

Arbitrage," which is the business model that I used in that editing company. For me it was the real statement that I could call myself an entrepreneur because I was living on money I made from a business and the business was running without me. I built it from scratch. I built the website myself and it was fantastic.

The other major breakthrough was I did my first ever online course launch, much later in 2007 after I'd been blogging for a while and I'd grown my email list and I had an audience. It wasn't huge—I had maybe three thousand subscribers—but I launched this course and it was the first time I ever sold anything that I personally created. And it was a very scary thing to do but I was rewarded and you know I did a proper launch and I had 400 paying members. It was sort of structured as a membership site the first time I launched it and that was the first time I made over $100,000 in one year from my blogging business.

I bought my freedom and freedom was the most important thing. So to be able to do that twice with two different businesses and very different types of businesses was very exciting.

HOW LONG DID IT TAKE YOU TO REACH 100% DIGITAL FREEDOM?

There were two times where I experienced this. The first time was my editing company. I didn't actually go full time until 2002 into the business because I was still studying at university. I probably quit my job around 2004 and that was the point where I no longer needed the money and I felt like my business was consistent enough. So to be fair I would say it took four years, but probably two years of full time focus to get to what I considered a safe full time income. It was the same story with my blog. I pretty much spent the first year building my audience and making a little bit of money from advertising. And in my second year I started growing my email list, and then the third year, 2007, was when I launched the course and took in over six figures.

WHAT WAS YOUR BIGGEST MISTAKE?

It was an English school I actually started at the same time as I was running my editing company. The reason was quite bizarre. I went on a business grant provided by the Australian government designed to support people like me, entrepreneurs who are trying to get their own small business up and running. I was concerned because my editing business had seasonal downturns, in particular summer in Australia, which is where most of my customer base was at the time. So I actually started doing some private English tutoring, just me like a freelancer basically. I was charging $15 an hour sitting down with kids in Brisbane and doing one on one tutoring. I didn't want to do it but I felt that I needed to do it. Typical entrepreneur, I saw a gap in the marketplace that these kids want tutoring, but what they really want is a one on one conversation with a local Australian because that's a real experience for them. So I thought I was going to invest and create a full blown English tutoring service connecting Australian teachers with the students and I signed a three year lease on an English school, basically an office on the third floor of a building very close to Brisbane. I set up my school, I bought some furniture, some computers, paid like $500 for a sign to put up in front of the English school, hired a couple of my friends who are English teachers who were recently back from teaching in Japan.

I went all in and I hated it. It was crazy because I sat there in this English school from 10 a.m. to 5 p.m. because I needed to be at the office in case someone walked up the stairs and in the door to purchase or inquire about tutoring and it almost never happened because no one knew about my business. Meanwhile I was running this successful editing company online so I was basically throwing

$1,100 a month in rent down the drain for an English school that was not really going anywhere. It was a cash burner, and I had created a job. I wanted to have freedom and instead I created something where I had to go somewhere every day. Completely the opposite of the laptop lifestyle that I was looking for and today live.

So it was a pretty much a failed experiment and after 10 months I got out of my lease. I had to pay them in advance to break it. Yeah, big mistake, a year long mistake, cost me a lot of money—pretty much all the profits of my editing business. The biggest lesson there is don't start a second business when you've got one that's successful.

WHAT IS THE SINGLE MOST EFFECTIVE TACTIC YOU DISCOVERED?

Blogging, maybe blogging and podcasting, but blogging by far is the single greatest source of audience building, of trust building, of new customer acquisition and of lead generation. It has absolutely changed my life. It's the first business that I've made over a million dollars with; in fact we're almost at 2 million dollars in sales. It's allowed me to support my family, travel the world, buy investment properties, and live anywhere in the world, and it's all come from me spending the time to produce valuable content on a blog and as a result be rewarded with searches and traffic. It's social traffic but mostly long term, ongoing search traffic, because I spent years growing a quality blog and that's what I teach people to do today. And most of my successful graduates, the coaching clients I've had, have gone on to make millions themselves. Their basis for their success is the content they put in their blog that it's always been the starting point. It's not necessarily the quickest path but they build real authority through successful blogging and that's rewarded with traffic, free traffic from Google, and free traffic from sharing their articles. That leads to anything from book deals, to product sales, to speaking on stage. Anything you can think of it can come from that success you get from building your brand, but most importantly it's a great way to grow a business.

WHAT ADVICE WOULD YOU GIVE SOMEONE WANTING TO ACHIEVE SIMILAR SUCCESS?

It's important to leverage your strength. I evolved to discover that writing is my strength and it's the thing I do the most today, It's the basis for my most profitable business. I write and I teach and even my teaching is basically writing or speaking. So you don't want to go and try and force yourself to develop a skill set based on a weakness. Develop a skill set based on a strength. Whether you have a genetic gift or you've acquired a skill through years of practice, there should be something in your business that you can leverage and develop into what I would call super power, or some people call it your zone of genius. It's the thing you are already good at that you could become great at, simply by making it the center point to your business.

So if you're great on YouTube and talking, that's where you should spend your time. If you're great at writing, then write books and blogs. If you're great at interviews and talking, do podcasting. If you don't want to do any of that sort of stuff, if you just want to innovate and create amazing products, focus on product creation and do e-commerce. If you love software and or mobile apps, go there, but make sure you're tapping into something that's a strength of yours. To me it's the most important thing because I've seen people do really well in business and the fundamentals are always the same—there's some great product or service with great marketing, and it's some person behind it who has actually done something long enough to get really good at it. It's usually based on something they love, and because they love it was something that they are naturally good at or have built into something good. It was never a weakness—that's the point– it was never something they forced themselves to do, because it's very hard to spend the next 10 years of your life building a business around something you hate. I'd hate to think anyone does that. I think maybe some people have but the best success stories I know are people loving what they do. That's why we grow businesses or do something we really enjoy.

Outside of that I think it's important to learn the fundamentals. There's no need to come up with something new when it comes to marketing. The education is there. I do what everyone else does and I teach it to people too: how to get traffic, how to narrow in on your niche, how to set up the technology you need. All these basic fundamentals that we all have to do as online entrepreneurs, that's a system that's already in place that we can all learn. There's no need to reinvent the wheel. You just have to get yourself educated and put it into place. The real magic sauce is what you uniquely bring to the table so that's what you do. You don't want to get caught up with the problems that have already been solved; that's where you can just buy solutions. Buy education, hire a coach, get someone to install the technology for you while you focus on that zone of genius that I was talking about earlier.

LEARN MORE ABOUT YARO'S BUSINESS:

My number one resource for anyone who wants to get started on turning your knowledge into digital products and services that you sell through the power of blogging and email marketing is my free report. You can get it at BlogProfitsBlueprint.com It's been downloaded over 150,000 times and it's responsible for the starting point for many bloggers whom you might know today. If you want to know how blogs work to get traffic, how that can be used to sell products and services, and how I personally use that, I've got plenty of case studies of some of my graduates using blogs in all kinds of really interesting ways: like skiing and fat loss and now independent book publishing, teaching women business, treating acne. It has all kinds of great examples you can follow and see it working for all kinds of different topics and different experts.

MARK VAN STRATUM, AUTHOR

www.amazon.com/Mark-Van-Stratum/e/B06XXYN8T2/

HOW DID YOU COME UP WITH THE IDEA FOR YOUR BUSINESS?

Affiliate marketing means that you're promoting products of other companies online that pay a commission for each sale or new member you bring them. What I like about the business is that there are low startup costs and you don't necessarily need your own product or brand. All you need is to be a good and creative marketer and you can start your business.

I met a guy who explained to me about affiliate marketing. He told me how the business worked and I realized it was a combination of being persuasive, creative, and having the nerve to take risks. This suited my personality and experiences in my previous jobs as a cartoonist and dating coach, so I decided to give it a chance and make the switch.

After being in the business for seven years, I have created global marketing campaigns for companies like Groupon and Amazon, but also lesser known companies. Now I have a team of people working with me. This is what gives me the most joy, being able to work with great people and help them develop.

WHAT WAS YOUR FIRST MAJOR BREAKTHROUGH?

In the beginning I started by promoting companies in the United States. I'm from the Netherlands myself, but in those days there weren't many affiliate marketers in my country. I struggled for months coming up with better marketing campaigns than my competitors, but the competition was very tough.

After struggling for a very long time, Groupon launched in the Netherlands, and that was my chance. There weren't many affiliates in the Netherlands so that gave me an advantage. Advertising in the Netherlands was still relatively cheap, and I could use the same ads I already developed in the U.S. And simply translate them to Dutch. It was an instant success. People in the Netherlands had never seen these type of advertisements, whereas in the U.S. they were already bombarded with them.

Luck = when opportunity meets preparation. I had already prepared myself. Then when the opportunity was there I was ready to take it. After my success in the Netherlands I expanded to bigger markets like Germany and France. Within six months my operation was worldwide and I became one of Groupon's highest earning affiliates.

After this it wasn't smooth sailing. Every new campaign is a new challenge. But I did have money in the bank and created a nice buffer for myself while I worked on coming up with new marketing angles for new products.

HOW LONG DID IT TAKE YOU TO REACH 100% DIGITAL FREEDOM?

This is very difficult question to answer. After about four months I was able to live off of it, but after this it was still a constant struggle keeping my head above water. It really took me a year to feel secure, and even then there always is the constant pressure. You're always a few bad decisions away from being broke. I'm lucky that I realized that in the beginning. So no matter how much money I was making, I wouldn't spend any of it because I never knew when I would need it. Nothing is worse then realizing you wouldn't have financial problems today if you wouldn't have bought that expensive car a year ago.

WHAT WAS YOUR BIGGEST MISTAKE?

There are too many to mention, actually. I think the biggest one was partnering up with the wrong person. I tried to include an old high school friend in the business because I wanted to help him and it always was my dream to have a business with a high school friend. However, he never put in the same effort as me and was slowing me down a lot. It cost me an insane amount of money, efforts, but worse of all... time! Nothing is more valuable than time. Now I'm a lot more careful who and what I spend my time on. This is a lesson I needed to learn though. It's all part of growing as a person.

The only way to learn is by making mistakes. So of course its smarter to observe other people's mistakes and try not to make the same ones. But in my experience it's better to make the mistake first, feel the mistake, and then learn how others solved this. Then make sure you won't make the same mistake again.

WHAT IS THE SINGLE MOST EFFECTIVE TACTIC YOU DISCOVERED?

First of all, I found the right mentor. Someone who had been in the business for long and was willing to share his knowledge with me, for a price.

Don't reinvent the wheel. you can spend a year testing new angles, waste lots of time and money. Or you can see how other people are doing it successfully, copy their tactics, and improve on that. After this I usually find an even better way of doing the same. But my starting point was where they ended. you can cut lots of corners like that.

Read as many books as you can. Learn as much as you can. I read books constantly. Whether its about marketing, entrepreneurs life-stories, or something unrelated as the evolution of farm animals, I'll take all the knowledge I can get.

Besides that it's perseverance. Just don't give up, no matter what.

WHAT ADVICE WOULD YOU GIVE SOMEONE WANTING TO ACHIEVE SIMILAR SUCCESS?

Get the right mentor. Work on your social skills. You need other people to become successful, and if you learn how to treat people with respect you have a great edge over others.

Let go of your ego. You're not trying to prove how good you are. You're not trying to get rich so you can show off your wealth. You're developing yourself as a person. If you become a more valuable person, you'll start making more money. You won't become a more valuable person by having a huge ego. Not one that I would want to be around anyway.

LEARN MORE ABOUT MARK'S BUSINESS:

Buy my book: "*Drug of Choice—The Inspiring True Story Of The One-Armed Criminal Who Mastered Love And Made Millions*" on Amazon: Amazon.com/dp/B06X9C6MJ6

JOHANNES VOELKNER OF NOMADCRUISE.COM

HOW DID YOU COME UP WITH THE IDEA FOR YOUR BUSINESS?

It was a complete coincidence. I discovered cheap travel for a cruise and simply asked, "Who else wants to join?" in a Digital Nomad Facebook group that I started a while ago. People loved the idea of crossing the Atlantic Ocean on a cruise ship together with other digital nomads, and over 100 people booked the trip within three weeks. Only when I saw the high demand, I explored the idea of really turning it into a business and Nomad Cruise was born.

WHAT WAS YOUR FIRST MAJOR BREAKTHROUGH?

In my very early beginnings I stumbled across AdWords. This was in 2008 when many clicks were still super cheap. With a little bit of experimentation I figured out how to use it to my advantage and promote products there. This allowed me to build up my passive income very quickly and so I had a lot more time focus more on passion projects.

HOW LONG DID IT TAKE YOU TO REACH 100% DIGITAL FREEDOM?

It took me less than two months. I was living in South Africa and working in tourism when I started. Since I had no clue about what type of work I could do online, I started as a virtual assistant doing basic administrative tasks and email support. My clients came from Switzerland and Germany, so I was able to charge a lot higher rates than in South Africa. After about two months I was able to quit my job and double my income thanks to geo arbitrage.

WHAT WAS YOUR BIGGEST MISTAKE?

I once started a small co-working space in Tarifa, Spain. Not that there is anything wrong with co-working spaces, but I simply realized that this is not the type of business I want to have because it tied me too much to one location. Eventually, when the Nomad Cruise took off, I decided very quickly to quit the co-working project but lost a lot of money along the way.

WHAT IS THE SINGLE MOST EFFECTIVE TACTIC YOU DISCOVERED?

There is no single tactic for me. Some things might work now but that doesn't mean they will still be working in a year. I think the most important thing for me is to take things step by step and then reevaluate. Most things and plans don't really turn out the way you want them, but if you take small steps and adjust your path you will reach your goal eventually.

WHAT ADVICE WOULD YOU GIVE SOMEONE WANTING TO ACHIEVE SIMILAR SUCCESS?

Take things step by step. Most people underestimate the amount of work it takes to become successful with something and will give up eventually. If you celebrate small achievements, take it step by step but still keep your big goal in mind, you're most likely to succeed.

LEARN MORE ABOUT JOHANNES'S BUSINESS:

My main project is Nomad Cruise. If you want to meet an incredible number of amazing people from all around the world while crossing the Atlantic on a cruise ship, you should definitely join us one day! Check out our trips and the video on NomadCruise.com

STUART WALKER OF NICHEHACKS.COM

HOW DID YOU COME UP WITH THE IDEA FOR YOUR BUSINESS?

My business is NicheHacks.com and I came up with it after deciding I wanted to move into the online marketing niche from other areas I was working in.

I knew I had to come up with something original that other people weren't covering. So I broke down the different areas of online marketing: e.g., niche research, traffic, SEO, content, blogging, etc., and analyzed which ones had the most potential. I saw that practically no one was focusing on showing people how to find profitable niches—let alone actually revealing profitable niches. So I went ahead and did just that. I talk more about the story here: NicheHacks.com/About-Me/

WHAT WAS YOUR FIRST MAJOR BREAKTHROUGH?

Still focusing on NicheHacks, the first breakthroughs were being linked to by major blogs in the niche and shared by authorities on social media talking about how good the content was, and making some initial early sales. It shows what we were doing was working.

HOW LONG DID IT TAKE YOU TO REACH 100% DIGITAL FREEDOM?

I messed around with online marketing for about three years, treating it like a hobby. After that I got serious with it and shipped myself off to Thailand with limited funds, a one way ticket, and told everyone at home I wouldn't be back until I had a successful business. There's nothing like running out of money in a foreign country to put the fire in you. I think I was more worried about having to go home and tell everyone I'd failed. It was a big motivator for me.

WHAT WAS YOUR BIGGEST MISTAKE?

Early on, before I really knew what I was doing, I spent hundreds of dollars on a custom theme from an inexperienced coder on Odesk for a website that never even got off the ground. I was convinced the type of theme I wanted didn't exist for the type of website I was created—but of course it did. I just didn't know what I was doing. It's only a failure if you don't learn from it and move on.

WHAT IS THE SINGLE MOST EFFECTIVE TACTIC YOU DISCOVERED?

Network with others and do outreach. You have to work *with* others and not against them. It can be beneficial for both of you.

WHAT ADVICE WOULD YOU GIVE SOMEONE WANTING TO ACHIEVE SIMILAR SUCCESS?

Be prepared to work hard, put in months on months of effort before even seeing any small progress, focus and stick with it. It's bleak to begin with but if you persist with it then it will work.

LEARN MORE ABOUT STUART'S BUSINESS:

You can find me at NicheHacks.com where we reveal and analyze profitable niches and share affiliate marketing strategies.

I'd recommend starting with one of our most popular posts like: NicheHacks.com/Commission-Black-Ops-Case-Study/

Chapter Two

SERVICE PROVIDERS AND PRODUCT DEVELOPERS

DIGITAL MARKETING SERVICES: AGENCIES AND CONSULTANTS

DERRIC HAYNIE OF VULPINEINTERACTIVE.AGENCY

HOW DID YOU COME UP WITH THE IDEA FOR YOUR BUSINESS?

As I was running my own flailing tech company, I started studying digital marketing like my business depended on it (because it did). As I got a little bit better, I had people reaching out to me with help on the digital marketing front and thus the agency was born. Our original concept, as stupid as it sounds, was to open up a storefront for digital marketing in downtown San Diego, where people could come in, learn about digital marketing, and buy "products" from us. That concept quickly pivoted a few different times, but that was the direction we started in.

WHAT WAS YOUR FIRST MAJOR BREAKTHROUGH?

The biggest a-ha moment for us was when we took an honest look at what we were doing and decided to stop doing about 80-90% of it. We went from a "full service" agency to being focused specifically in social media, and we created our own content tilt from that—being focused on the brand building and engagement side of social, rather than the typical big budget advertising side. Once we stripped away all the other components of the business, it became so much easier to scale. And clients started rolling in.

HOW LONG DID IT TAKE YOU TO REACH 100% DIGITAL FREEDOM?

So, my day job was playing high stakes poker, which typically means working two days a week from 11 a.m. to 3 a.m., then studying and strategizing away from the table a few hours a week on top of that. The agency absolutely sprung up as a side job, and it wasn't until I'd gotten a $50,000 investment (from a poker friend and successful entrepreneur) that I was able to take the leap into full time.

WHAT WAS YOUR BIGGEST MISTAKE?

At one point, we had succumbed to the "infoproduct" craze. We were convinced we needed to make online courses surrounding digital and growth marketing and sell them to the masses. This failed miserably for a lot of reasons. One, we knew a lot about digital marketing, but we didn't have any multimillion dollar successes under our belt to actually prove it, so from an outside perspective, why go with us vs. someone who is actually running a successful company? Two, we had a small community and following, but it was not nearly big enough to support us in monthly sales. Three, making courses is actually very hard and time consuming and it takes a long time to launch and monetize. Overall, this was a major distraction from getting clients and growing our business. But we still do have the courses, and we give them away for free. Plus we learned a lot about what not to do. So while it was a huge failure, I am proud of the learning that came from it.

WHAT IS THE SINGLE MOST EFFECTIVE TACTIC YOU DISCOVERED?

Give value first. And give way more value than you think you should have to. I now make it a point to meet with pretty much anyone, for free, in order to give them some advice on how to grow their business. If 30 minutes of my time can help send them off in the right direction, then I want to help. And I know that even if they aren't the right fit for my company, they will remember me, thank me, and some day something will come back around my way.

Speaking has helped our business. And expect about six months delay between the act of speaking and the impact on the business.

Make people feel as if working with you is "special." What I specifically mean is that, when I am in a sales call, I am specifically trying to disqualify them, and I'm telling them things that don't fit my business. I'm letting people know that we don't just take anyone and that it needs to be the right fit. And I'm not lying about it, but I'm doing it in such a way that it tends to make people want our services more.

WHAT ADVICE WOULD YOU GIVE SOMEONE WANTING TO ACHIEVE SIMILAR SUCCESS?

Focus on learning as fast as you can. Only do things that you have proven are contributing to the success of the business.

I also think people underestimate the value of revenue right away. And many people struggle with investing their money. Money is a tool that you use to make more money. You need to be comfortable throwing some of it around.

And one final thing. I did what I did, largely, without a mentor. But if you are just starting out, I would recommend actually spending two to three years underneath someone that you consider a guru, working for pennies, it doesn't matter. Take their expertise, absorb it, and start your own thing full force a little bit later. It will be a much smoother sail than what I went through.

LEARN MORE ABOUT DERRIC'S BUSINESS:

You can of course check out our site: VulpineInteractive.agency, or our sales deck: Derric.link/Sales-Deck.

Don't hesitate to email me at Derric.Haynie@gmail.com, or follow me on Twitter @SixPeppers: Derric.link/Twitter. I'm always happy to help.

JOSH HOFFMAN OF EPICFREELANCING.COM

HOW DID YOU COME UP WITH THE IDEA FOR YOUR BUSINESS?

In 2012 I was a senior at San Diego State University, studying journalism, and working part time as an assistant producer at NBC in San Diego. That summer, after I graduated and was offered a full time position, I declined the offer because it became clear the corporate culture wasn't for me. As I brainstormed ideas for how I could use my journalism skills—writing, storytelling and creating content—I decided to transition from traditional journalism to an emerging trend at the time called "brand journalism" (really just a fancy term for content marketing). Ultimately, I started a digital marketing consultancy, with a focus on social media and content marketing strategy and execution.

WHAT WAS YOUR FIRST MAJOR BREAKTHROUGH?

My first client. The first client is always the hardest part of getting a freelance business on its feet and moving in the right direction. My first client was a local Los Angeles restaurant where I used to work in high school. Upon quitting my job at NBC in San Diego and moving to Los Angeles, I approached the owners about digital marketing (which they weren't fully and strategically utilizing up to this point). Even though I didn't have any digital marketing experience at the time, I also made sure the owners knew I had emerging skills and talents, was creative and strategy-oriented, and did everything possible to continuously learn and improve along the way. In other words, I made the conversation more about myself—someone who is self-confident, an outside-the-box thinker, ambitious and highly motivated—and less about my experience.

HOW LONG DID IT TAKE YOU TO REACH 100% DIGITAL FREEDOM?

It took six months, but I was also living with my mom, so my monthly expenses were almost nothing. Had my monthly expenses been higher, the urgency of the situation probably would have compelled me to earn enough money and become 100% digitally free in less time.

WHAT WAS YOUR BIGGEST MISTAKE?

In 2015 I had my most successful year up to that point. I was growing extremely fast, attracting better clients with bigger budgets, and getting opportunities left and right. So, in the heat of the moment, I made far too many hasty decisions, like hiring a full-time employee and renting an office space for us. Instead of being diligent and thoughtful about reinvesting in my business and delegating certain tasks, I was trying to sprint toward the finish line—even though in business there is no such thing. (If anything, business is a marathon, so it's important to pace yourself.) The result was a business that all but crashed and burned, a nearly empty bank account and six weeks of serious depression from burning out.

WHAT IS THE SINGLE MOST EFFECTIVE TACTIC YOU DISCOVERED?

Proactively marketing myself and developing a personal brand. Many businesses, whether they're freelancers or larger-scale organizations, only rely on word-of-mouth to market themselves. Word-of-mouth is great, don't get me wrong, but what many people don't realize is that word-of-mouth is not a marketing strategy, because you can't scale or control it. As soon as I started to proactively market myself and develop a personal brand through online (social media and content marketing) and offline (hosting lectures) means, my income nearly doubled within four months. I was also able to raise my hourly rate from $40 an hour, to at least $100 an hour based on the supply and demand of my time.

WHAT ADVICE WOULD YOU GIVE SOMEONE WANTING TO ACHIEVE SIMILAR SUCCESS?

Proactively market yourself and develop a personal brand. It takes time and effort, but what doesn't in a successful business that's built to last?

LEARN MORE ABOUT JOSH'S BUSINESS:

You can visit Joshoffman.com (my personal website) and EpicFreelancing.com (a website I run to help freelancers achieve financial success, creative freedom and lifestyle design.)

DANIEL KNOWLTON OF KPSDIGITALMARKETING.CO.UK

HOW DID YOU COME UP WITH THE IDEA FOR YOUR BUSINESS?

I followed my passion. I've had various jobs throughout my career, some I liked, some I disliked, but the lightbulb moment was when I realized I could create a business around my passion, digital marketing. I've always been interested in marketing. I learned about it at school, studied it at university and applied it within a large blue chip organization I worked for. I used to read various digital marketing publications in my spare time and thought it would be an exciting challenge to apply them to my own personal brand. After growing a small but highly engaged audience, and gaining my first couple of marketing consultancy clients, I knew this was the path I wanted to go down.

WHAT WAS YOUR FIRST MAJOR BREAKTHROUGH?

My first major breakthrough was being accepted to write as a contributor for Social Media Examiner. This grew the exposure for KPS Digital Marketing more than I could ever imagine. This was such a big achievement for me as I had only started writing my own blog six months prior to being accepted, and Social Media Examiner is (in my opinion) the best and most credible social media marketing publication in the world.

After I achieved this, I knew I could achieve anything I put my mind to. I invested every spare minute I had in creating educational marketing content for my own blog and other big publications. Within a few months I was named as #12 Most Influential Digital Marketer on Twitter in the world in 2016—I couldn't believe it!

HOW LONG DID IT TAKE YOU TO REACH 100% DIGITAL FREEDOM?

Ok, this is going to be a short answer. I quit my job and went traveling around Thailand before I started KPS Digital Marketing. It was a huge risk starting a business from scratch with no other job, but I put my everything into it and made it work!

WHAT WAS THE BIGGEST FAILURE, WASTE OF TIME OR MONEY, AND MOST EMBARRASSING MISTAKE YOU MADE ALONG THE WAY?

I've made a lot of mistakes over the last year and a half since starting KPS Digital Marketing, but there's one that sticks in my mind the most. I always love testing out new digital marketing strategies; it's what keeps us at the cutting edge in the marketing world. When I first started KPS I used to test strategies in a more risky way. Rather than testing things in a small way, seeing if it worked and then scaling it, I would go all guns blazing with an all or nothing approach.

One strategy I tested was automating outreach to influencers on Twitter whom I thought would be interested in a blog I had written.

After tweeting 50 or so influencers in the space of two minutes I received a message from a huge marketing influencer I look up to. He basically named and shamed me from spamming everyone and said it was not the way to do things. This was incredibly embarrassing for me at the time and quite heartbreaking to be honest! Since then, I have learned a lot!

WHAT IS THE SINGLE MOST EFFECTIVE TACTIC YOU DISCOVERED?

It's so difficult to pinpoint a single strategy because I truly believe that a highly effective business growth strategy incorporates a variety of elements. First, building relationships via networking is an absolute must. If I hadn't gone out in the real world and built strong relationships, the business would be nowhere near where it is today.

Second, creating and promoting value-adding content via our blog, social media, video and email list has been crucial and we've gained a lot of business from this. Also, building relationships via these platforms, in conjunction with face to face networking has been crucial.

Finally, speaking at events and writing for a variety of big publications has helped grow the business dramatically. There is a variety of other things we've done, but the ones I have mentioned above have provided the best results.

WHAT ADVICE WOULD YOU GIVE SOMEONE WANTING TO ACHIEVE SIMILAR SUCCESS?

Follow your passion and work your face off to achieve whatever it is you want to achieve. If you're looking for tangible tactics to help you grow your business, you should check out our blog where I share all the secrets of how we have grown in step by step tutorials for you to follow: KPSDigitalMarketing.co.uk/Blog

LEARN MORE ABOUT DANIEL'S BUSINESS:

Our best-selling service is completely free and provides a huge amount of value. It's our blog (kpsdigitalmarketing.co.uk/blog). Within the blog we regularly post step by step digital marketing and business growth tutorials which hold your hand through the process of executing the strategies our authors have had success with. We have some of the most influential digital marketers in the world contribute original content to the blog including the #1 digital influencer in the world, Sam Hurley.

The best places to keep in touch with me are Twitter and Snapchat, but you can catch me on various channels outlined below. Once you've read this, take a photo, post it on social media, tag me and say hey!

Website: KPSDigitalMarketing.co.uk

Snapchat: Danknowlton1: Snapchat.com/add/DanKnowlton1

My Twitter @Dknowlton1: Twitter.com/DKnowlton1

KPS Twitter @KPSDigitalMktng: Twitter.com/KPSDigitalMktng

Facebook: Facebook.com/KPSLtdDigitalMarketing

LinkedIn Daniel Knowlton: LinkedIn.com/in/DanielKnowlton1/

YouTube: KPS Digital Marketing

RICH LATIMER OF RICHTRAINING.COM.AU

HOW DID YOU COME UP WITH THE IDEA FOR YOUR BUSINESS?

it came from my 15 years as a rock musician honing my skills in social media and email marketing, combined with my need to fund a youth mental health music passion project. I had been looking for this new method to generate income and actually turned to asking millionaires in my region for help. This was tough but I was bold and fearless and just asked each for $1 million. None gave. One, however, offered to show me how to make $1 million myself and I took the challenge of diving deep into what was stopping me from creating money in my life.

WHAT WAS YOUR FIRST MAJOR BREAKTHROUGH?

As with lots of things it was that lucky break, I built an email system and social media setup for a family member who showed it to a business coach who then trialled it on a few clients and that's how I got the break. It took me six months to contact him! Once we were in touch he started vetting me, making sure I was the real deal, and slowly I built trust. He let me in then to the presentations where he speaks to building clients and I was able to pitch directly to them. This was slow to start; the products were not clear and my pitch was bad but we had some results and from those we grew.

HOW LONG DID IT TAKE YOU TO REACH 100% DIGITAL FREEDOM?

Around three years to hit a point where I could be free, but along with this came the team that helped me get there so I realized very quickly it is about the team, not me. In fact that is the number one mistake I feel entrepreneurs make: they want to fulfill their needs but will soon see a team is required.

WHAT WAS YOUR BIGGEST MISTAKE?

Trying to run and control everything myself would be the issue and leads in from my words above about the team. I tried this path but it was not scalable nor satisfying. It's a great thing to be in a team and my team loves and respects my leadership and I them. This is a key factor, I think, in long term successful businesses, to make sure you have the right people in the right place and *use* them. I learn this the slow, hard way.

WHAT IS THE SINGLE MOST EFFECTIVE TACTIC YOU DISCOVERED?

Finding the right people, getting the products and numbers right, effecting delivery, then cementing yourself as the best of the best in your niche. That would be the nutshell but often you find others who are already successful in some way with your client base and can approach them for a joint venture.

WHAT ADVICE WOULD YOU GIVE SOMEONE WANTING TO ACHIEVE SIMILAR SUCCESS?

Be prepared to work harder than you have ever worked in your life, for less money than you have ever worked, and for longer than you have ever worked—and expect nothing and be grateful for every part of it. That's the guru speaking—no, really it's actually the ability to connect it to a higher purpose and never stop moving forward.

LEARN MORE ABOUT RICH'S BUSINESS:

We are launching a new website soon—RichTraining.com.au to show you what we do in the world.

SUJAN PATEL OF WEBPROFITS.AGENCY

HOW DID YOU COME UP WITH THE IDEA FOR YOUR BUSINESS?

I've always been entrepreneurial-minded, back to when I was seven years old and flipping bags of popcorn from Costco (my mom says that's the first time she figured out how hard I was willing to hustle). After dropping out of UC-Irvine and leaving a position as the head of SEO for Oversee.net, I started my first agency, which I sold back in 2014.

I was pretty burned out from agency work at that point, so I took a step back and went to work as the VP of Marketing for a SaaS program called When I Work. While I was there, I soaked up everything I could about how software and apps work, giving me the tools I needed to launch my own projects, including Mailshake (a program I built to help marketers send better cold emails) and LinkTexting (a mobile app download tool for converting desktop traffic).

I actually recently went back to agency work as the co-founder of Web Profits. While I was focused on my SaaS companies, I realized that not only was I referring out millions of dollars in consulting leads, but that I also wanted to put everything I'd learned about scaling businesses to use with client engagements. That really put the idea in my head about going back to an agency model.

WHAT WAS YOUR FIRST MAJOR BREAKTHROUGH?

One of my biggest breakthroughs was back in 2009. I'd been taking on SEO consulting gigs on the side while I was working for Oversee.net, but I wasn't sure if I'd be able to turn that into a full-time business. I wound up giving myself one year to make it work by gaining as many clients as possible.

I actually did meet my goal, ending the year with great revenue and my first official employee (thanks in part to Oversee signing on as a client!). But more than that, testing myself proved that I had what it'd take to make it—that I could make entrepreneurship sustainable. I've always had hustle, but that was one of the first times I remember feeling like I was on the path to success.

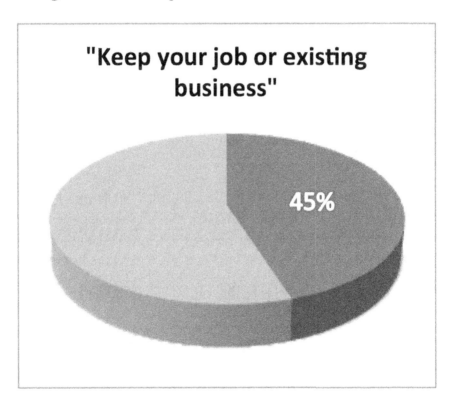

HOW LONG DID IT TAKE YOU TO REACH 100% DIGITAL FREEDOM?

Going from a job to being on my own with my first agency was actually pretty smooth. I was making a lot of money at Oversee. net, but I'd also been working SEO consulting gigs on the side, so I knew what kind of demand there was for the services I'd be offering (and roughly how much I'd be able to make doing it full time). I also knew that I could live pretty cheaply if I needed to, so I wasn't too worried about going out on my own.

WHAT WAS YOUR BIGGEST MISTAKE?

Oh man, I've failed so many times, this section could get long. I've had entire businesses fail (ask me about my weather app!), but I think one of the failures that affected me the most was staying with my first agency too long.

I did a lot of things to try to beat the burnout I was feeling. I tried new hobbies, I changed up my work environment, and I took vacations (when I could). I did all the things you're supposed to do, but they didn't work. It took me a long time to really look inside and realize that I wasn't excited about the work I'd been doing 24/7 for the last five years.

Eventually, I did wind up selling the company, but I wish I could go back in time and tell myself to make the call sooner, rather than wasting so much energy trying to make the wrong situation work.

WHAT IS THE SINGLE MOST EFFECTIVE TACTIC YOU DISCOVERED?

I'm a huge believer in content marketing. I publish a lot of content on my blogs and on sites like Entrepreneur, Inc, Forbes, Huffington Post, Search Engine Journal, Content Marketing Institute and others. I actually get asked all the time how I manage to keep up with my writing schedule, but the truth is I wouldn't spend so much time on it if I wasn't getting such good results.

WHAT ADVICE WOULD YOU GIVE SOMEONE WANTING TO ACHIEVE SIMILAR SUCCESS?

Start putting yourself out there now. I've been in this business for a long time, and the people I see succeeding are the ones who are investing in building personal brands for themselves. There's so much competition out there, that anything you can do to differentiate yourself helps.

Start publishing content under your name, on your site and as guest posts on others. Answer questions on sites like Quora or Inbound. org (if you're in digital marketing). Do whatever you can to get your name in front of others in your industry. It'll take time to see results, but every action you take is cumulative.

LEARN MORE ABOUT SUJAN'S BUSINESS:

I blog on my personal site (SujanPatel.com) and my agency site (WebProfits.Agency). I share marketing info on my app sites (including Mailshake.com and LinkTexting.com) and on my contributor pages at the sites listed above.

On Twitter, I'm @sujanpatel: Twitter.com/SujanPatel.

My LinkedIn page is LinkedIn.com/in/SujanPatel.

You can also pick up a copy of my latest book at 100DaysOfGrowth.com.

RACHEL PEDERSEN OF RACHELPEDERSEN.COM

HOW DID YOU COME UP WITH THE IDEA FOR YOUR BUSINESS?

My business idea hit me over a set of highlights—literally! I was working as a hairstylist and my hair client mentioned she needed help with social media. As I was giving her a set of highlights, we brainstormed how I could help her out! I knew very little about social media. I just knew enough to help her. Several years later I decided it was time to get serious about social media and began reaching out to business owners. The response was overwhelming—within just five months I was able to leave my 9-to-5. One month later I was fully booked!

WHAT WAS YOUR FIRST MAJOR BREAKTHROUGH?

The first major breakthrough for me was securing my first client at a premium monthly price. It was more than I had made in a month in previous jobs! That moment was unreal, and showed me that there was a market in need of my services.

HOW LONG DID IT TAKE YOU TO REACH 100% DIGITAL FREEDOM?

I hustled like a maniac—and left my 9-to-5 within five months. Several months later I retired my husband from his 9-to-5 as well. I wasn't going to dive in and take the plunge before seeing that I could secure income that matched my 9-to-5, and I'm so glad that I actually did wait for that milestone.

WHAT WAS YOUR BIGGEST MISTAKE?

One of my early mistakes was to work with someone that didn't fit with my business goals and communication style. On one of the first calls there were indications that it wouldn't be a great fit—but we both ignored those discrepancies. It's absolutely essential to make sure your goals for your business, communication, and future partnerships align well with your clients. Ignoring these warning signs will lead to a deteriorating relationship—and causes both parties to question their own abilities. Thankfully the relationship was quickly mended and we laughed about our poor communication together— but it doesn't always end that way. I recommend only taking on clients and projects that align with your "why" and fit into the plans for your business and goals.

WHAT IS THE SINGLE MOST EFFECTIVE TACTIC YOU DISCOVERED?

Hands down, being social was the best growth tactic I discovered. It sounds silly, but it's true! As a social media manager and strategist it can be easy to find yourself hiding behind a computer... Actually taking the time to get to know people and sharing conversations

WHAT ADVICE WOULD YOU GIVE SOMEONE WANTING TO ACHIEVE SIMILAR SUCCESS?

The best way to achieve big results is by partnering with a mentor who can help you to reverse engineer your goals. Create a clear plan for action, create the steps to achieve those goals, and then take action every single day. A mentor or a coach can help you to determine the mindset you need in order to achieve success!

LEARN MORE ABOUT RACHEL'S BUSINESS:

Everything about me, from Social Media United to my 1:1 services can be found at my website—RachelPedersen.com—I look forward to getting to know you more. Let's do this!

JOHN RUHLIN OF RUHLINGROUP.COM

HOW DID YOU COME UP WITH THE IDEA FOR YOUR BUSINESS?

It was a natural progression over time. I originally started off selling Cutco knives to put myself through college. My first major mental shift in business gifting came as a result of witnessing it done first hand through my first mentor, Paul Miller. He was an attorney whom referrals flocked to because he was so radically generous and always giving things away. For example, the one time Paul got a really good deal on noodles he purchased an entire truckload of them and gave them away to people at his church.

When I first started selling Cutco knives, Paul was the one who gave me the idea to tailor gifts to the spouse, not the client or employee. When I suggested giving engraved pocket knives to each of his clients, he asked if we could engrave paring knives for their wives instead. He always taught that you take care of the inner circle. If the family is happy, then the individual is happy. Thanks to Paul, I realized it wasn't about the knife. Rather, he understood the psychology of relationship building. He was top of mind, well loved, and just attracted deal flow like never before. I modeled those practices and over time I learned through trial and error.

WHAT WAS YOUR FIRST MAJOR BREAKTHROUGH?

Back in 2007, I met Cameron Herold at a conference for the Entrepreneur's Organization. After waiting for over an hour just to get a chance to talk to him, he mentioned that he was scheduled to speak at my local EO chapter in a few months. I said that I was a season ticketholder to the Cavs and offered to take him to a game the night before the event. As we were talking he casually mentioned that his favorite store was Brooks Brothers, which started a crazy idea brewing in my mind. I asked him what his shirt size was so that I could send him a shirt. Even though I could tell he thought I was crazy by the look on his face, he was a good sport and told me anyway.

On the day that he was supposed to arrive in town he was having a really rough day. His flight had been delayed, and he missed his connector flight so he was arriving several hours later than expected. When I heard that he was delayed I came up with the insane idea to go to Brooks Brothers and purchase one of everything in his size. I ended up purchasing $7,000 worth of clothes and putting it on my Amex. I then convinced the general manager of the hotel he was staying at to help me brand his hotel room like a Brooks Brothers store.

When Cameron finally arrived several hours late, I could tell he was exhausted. I told him to take his time getting ready and that I would be waiting in the lobby. When he came back down, his face was glowing. He couldn't believe the lengths I had gone to and told me that he was willing to talk about whatever I wanted for as long as I wanted.

My grand gesture didn't end up costing me a dime. Cameron generously reimbursed me for all the clothing he kept, and has become a great friend and business ally. He has opened doors for me with CEOs of billion dollar companies. All because I took the time to do something genuinely nice for him with no expectation of receiving anything in return.

HOW LONG DID IT TAKE YOU TO REACH 100% DIGITAL FREEDOM?

My situation is a little unique because I have never really had a job. I interned with Cutco and started the business out of that as a business gift strategy and service. I thought about quitting college as a result but finished anyway.

WHAT WAS YOUR BIGGEST MISTAKE?

By far my biggest mistake was trying to do it all on my own for the first eight years and not staying in tune with the numbers. I had turned over all the financial aspects of my business, including my taxes, to my right hand person, who served as both my assistant and CPA. She ended up stealing from me which almost crushed the business, and since she also handled my taxes, it led to a very unpleasant IRS audit.

I would also say I was mistaken in investing in too many things at one time and thinking I was good at any business. I had made several investments in areas that I wasn't particularly knowledgeable in, and they turned out badly. During 2007-2008 this, along with the theft, almost sunk me.

WHAT IS THE SINGLE MOST EFFECTIVE TACTIC YOU DISCOVERED?

Without a doubt, our most effective growth tactic has been to model firsthand what we teach. We send out $250,000 gifts in year, and none of them are branded with our company logo. We focus our gifts on the recipients as opposed to trying to use them as part of a marketing campaign. We strive to be radically generous and eat our own dog food so to speak. When you walk the talk and show people first hand the experience of being appreciated in a genuine way, it can't help but develop relationships and open doors.

WHAT ADVICE WOULD YOU GIVE SOMEONE WANTING TO ACHIEVE SIMILAR SUCCESS?

Be bold. Give and do more than is reasonable. Don't hold back 5%. When you go "all in" and follow through, people feel the difference and respond accordingly. That is not just with gifts, it's with everything you do. When you do things with a standard of excellence you stand out.

LEARN MORE ABOUT JOHN'S BUSINESS:

You can learn more about our firm and our proven process for gift giving at RuhlinGroup.com. Our website will allow you to see examples of successful gifting programs and give you a basic overview of how we operate. You can contact us through the website if you would like to get more information on partnering with us for your own strategic gifting needs.

You can also purchase my book, *Giftology: The Art and Science of Using Gifts to Cut Through the Noise, Increase Referrals, and Strengthen Retention* on Amazon: Amazon.com/gp/product/1619614332/

It offers further insight into what to do and what to avoid when gifting, and establishes best practices for using gifts to open doors and develop relationships.

You can also follow me on:

Facebook: Facebook.com/JohnRuhlinJr

Or Twitter: Twitter.com/Ruhlin

JAMIE STENHOUSE OF JAMIESTENHOUSE.COM

HOW DID YOU COME UP WITH THE IDEA FOR YOUR BUSINESS?

It happened originally. Being a high school dropout with a speaking stutter, I pursued a career in IT multimedia so that I would never have to use my voice again and simply work behind a keyboard for the rest of my days. After spending three years in TAFE doing IT multimedia, I quickly found that when I tried to get employed, every employer wanted me to "speak to clients, handle help desk, or man the phones"...to which my natural response was no. That led me to take my skill set and try to figure out how to generate an income online without using my voice. I began to learn everything I could about email marketing, funnels, advertising, copywriting and so on.. I picked up my first client which led to my second, then my fourth and it just grew from there.

WHAT WAS YOUR FIRST MAJOR BREAKTHROUGH?

I don't think there ever was a "major breakthrough." It was a series of small wins and even then, those wins were simply completing the daily tasks that I didn't always like doing but I knew I should do in order to get to where I wanted to be. The only time success is a light switch flick effect, that is, when its a single moment, is when your goals are too small. Any goal is a climb, a process, a journey, never a moment.

HOW LONG DID IT TAKE YOU TO REACH 100% DIGITAL FREEDOM?

Almost right away. Being 18 when I started my first and then my second business, I didn't have many overheads so it was easy for me to go all in. I say to people who are wanting to start out that are older than I was when I started, they should strip back their lifestyle as much as they can in order to go all in. The older you get, the harder it can be to become 100% digitally free due to the amount of financial responsibilities that you take on.

WHAT WAS YOUR BIGGEST MISTAKE?

Nothing strikes me as a big failure. From my design agency to my clothing line to client jobs and my training brand, I had many slip ups and "whoops" moments, but they never screwed me over for the long term. I learned, rolled with them and figured out how to keep all parties happy. If anything, I wish I had learned about tax and personal earnings a bit earlier. If you treat every obstacle as an opportunity to better yourself then you can never really fail. If you slip up three times with the same mistake then yes, I consider that a "failure," not in the task but in the opportunity to grow from it the first and the second time.

WHAT IS THE SINGLE MOST EFFECTIVE TACTIC YOU DISCOVERED?

Sell. As basic as it sounds, hardly anyone does it. In a world of social media and feel good projects hardly anyone is doing the number one thing that a business needs to survive. And that is to sell, to generate sales. Many people get caught up in product development or research or client work or jumping from course to course when in fact, they just need sales to get the wheels turning. Sales can fix any problem in any business at anytime anywhere in the world. If you take anything from this, aim to spend at least two hours per day on sales related tasks. Not content, not social media, not client management, not design and not networking—actual sales where you are sending quotes or showing proposals to prospects.

WHAT ADVICE WOULD YOU GIVE SOMEONE WANTING TO ACHIEVE SIMILAR SUCCESS?

Start now. Move quickly and have a single project with a single product to focus on. If anything I've learned over my past three businesses it's that the power of a single focus is incredible. In my past brands I may have focused on too many product lines, or clients, or projects within the projects where my focus was split. Sure I was enjoying being creative and giving birth to my ideas but I was not making progress in the form of sales. Now while money isn't everything, it's everything in business. The ability to generate sales allows you to further your message and impact. I speak to upcoming people in the game and they have this product and that product and this idea when in fact they have no or very few customers to sell to. Focus on one product, make it as quickly as you can or ideally, presell it, and perfect it and grow it to at least six figures, and then maybe, if it's viable, start a new project or a different product line. Too many people pick something up and put it down when it doesn't give a result after 15 months. This is your life's work, be patient, show it respect and focus on the one thing.

LEARN MORE ABOUT JAMIE'S BUSINESS:

MarketTitans.com.au is where we generate customers online in any industry for our clients, or JamieStenhouse.com where I show entrepreneurs how to do it themselves through my online programs.

VIRTUAL ASSISTANTS: CAN'T DO WITHOUT 'EM

MICHELLE DALE OF VIRTUALMISSFRIDAY.COM

HOW DID YOU COME UP WITH THE IDEA FOR YOUR BUSINESS?

I'd literally just landed in Egypt from my home country of the UK on a one-way ticket with a laptop and no idea how to make money. I knew I wanted to travel and not be reliant on needing to find a job, so I began researching online and went through considering every possible option I could for a location independent business. Eventually virtual assistance came up. It seemed like the best fit for me, and I ran with it.

WHAT WAS YOUR FIRST MAJOR BREAKTHROUGH?

I'd say it was the moment I began teaching virtual assistance and how to operate an online business. Once people pay for your knowledge, to learn what you've learned and gain from your experience, it's quite remarkable. Building a business, especially online, is tough. You face challenges you wouldn't normally have considered, but it's just an incredible feeling when you can really begin to give back to your colleagues, and you just think "yep, it's all been worth it."

HOW LONG DID IT TAKE YOU TO REACH 100% DIGITAL FREEDOM?

I went completely cold turkey and actually quit my job before I started the business. It was bold, but I'm an all-or-nothing kind of woman. I left the UK to go to a country where I knew my costs of living would be low (about 50 GBP per month for a flat and food cost next to nothing). I've never been afraid to make changes or sacrifices to move forward. I know they are only temporary for potentially much quicker results, and what that did was literally buy me more time through keeping my living expenses extremely low.

Within two and a half years I was traveling and living in first world countries again, but with a little surprise along the way: I met my husband and we had a baby, so the business at that time wasn't just supporting me, but my little family as well. We've now had three children in three different countries and my husband works with me in the business, along with around 20 team members.

WHAT WAS YOUR BIGGEST MISTAKE?

Not following my instincts when it comes to things like who I work with, and how I work. A good example would be working with the wrong clients, and not having the guts in the early days to say no to people. You realize quickly that even paying clients can drain your energy and resources if they aren't properly managed or they simply aren't a good match. I've also had my fair share of technical disasters, but that also taught me a valuable lesson in really investing in good systems. I tend to see short term failures as long term saviors.

WHAT IS THE SINGLE MOST EFFECTIVE TACTIC YOU DISCOVERED?

If we're talking tactics, I'd say videos—for sure. The moment I got over myself and started to make videos on YouTube and put myself out there, then it became so much easier to get that rapport with people that I wouldn't normally be able to achieve from behind just a blog post or email. Those are good and all, and for sure we can communicate well through the written word, but nothing shows authenticity to your audience digitally like being face-to-screen with them.

WHAT ADVICE WOULD YOU GIVE SOMEONE WANTING TO ACHIEVE SIMILAR SUCCESS?

Don't dismiss self-development and working on your mindset and beliefs. This may sound a bit more "woo woo," but it's absolutely true—as soon as I got out of worry mode, everything transformed. I was always concerned about money, being good enough, things going wrong, you name it, and I would repeatedly attract the same cycle of circumstances into my life, without realizing, they weren't happening by chance—I was putting all my energy into things I didn't want to happen. As soon as I shifted my thoughts and feelings and began contemplating all the things that could actually go right, for instance all the ways money could come in (instead of go out) and basically put myself in this frame of mind, then literally the flow of the tide turned and I was getting creative ideas, opportunities and energy to take action and move forward out of nowhere. I went from doing $20,000 to $30,000 launches which left me feeling stressed, to $80,000 which was smooth sailing in a matter of months.

Seek out people like Tony Robbins, John Assaraf, Vishen Lakhiani and T. Harv Eker—just keep an open mind!

LEARN MORE ABOUT MICHELLE'S BUSINESS:

My website is VirtualMissFriday.com—I help clients and colleagues to create their dream online businesses through carefully designed strategies and incredible Internet-based support which I call 1nSourcing, where we're reinventing the way to outsource!

SOFTWARE, APPS, AND SOFTWARE AS A SERVICE (SAAS)

AKSHAT CHOUDHARY OF BLOGVAULT.NET

HOW DID YOU COME UP WITH THE IDEA FOR YOUR BUSINESS?

One of Stack Overflow's founders, Jeff Atwood, had a blog called Coding Horror that I used to follow voraciously. One day, unfortunately, his blog crashed, and he lost all the data on it, but fortunately, his blog was so popular that he was able to recover most of the content on it from cached pages, and with help from Google.

Reading about his experience made me realize that website crashes and data loss could happen to anyone, if it could happen to a tech-savvy guy like Jeff. It also showed me that there wasn't a solution available to fix it quickly enough. This is what sparked the idea of BlogVault, the tool I created to back up entire WordPress sites.

WHAT WAS YOUR FIRST MAJOR BREAKTHROUGH?

Though I'd created BlogVault mostly as a service to the WordPress community (it was priced at US$29/year), I never thought I could actually make money off it. The subscription rate just covered the storage expenses for maintaining a Linode cloud server that came at US $28/month, and an Amazon S3 account for storage. However, more and more customers got wind of us (I don't even know how,) and kept signing up. Then it dawned on me that the annual charge was too little. I tried increasing the price, and nothing changed. This confirmed my theory that users preferred BlogVault's backup-as-a service model that kept an active eye on the system, because many things can go wrong, even while transferring data to a remote site.

HOW LONG DID IT TAKE YOU TO REACH 100% DIGITAL FREEDOM?

It took me more than a year to quit my job. After all, I had a lot to learn with respect to WordPress. I came from a background of writing in C and for a kernel and network programming. A lot of people I followed in the blogosphere said it was very, very technical, but I tried managing on my own. Eventually, I got enough positive feedback to take me to a point where I thought it was worth trying without a safety net.

WHAT WAS YOUR BIGGEST MISTAKE?

Oh there were a couple of big mistakes we made. I think the most painful was when VaultPress, Automattic's own paid backup service, launched two weeks after BlogVault. I'd known that there was a need for a backup service, but now I couldn't even say that we were the first backup service for WordPress because we were fresh off the boat and hadn't focused on marketing. Nobody knew us. What's worse, I'd not even realized that our payment system wasn't working for the first six months! I was working at Citrix at the time, and BlogVault was a side project of mine, so I didn't really bother to check. It was a user who alerted me about the issue. That was a really bad time for us. But like they say, every dark cloud has its silver lining. Ours was that people who found VaultPress looked for other options, and found us. It was really strange, since BlogVault couldn't call itself a competitor... and yet users thought to try us. I realized then that VaultPress was probably the best thing that could have happened to us. Competition actually validates your market more than anything else. My stumbling block was marketing, and VaultPress took care of that for me.

WHAT IS THE SINGLE MOST EFFECTIVE TACTIC YOU DISCOVERED?

Meeting people, I've discovered, is what makes things work. I had to learn that the hard way since I usually shy away from new people, but the WordPress community is so open and friendly! In the initial days, I thought I'd do some marketing (by which I mean write a couple of blog posts), but I ended up coding the entire time. I learned to ease up a little in the WordPress community over time though, and in 2014, I met with Vineeta and Tom, the founders of Wholegrain Digital (a popular UK-based WordPress design agency) in the U.S. We ended up hitting it off, and as fate would have it, they recommended us to the CEO of WP Engine, Heather Brunner, and then to Jason Cohen, the company's founder and CTO. I'd shyly reached out to Jason a couple of times over email before, but hadn't gotten a response. In his defense, BlogVault had no brand-recall, no marketing. He had no reason to check us out, and even if he did, he only would have a couple of blog posts I'd written. Since we got recommended so highly though, Jason looked at the product, saw the value in it, and we got working on a specialized product just for WordPress migrations to WP Engine's platform. After the meeting, things happened really fast for us. WP Engine's customers migrated to their hosting service with ease, and we became their official partner for all onboarding. That partnership really took us to new places and established us as a reliable service.

If I could name another selling point of ours though, I'd say that it was our customer service and support. I'm really proud of it and I have talked about it in other interviews as well. I strongly believe in treating others in the same way I'd like to be treated. I've seen that when you practice this principle, it becomes personal (in a good way) and it really counts. When you're nice and go out of your way to solve problems that people bring to you then they trust you and enjoy talking to you.

WHAT ADVICE WOULD YOU GIVE SOMEONE WANTING TO ACHIEVE SIMILAR SUCCESS?

The only advice I'd give someone looking to start a business related to WordPress, is to get involved with the community. Helping out and being remembered as someone who adds to the community takes a lot of time (and patience), but it makes a great difference. WordPress is built around the idea of community so much so that I think it comes close to being a family. It's that open, close-knit, and helpful. So if you're an entrepreneur eyeing WordPress, I'd suggest that you make sure that what you have to offer focuses on serving the community. If you're good, not only will customers stick around, but they'll talk about you to their friends, and everybody else as well. A lot of WordPress is do-It-yourself, so I think there's a real need for support, and for software as a service (SaaS) products in the community. Besides, since it helps everyone out and allows even novices to navigate the WordPress community with ease, it ties in with the spirit of WordPress.

LEARN MORE ABOUT AKSHAT'S BUSINESS:

We maintain a blog where we post regularly about WordPress best practices with a focus on backup, security and management. BlogVault.net/Blog/

We also post what we're up to at the moment on our Facebook page: Facebook.com/BlogVaultNet/ and Twitter feed @blogVault: Twitter.com/BlogVault.

If you'd like to get in touch with us, or ask us question about our service, we respond to every entry that comes in through the contact form on our website too: BlogVault.net/contact

KEITH BLOUNT OF LITERATUREANDLATTE.COM

HOW DID YOU COME UP WITH THE IDEA FOR YOUR BUSINESS?

I was both trying to write a novel and researching for a Ph.D., and my messy way of working involved a combination of chapters and notes in Word, outlines in Excel and on index cards, and research all over the place. It occurred to me that there must be a better way of tying together these various aspects of writing a long text, and that outlining, writing and research-gathering were exactly the sorts of things that good software could integrate. I therefore set about trying to find such software, but found nothing that did what I needed—so I taught myself to code and wrote it myself, which is how Scrivener was born.

WHAT WAS YOUR FIRST MAJOR BREAKTHROUGH?

I think the first breakthrough was getting a community of writers interested in Scrivener. I posted a very early version of Scrivener on the National Novel Writing Month forums back in 2005, asking for writers there to test it and give me feedback. At the time, I was mainly writing Scrivener for myself, and thoughts of selling it were secondary. But the response I received made me realize that I wasn't alone in my desire for such a piece of software. Those early users gave me lots of great ideas (I went on to rewrite the app completely before its release in January 2007) and, amazingly, they were so excited about the software that they went on to tell other people about it on blogs and forums (this was before social media had taken off). That virtual word of mouth had an incredible effect. I had expected to sell only a few copies here and there, but without any advertising, not long after Scrivener's release I realized it could pay as a full-time job.

HOW LONG DID IT TAKE YOU TO REACH 100% DIGITAL FREEDOM?

It took just over a year. I was a primary school teacher when I wrote Scrivener, but it so happened that in the summer of 2008—a year and a half after Scrivener was released– I moved with my family from London to Cornwall. I was told by a head teacher that it would be difficult to get a teaching job in Cornwall without first moving there, so the plan was to find a position after we'd moved. But over the previous year or so, Scrivener had earned quite a bit more than I made as a teacher, and sales showed no signs of slowing down. So, as much as I loved teaching, I decided not to look for another post, and to instead concentrate on running my own business.

WHAT WAS YOUR BIGGEST MISTAKE?

That one's easy—the way we handled our iOS version was our (my) biggest mistake. I wrote Scrivener for the macOS platform. A year or two into Scrivener being on sale, I was approached by an enthusiastic Australian, Lee Powell, who wanted to build a Windows version. We worked out a profit share agreement and he built Scrivener for Windows over the following two years. This worked out well, and resulted in Scrivener being available to many more users.

When it came to building an iOS version, then, I went a similar route. Users had been asking for an iOS version ever since the iPhone was announced, and once the iPad was released, it became a daily request. I didn't have time to write it myself, though, as the macOS version was a full-time commitment, so I set about finding developers who could work on it independently, as Lee had done with Windows. It was a disaster. There were numerous problems. One was that, because I was concentrating on the macOS version, I was not setting and checking deadlines for the iOS developers, and I was not checking the code being written as closely as I now realize I should have been. As a result, I only realized much too late that the code was never going to be in a shape that could be released. (I ended up taking over the project and rewriting the whole thing myself—I was a more experienced coder by this point.)

But perhaps the biggest mistake was this: I told our users that we were working on it. And then I kept saying, "It will definitely be released next year." And I kept turning out to be wrong. That last year, before we finally released our iOS version, was not much fun, because it seemed as though everyone else and their dog had released an iOS app, and we felt our users' frustration and impatience for something we had promised years ago. Fortunately, the iOS version is now out and is doing well!

WHAT IS THE SINGLE MOST EFFECTIVE TACTIC YOU DISCOVERED?

Well, we've never found advertising to be very effective for us, for some reason. The growth of our business has always been driven by word of mouth. This has come about in different ways. An enthusiastic group of early adopters was invaluable, as were good reviews from the various magazines and websites. These days, social media is great—we are very active on Twitter and Facebook, and you can get an uptick in interest if someone with a lot of followers mentions you.

We have also had some success with sponsorships. We're now one of the sponsors of National Novel Writing Month, for instance, offering a 50% discount to anyone who writes 50,000 words during November as part of that event, and this always brings us a lot of new users.

Actually, though, I'd say the most effective tactic is simply not losing sight of the product. We continue to concentrate on making Scrivener the best software it can be, and providing our users with great support to the best of our abilities. I think that if you do that, then people will recommend you.

WHAT ADVICE WOULD YOU GIVE SOMEONE WANTING TO ACHIEVE SIMILAR SUCCESS?

If you build something you truly need, and that you are really passionate about, there are going to be other people out there who need it too, and who will also be passionate about it. Not just "build it and they will come," but "build it *well* and they will come"—we hope!

LEARN MORE ABOUT KEITH'S BUSINESS:

Scrivener is what we're known for—a writing app built specifically for working on long or difficult pieces of text, from novels to nonfiction, from theses to screenplays. It allows you to write in any order, bring in research, zoom in on the details or step back to get an overview. You can find us at LiteratureAndLatte.com.

DAVIDE DE GUZ OF CLICKMETER.COM

HOW DID YOU COME UP WITH THE IDEA FOR YOUR BUSINESS?

Five years ago I used to run my own digital agency. It was a small, kind of a boutique one with few very select clients. To monitor their online marketing spending and be sure that the publishers' reports were accurate we developed an internal software.

WHAT WAS YOUR FIRST MAJOR BREAKTHROUGH?

That software was so good that most our clients loved it. One day a marketing manager from our biggest client, a multinational food company, requested the access for some members of the team overseas. In that moment we realized this could have been a great success and ClickMeter as a SaaS (software as a service) was born.

HOW LONG DID IT TAKE YOU TO REACH 100% DIGITAL FREEDOM?

I worked for 12 months part time as the agency director and with my personal money hired a full time developer to work on ClickMeter. I also reserved some servers on Amazon AWS and spent some thousands of dollars in marketing campaigns. I was the classic multi-hats entrepreneur, taking care of everything except for coding. After 12 months we were cash-positive and I had enough money to pay my salary and other three full-time engineers. So I quit the agency and started to work 12 hours a day for ClickMeter. From that point on our income doubled every year.

Things are going so well that in November 2015 we decided to create another startup called Rebrandly (Rebrandly.com). With that you can create short links that include your name or brand. Practically, you register a domain name with us and you use it to create your branded short links like davide.link/10books. A branded link is trusted, pronounceable, memorable and cool! Rebrandly is going even better than ClickMeter.

WHAT WAS YOUR BIGGEST MISTAKE?

Everything should have been made faster. I should have left the agency earlier, invested more money, thought bigger. Being prudent just extended the timeframe. In life you need to make choices. I firmly believe in the mantra: fail fast. If you have to fall it's better not to lose time.

WHAT IS THE SINGLE MOST EFFECTIVE TACTIC YOU DISCOVERED?

There is no "single tactic." The combination of a great product, a sincere passion and great content marketing has been the formula for our success. But if I would have to choose one, I'd say that our most brilliant move has been the "refer a friend program." From your ClickMeter dashboard you can contact your friends, colleagues, partners and tell them about ClickMeter. For every new free subscription you receive an update of your plan and so does the new member.

WHAT ADVICE WOULD YOU GIVE SOMEONE WANTING TO ACHIEVE SIMILAR SUCCESS?

We are living in a moment of incredible opportunities. If you have enough strength to be a web entrepreneur, just think big, think global and create an innovative venture. Do not copy—innovate. This is the time.

LEARN MORE ABOUT DAVIDE'S BUSINESS:

ClickMeter (ClickMeter.com) is the tool for every digital marketer. With ClickMeter you can monitor, compare and optimize all your marketing links in one place and increase the conversion rate. ClickMeter counts more than 150,000 customers; they are marketers from 200 different countries in the world including Fortune 500 companies.

CHRIS GUTHRIE OF UPFUEL.COM

HOW DID YOU COME UP WITH THE IDEA FOR YOUR BUSINESS?

For every business I create they all come from trying to solve the problems I personally experience. For example, years ago I got started building my online business by doing Amazon affiliate marketing. One of the pains I experienced was manually going to Amazon.com, finding the product I wanted to create a link for, going through the steps to create the link and then reopening my WordPress website to paste the link into the content editor. I thought that if I was annoyed by the time it took to do this, that other bloggers that use Amazon's affiliate program would probably be annoyed too. So I set out to create a WordPress plugin that allows affiliates to create links inside of WordPress instead of being forced to go to Amazon to do it. The result was EasyAzon.com and we've been selling our plugin for over five years now.

I replicated this same model for every other business or project that I've taken on, including my blog UpFuel.com, Salesbacker.com, AmaSuite.com and others.

WHAT WAS YOUR FIRST MAJOR BREAKTHROUGH?

The first breakthrough was when I built an Amazon affiliate website in the product review space. That's where I was able to earn my first $1,000 per month after trying in the past to build a larger income by creating forums in the video game space (the best I ever did there was $500 a month with AdSense). Ultimately the breakthrough came by trying to take a step back and really walking through any project that I was about to undertake and see how I'd create something that would provide value for the people who would use it and how I could be compensated for the value I created.

HOW LONG DID IT TAKE YOU TO REACH 100% DIGITAL FREEDOM?

It took about a year to replace my income (after spending several years failing at other things before that). I was fired from my job on Oct 13, 2009, and fortunately I was already making more money than my day job by that point and so I decided to focus full time on growing my online business.

WHAT WAS YOUR BIGGEST MISTAKE?

I wasted a ton of time working on projects that had no hope of every being successful enough to provide me a full time income because I failed to take the time to look at the big picture. For example, I used to run a variety of forums in the video game niche. It wasn't until I was generating 500,000 page views a month and earning only $500 a month that I realized that all the time I spent on my forum wasn't going to work out. That lead me to thinking that getting traffic, while important, isn't the most important thing to do. Getting the right traffic is far more important. That's what lead me to creating websites that were focused on product reviews and getting traffic from people that were interested in making a buying decision.

WHAT IS THE SINGLE MOST EFFECTIVE TACTIC YOU DISCOVERED?

How to get free traffic from Google. Learning how to get free traffic from organic SEO is really valuable as it helps provide a base of traffic and revenue that you can use to go out and scale whatever you're trying to build.

WHAT ADVICE WOULD YOU GIVE SOMEONE WANTING TO ACHIEVE SIMILAR SUCCESS?

Find something you're interested in but make sure that you can look at your idea from a big picture perspective and see how you can earn the amount of money you'd like to make. If you don't see a clear path to eventual success after putting in hard work, it's not worth going with that idea.

LEARN MORE ABOUT CHRIS'S BUSINESS:

Visit my blog at UpFuel.com to learn more about how I'm building online businesses. You can join my free private mastermind group on Facebook by going to UpFuel.com/fb.

KYLE JAMES OF RATHER-BE-SHOPPING.COM

HOW DID YOU COME UP WITH THE IDEA FOR YOUR BUSINESS?

I was slinging drugs as a pharmaceutical rep back in 2001, very tired of all the travel. I came up with a website that listed coupons and deals for a slew of different online stores. At the time, I had no idea what I was doing, but knew I wanted to work for myself at some point. Rather-Be-Shopping.com was born. After a huge learning curve, the site started to gain popularity due to some good publicity and I was able to run it full time starting in 2003.

WHAT WAS YOUR FIRST MAJOR BREAKTHROUGH?

Getting really lucky and ranking well with this new search engine with a really strange name...called Google. This was in 2002.

HOW LONG DID IT TAKE YOU TO REACH 100% DIGITAL FREEDOM?

It took me about two and a half years before I went full time.

WHAT WAS YOUR BIGGEST MISTAKE?

A few years ago I hired a PR company to try and take Rather-Be-Shopping.com to the next level. I spent thousands of dollars on things I could have done better myself, namely media outreach and content marketing. Make sure you know what you're getting when hiring a PR company and see if you can do it internally in the beginning. After all, be aware that most reporters and journalists would rather hear from you than a PR firm.

WHAT IS THE SINGLE MOST EFFECTIVE TACTIC YOU DISCOVERED?

Be the face of the business and make your relationships with your customers personal and engaging. My idea with RBS was if somebody's looking for coupons, instead of saying "Oh, I wonder what Coupons.com or Coupon Cabin has?" I wanted them to think "Oh, I wonder what Kyle has?" It's paid off big time and it's a great tactic for all new businesses to follow.

WHAT ADVICE WOULD YOU GIVE SOMEONE WANTING TO ACHIEVE SIMILAR SUCCESS?

Only you know your business and have the passion for it, especially in the beginning. Stick to your values and trust your gut instinct. Be willing to work harder than anyone else and don't accept mediocrity on anything. In the end, this dedication will show through to your customers, and believe me, they'll become very loyal.

LEARN MORE ABOUT KYLE'S BUSINESS:

Come by our site at Rather-Be-Shopping.com and say "What's Up?" Also be sure to follow Rather Be Shopping on:

Facebook: Facebook.com/RatherBeShopping

Twitter: Twitter.com/RatherBeShop

and Pinterest: Pinterest.com/KJames7475/

SERGEY KOTLOV OF WORKSHOPBUTLER.COM

HOW DID YOU COME UP WITH THE IDEA FOR YOUR BUSINESS?

I'm a creator of Workshop Butler—a platform for trainers and teachers to automate their organizational activities before and after training events. I came up with the idea of Workshop Butler while helping a quite big training brand, Management 3.0, to manage its events and facilitators. I was a part of Management 3.0 team for two years, developing a service which later became Workshop Butler.

WHAT WAS YOUR FIRST MAJOR BREAKTHROUGH?

My first major breakthrough was the acceptance of our team to THINK accelerator program in Sweden. During three months full of educational activities, hard work and mentoring sessions, I could clarify my vision for Workshop Butler and made appropriate steps to get our first paid clients on board.

HOW LONG DID IT TAKE YOU TO REACH 100% DIGITAL FREEDOM?

It wasn't about earning enough money. It was more about making the decision to start doing it. As a developer, it was quite easy to me to start working remotely. I quit my job about three years ago and after few experiments, I joined a distributed team. From that moment, I was 100% digitally free.

WHAT WAS YOUR BIGGEST MISTAKE?

Not concentrating enough on the selected type of clients. When I started Workshop Butler, we had three paid clients. Yet I decided to change the direction of the product and target another type of clients first—independent trainers. It was a right choice. However, we invested too much time and money in making our old clients happy. We made features only they needed. As a result, we couldn't deliver a solid product for trainers in a required time frame and I had to find additional investments.

WHAT IS THE SINGLE MOST EFFECTIVE TACTIC YOU DISCOVERED?

Make the client happy. One at a time.

WHAT ADVICE WOULD YOU GIVE SOMEONE WANTING TO ACHIEVE SIMILAR SUCCESS?

You should be prepared that your experiments fail many more times than they succeed. And that's normal. Scientists run hundreds of failed experiments before they get a successful one. Toddlers fall many times before they take their first step. Investors put money in several companies at once, expecting only one of them makes a good return on investment.

LEARN MORE ABOUT SERGEY'S BUSINESS?

Visit WorkshopButler.com and follow me on Twitter (Twitter.com/SKotlov) where I share some insights on my journey as an entrepreneur and our findings how to run your training business more effectively.

RYAN KULP OF USEFOMO.COM

HOW DID YOU COME UP WITH THE IDEA FOR YOUR BUSINESS?

Fomo was originally a Shopify app called Notify, which I acquired in March 2016. My business partner and I, just friends at the time, struck a great deal with the solo founder of Notify and immediately began to rebuild it from scratch.

Notify was a tool that let Shopify store owners show recent purchases on their website, as visitors browsed in real time. This helps increase conversions, because a store's prospects are inclined to think "wow, this store must be great!"

But we saw a much bigger opportunity than Shopify-only and recent sales. We wanted Notify to work on any website, for any type of business (not just ecommerce), and we wanted to let users show off any kind of activity, including signups, blog comments, product reviews, and more.

So we spent three months rebuilding Notify, and we came up with a new name: Fomo. This is an acronym for "fear of missing out," which helps propel our brand forward as a leader in social proof technology.

Fomo launched on August 9, 2016, and we've been growing since.

WHAT WAS YOUR FIRST MAJOR BREAKTHROUGH?

Realizing what channels work best, and then doubling down on them, is everything. At the beginning it's good to try all types of digital marketing: content, ads, SEO, events, email, etc. But if you're paying attention, you should learn pretty quickly which channels actually work.

Alternatively, it may be the case that you try lots of things and none of the channels seem to work. (By the way, "working" means that the cost to acquire a customer on a given channel is less than the value you get back from the customer).

If you get the feeling that "we've tried everything, and nothing works," then maybe it's a product problem. The market is rejecting your solution. And that's OK, because it's generally easy to fix products. You cannot, however, easily create new markets or convince people they need something that they don't.

For us, we realized that despite building Fomo to work on any website and fit any business model, ecommerce stores are still our #1 customer persona. We spent a few months fighting this, because we wanted to be customer-agnostic.

Today, I'm glad we are focused on ecommerce, because it lets us tailor our messaging to that business type. Instead of "use social proof to boost conversions," for example, we can boldly announce "increase sales on your ecommerce store." So, build your messaging around the core audience, even when it's tempting to attract everyone.

HOW LONG DID IT TAKE YOU TO REACH 100% DIGITAL FREEDOM?

Luckily, Notify was already making money (more than $10k/month) when we acquired it. While we didn't pay ourselves anything (and I still don't, 100% bootstrapping as I write this), we've been fortunate to freelance with other companies part time to pay the bills.

It's tough to work full time and build a company on the side. It's also tough to quit your full-time job, have no income, and try to build a company on the side. So the best option, in my opinion, is somewhere in between: cut expenses aggressively, work part time for a higher hourly wage, and prioritize revenue above all else.

Many founders like shiny objects and vanity metrics, like household name customers or X number of users. Instead, find the easiest-to-close customers, as quickly as possible, and start billing them. The other aspects of strategy, like bigger customer personas and viral growth, can come later.

WHAT WAS YOUR BIGGEST MISTAKE?

Immediately after launching Fomo, we hired a business development rep. He came from a couple of very successful, later stage startups, so it felt like a home run.

However, we were nowhere near ready to integrate with big platforms. From a product perspective, we weren't mature enough. From a sales and strategy perspective, there was very little value we could add to the other company's audience.

So we let that person go, but it cost several thousand dollars and was a mistake.

WHAT IS THE SINGLE MOST EFFECTIVE TACTIC YOU DISCOVERED?

For us, insanely aggressive customer service and writing long-form content has worked best. We pay our support team extra to work on the weekends, and I'm typically on live chat with customers in Europe or Asia as late as 3 a.m. on weeknights. Our very first piece went viral on reddit, which was about how we acquired Notify and turned it into Fomo.

We're fortunate to be part of a well defined niche, "social proof marketing," and have begun to rank for related keywords in search.

WHAT ADVICE WOULD YOU GIVE SOMEONE WANTING TO ACHIEVE SIMILAR SUCCESS?

Don't quit your job (yet), build an MVP (minimum viable product), get your first 10 paying customers. You can skip complex market research, focus groups, etc., if you are your number one user. If you won't use your own product, maybe do more research, or reconsider the problem you're solving.

As founders become more serial in nature, you develop intuition about what people want. But in the beginning, being your best customer and intimately knowing the ins and outs of a pain point is a lot more valuable. This is more valuable than knowing how to code, knowing how to design, etc. All of those aspects are just functions that serve your expertise.

LEARN MORE ABOUT RYAN'S BUSINESS:

If your conversion rates could use some help, consider plugging Fomo (UseFomo.com)into your website. Setup takes less than 10 minutes and you'll immediately begin collecting data that will help you determine if it's adding value to your business. Further, I write a couple times per month on my blog (RyanCKulp.com) about marketing and sales.

You can also follow me on Twitter: Twitter.com/RyanCKulp

ADAM ROTMAN OF GETSTENCIL.COM

HOW DID YOU COME UP WITH THE IDEA FOR YOUR BUSINESS?

Stencil actually started out as a tool strictly for creating and sharing text-based images on Pinterest. It quickly evolved to become a product that businesses can use on any social network, blog or email marketing app to create branded visual content. The idea came from seeing all these text-based images on Pinterest and wondering, "How the heck are people making these?" That sparked the idea for a browser-based application that could instantly turn text on any webpage into an image. People loved the concept right away. We reached out directly to any blogger that was writing about Pinterest to see if they would write about us. A bunch of them did and that was the jump off point we needed.

WHAT WAS YOUR FIRST MAJOR BREAKTHROUGH?

I'd have to say this was partnering up with our friends at AppSumo. Strategic partnerships are amazing when the audiences overlap well. This was also a way for us to get exposure to a ton of new potential customers. Word of mouth is an amazing thing.

HOW LONG DID IT TAKE YOU TO REACH 100% DIGITAL FREEDOM?

It took about two years before we were making enough income to be able to quit our day jobs.

WHAT WAS YOUR BIGGEST MISTAKE?

At one point we tried to be everything to everyone. That didn't work out so well. At one point we had a "publisher" version of Stencil that people could install on their own websites. It was a fun idea, but full of technical debt and very little upside in terms of revenue, as this wasn't something most publishers were willing to pay for. In the end, we abandoned the publisher version and focused completely on the browser tool for end users. It was the right move. The takeaway: find out what works and focus on that. Spreading yourself too thin—especially in the early days—can be really distracting and counter-productive.

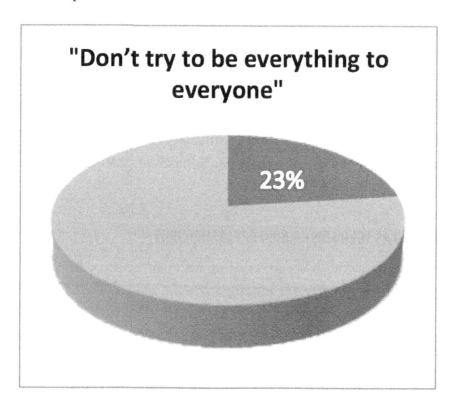

"Don't try to be everything to everyone"

23%

WHAT IS THE SINGLE MOST EFFECTIVE TACTIC YOU DISCOVERED?

Strategic partnerships can be incredibly powerful. Trying to come up with cool cross-promos to do with brands in a similar space can be a win-win for everyone and a great way to tap into a new audience.

WHAT ADVICE WOULD YOU GIVE SOMEONE WANTING TO ACHIEVE SIMILAR SUCCESS?

I'm sure you've heard this before, but it's invariably true in business: *persistence pays off.* The temptation to give up can sometimes be totally overwhelming, but the trick is to charge through. It helps if you have a business partner to keep you motivated when you're down and to do the same for your team when they're feeling lost.

LEARN MORE ABOUT ADAM'S BUSINESS:

The best way to find us is at GetStencil.com and reach out to us any time on:

Twitter: Twitter.com/GetStencil

Facebook: Facebook.com/GetStencil

Pinterest: Pinterest.com/GetStencil

Instagram: Instagram.com/GetStencil

FRED STUTZMAN OF FREEDOM.TO

HOW DID YOU COME UP WITH THE IDEA FOR YOUR BUSINESS?

Freedom is a application that allows you to be productive by locking yourself away from digital distractions. When I was in graduate school working on my Ph.D., I studied social media. And just like anyone else, I was distracted by social media. I would go to a coffee shop to work; the reason I went to this coffee shop is that it didn't have wi-fi. I found that being locked away from digital distractions helped me be more productive. One day, the coffee shop added a wi-fi access point, and my productivity system started to fail. I went home that night and wrote the first version of Freedom. At the time, it was very simple—just a button that locked you offline! I shared it online, and it went viral. Over the past few years, 1.5 million people have tried Freedom, and we've been featured in great media outlets like the *New York Times* and *Oprah* magazine.

WHAT WAS YOUR FIRST MAJOR BREAKTHROUGH?

I come from an entrepreneurial family, and I've always considered myself an entrepreneur. I've started companies and significant internal products at companies where I've worked, so I'm always looking to build products with impact. With Freedom, it was obvious pretty quickly I was building a product with impact that affected people in a positive way. In technology, the cliché is we are all building products to improve people's lives—but this was very tangible immediately. So I realized that I was working on a good idea and in a positive direction. Of course, lots of people have good ideas, and ultimately your success is all about execution—so once I had the "breakthrough" of the product being validated, I had to figure out how to execute on the company (which was much harder and more complicated—my real breakthrough!).

HOW LONG DID IT TAKE YOU TO REACH 100% DIGITAL FREEDOM?

I worked on Freedom as a side product for almost five years before I left my job! In the beginning, Freedom was a very simple one-button app that I gave away for free. However, people very quickly started asking for more features, compatibility for different operating systems, etc. To invest time in building these products, I started charging for the products. Over the years, I became a better developer, figured out how to market the product, and eventually developed the idea for our current business model (a SaaS product). The SaaS product was a considerably bigger undertaking than the business model that came before, and I knew I'd need to work on it full time. So in 2013, I left my job to work on Freedom full time. The first year or two was pretty touch and go, but with increased sales, grants, and eventually with some angel investors we were able to scale the business and get cash flow positive and growing!

WHAT WAS YOUR BIGGEST MISTAKE?

Where do I begin? Of course, a big part of being an entrepreneur is making mistakes and learning from them. So I've made plenty of mistakes - bad hires, poor product decisions, etc. But I think the biggest problem is time wasted focusing on the wrong things. When you are getting a company going you have to be incredibly focused on execution, but there are so many opportunities for distraction. Meeting with potential investors, pitch events, networking constantly, etc.—all of these things feel like work, but for the most part they aren't actually work. And I'm guilty of spending a lot of time on this. What makes our company successful is executing on the idea of helping people be more productive by reducing distraction—realizing that gave me focus and clarity, and the ability to work without distraction on the most important things.

WHAT IS THE SINGLE MOST EFFECTIVE TACTIC YOU DISCOVERED?

If you ask a VC, we are probably doing things the wrong way. For example, desktop software is a big part of our business. And we use email to engage with our customers. But what I've learned is that when the market is entirely moving toward a business model (e.g. mobile first), there are big opportunities for those forgotten consumers. So my advice would be to look for your opening—and those openings are often non-obvious because all of the market and your peers are moving in a single direction. But if you can figure out your underserved area and gain a foothold, you can grow reliably from that position.

WHAT ADVICE WOULD YOU GIVE SOMEONE WANTING TO ACHIEVE SIMILAR SUCCESS?

I am definitely hesitant to say I've achieved success! We have so much more work ahead of us—so my advice applies to me as well. And my advice is—do the work. There is such a vast gap between those with ideas, and those who actually execute on ideas. So you need to start doing the work - actually executing on ideas. And your first few ideas won't work out, so you also need to prepare for that and learn from it. Eventually, you will execute on a successful idea, but only if you do the work.

LEARN MORE ABOUT FRED'S BUSINESS:

You can find Freedom at Freedom.to, and follow us on Twitter at Twitter.com/Freedom or Facebook at Facebook.com/FreedomApp

DOMINIC WELLS OF HUMANPROOFDESIGNS.COM

HOW DID YOU COME UP WITH THE IDEA FOR YOUR BUSINESS?

After I had been having some success with my first few niche sites, I started looking on marketplaces like Flippa because I wanted to see if I could flip sites quickly, or if I could buy any in the future. One thing stood out: people were paying money for starter sites that were pure garbage. I realized that if they were buying junk sites, I could offer them something better, and that's how I came up with the idea for HumanProofDesigns.com.

I initially started selling these sites on Flippa too, but eventually moved to only selling them on my own site. I wanted to be able to control the content and build a brand, and I didn't want to keep competing with scammers. Over time, we also started adding training, and a membership to the site, so that we've become the leader in this corner of the industry.

WHAT WAS YOUR FIRST MAJOR BREAKTHROUGH?

I think the first major breakthrough came from outreach and networking with other marketers. Ironically enough, I wrote a review of Flippa on my site where I criticized a lot of the junk sellers on there. Through that, I started getting attention from other people in the industry who agreed with my thoughts, and one of them was Justin Cooke from Empire Flippers.

We ended up exchanging emails and I asked if they'd consider pointing any of their audience members who wanted started sites in my direction, and to my delight, Justin agreed.

Over time, I started networking with a lot of other people in the niche site space, and now I get a lot of attention and authority without even having to proactively network with people. Much like this article, they come to me now.

As well as getting more traffic and attention, networking lends you a lot of social proof and trustworthiness, which makes it a lot easier to make sales and demonstrate your value. Referral traffic is our best converting traffic source.

HOW LONG DID IT TAKE YOU TO REACH 100% DIGITAL FREEDOM?

I actually started quite slowly and only earned enough to quit my job at the beginning of the second quarter of 2014, after having started out online in August 2012. One thing I noticed is that once I got traction, things moved a lot quicker. It took 18-20 months to earn $1,000 per month online, but it only took another 10 months to get to $10,000, and then another six months to get to $15,000.

WHAT WAS YOUR BIGGEST MISTAKE?

I can only pick one?!

Hmm, it's actually a tough question. I think I have had a few failed experiments, joint ventures, or business ideas that didn't quite pay off. The thing is though, I've had just as many of these that worked out really well, so it's just a case of keeping on trying new things, and accepting that some things won't work out how you had hoped.

It's pretty embarrassing when you launch a new product and it falls on deaf ears, so it's just a case of going back and doing more research and then improving your offer and pivoting to something different.

WHAT IS THE SINGLE MOST EFFECTIVE TACTIC YOU DISCOVERED?

As mentioned earlier, networking with other influencers and working your way up the ladder. This is hands down the best.

WHAT ADVICE WOULD YOU GIVE SOMEONE WANTING TO ACHIEVE SIMILAR SUCCESS?

Keep evolving and keep improving, and be real. While networking with others is the easiest way to get success, it's amazing how many half-hearted networking attempts there are. Some people never get replies and they probably have no idea why. You need to think about how your selfish (and that's what they are really) attempts at networking come across to the other person, and instead just try to be their friend. Always give before you ask as well.

LEARN MORE ABOUT DOMINIC'S BUSINESS:

Visit HumanProofDesigns.com as often as you can, and you'll stay in touch with our projects. I'm pretty active replying to my email subscribers as well, hint hint.

Chapter Three

AUTHORS, CRAFTERS, AND OTHER ARTISTIC TYPES

WRITERS: SCRIBBLE, SCRIBBLE, SCRIBBLE

STEVE ALCORN OF WRITINGACADEMY.COM

HOW DID YOU COME UP WITH THE IDEA FOR YOUR BUSINESS?

I've always been very entrepreneurial, from selling comic books as a kid to operating my own sound recording studio as a teenager. After college, my wife and I became involved in designing theme parks. She worked as an Imagineer at Disney for almost 38 years, and I founded Alcorn McBride (Alcorn.com), the company that provides audio, video and control products to all the world's theme parks.

But that's my day job. My online pursuits started as a hobby but have also turned into a collection of thriving enterprises. I teach an online class in imagineering at ImagineeringClass.com, have two online restaurant review sites that I've not yet monetized, ForkingOrlando.com and ForkingChicago.com, and have helped more than 30,000 students write their novels through WritingAcademy.com.

All of this certainly keeps me busy, but I enjoy it. In the material that follows I'll focus on how Writing Academy was created and came to be a major online educational resource for aspiring authors.

WHAT WAS YOUR FIRST MAJOR BREAKTHROUGH?

I began writing novels 20 years ago, and in the process I met a Hollywood screenwriter who had taken up teaching online classes through college extension programs. He convinced me to create my own classes, which are still distributed through nearly 2,000 colleges and universities worldwide. This was quite a profitable endeavor.

In 2010 I was reading an airline flight magazine about MOOCs (massive open online courses) and wondered if my material would lend itself to those. I contacted one of the providers and created a video-based class about novel writing. The next month they offered it through Living Social and sold $80,000 worth in two weeks.

That convinced me there was something worth pursuing in a big way, so I created a succession of classes, some with my daughter, who is a screenwriter. I quickly realized that it made more sense to host my own school rather than provide the classes on other people's platforms, and that was how the website WritingAcademy.com became a thriving educational market.

Since then, partnerships with Groupon have extended Writing Academy's marketing reach considerably, and I also allow the courses to be hosted on a select set of affiliate sites, particularly overseas.

HOW LONG DID IT TAKE YOU TO REACH 100% DIGITAL FREEDOM?

Because I am an entrepreneur, I've never had a job I could quit. I work seven days a week, but as far as I'm concerned my work is play; I don't know what I'd do without it.

Many people regard modern technology as a digital leash that keeps them tethered to their job wherever they are, but I see it as the opposite. I love the fact that I can market, moderate and event create new classes from anywhere, at any time. That digital freedom allows me to travel the world while doing what I love.

WHAT WAS YOUR BIGGEST MISTAKE?

Successful business consists of doing what you do as well as you can, and trying new things to discover what else you can do. Some of those new things will work, and some won't, so the secret to success is to experiment carefully, never putting all your eggs in one basket.

Each unsuccessful experiment is a valuable learning experience, so I don't regard them as failures.

One of the things I've learned that doesn't work for me is advertising. I've tried a variety of approaches, and none have returned more than their cost.

On the other hand, affiliates and cross marketing work well, and I try to do as much of that as I can. My biggest weakness is that I really don't like marketing; to me, the joy of the business is creating content and sharing it. So I could be doing vastly more business if I spent more time on marketing, or hired a dedicated person to do it. Someday I may, but right now that sounds a bit too much like work to be fun.

WHAT IS THE SINGLE MOST EFFECTIVE TACTIC YOU DISCOVERED?

Partnering with Groupon was a big deal for us. Not only did it generate $100,000 in sales in a short period of time, but it allowed us to build a huge email list consisting entirely of people who had already bought something from us. As a result our click-through rates and conversion rates are amazing.

WHAT ADVICE WOULD YOU GIVE SOMEONE WANTING TO ACHIEVE SIMILAR SUCCESS?

Don't expect to be able to generate a six figure income without putting in long hours. Having the freedom to quit one job doesn't mean you can quit working. You're just working in a different way. So be sure to pick something you love, or you're not achieving true freedom.

LEARN MORE ABOUT STEVE'S BUSINESS:

The key to success in any business is clear and effective communications. That means knowing how to write compelling copy that involves your readers, and incorporates an effective call to action. Additionally, online businesses need to build their email list of prospects, and the best way to do that is to give something away in exchange for contact information. But what should you give away? Something that costs you nothing, but is of great value. That means the written word. Both of these requirements involve writing. Not just any kind of writing, but effective, impactful nonfiction.

At WritingAcademy.com we can show you how to create writing that will turn your prospects into paying customers. Whether it's through self-publishing a best selling book, or creating rich online content, writing is the key to your success. Our best-selling non-fiction writing course is an ideal place to start on your road to success. You can learn more about it here:

WritingAcademy.com/p/Non-Fiction-Writing-Workshop

Facebook.com/WritingAcademy

DEREK DOEPKER OF EBOOKBESTSELLERSECRETS.COM

HOW DID YOU COME UP WITH THE IDEA FOR YOUR BUSINESS?

It all started with a package that arrived in the mail back in 2012. I had won a Kindle e-reader for posting a comment on a blog. As soon as I saw the Kindle, I remembered hearing about people self-publishing books on Kindle.

At this point I was a serial online entrepreneur chasing shiny object after shiny object. I was blogging, creating YouTube videos, writing books and online courses, and whatever else I could find as a way to make money. All I did was burn a hole in my already empty pocket.

Kindle books seemed like a great way to get more exposure to a new audience and build a list without spending much money.

WHAT WAS YOUR FIRST MAJOR BREAKTHROUGH?

I was vacationing with my family over Christmas when I launched my third book *50 Fitness Tips You Wish You Knew*. Up to this point, my prior two books had barely sold, earning me less than a couple hundred bucks not counting expenses.

After throwing everything I had into a free promotion, what happened next "shouldn't" happen. I was a dead broke valet parker and no name author, so imagine how surprised I was to wake up after the book came off the free promotion and saw it starting to sell hundreds of copies.

With a few days of sales continuing to pour in, I knew my life would never be the same. I also knew right away I was going to teach other authors what I had discovered.

HOW LONG DID IT TAKE YOU TO REACH 100% DIGITAL FREEDOM?

I quit my job about three months after the launch of my first successful book. Not from the book royalties, but from creating an online course teaching other authors what I had discovered. By building up a large 1,000+ person buyers list, I was able to both support myself with course sales and ongoing affiliate sales.

Since then, I've continued to grow my business with more kindle books, training courses, and my personal favorite passion of coaching.

WHAT WAS YOUR BIGGEST MISTAKE?

It's hard for me to even see things as mistakes at this point because it all seems so necessary looking back.

The most frustrating experience for me was creating 18+ hours of video and a 350+ page book to sell. I launched it on my own website and was only able to sell a few copies to friends and family at "name your own price." I spent about four months creating it only to have it seem like a complete waste of time.

Luckily, I've salvaged and repackaged much of that content into the books that have now become bestsellers. #winning

WHAT IS THE SINGLE MOST EFFECTIVE TACTIC YOU DISCOVERED?

I don't know if I'd call it a tactic as much as a way of being. It's to form genuine relationships with others and see my competition not as competitors, but as collaborators.

It's much quicker to network with 10 influencers and have them share my work with their thousands of followers than to try to build up tens of thousands of followers of my own from scratch.

WHAT ADVICE WOULD YOU GIVE SOMEONE WANTING TO ACHIEVE SIMILAR SUCCESS?

There are so many things I couldn't cover it all, so my advice would be to learn it all by getting my book *Break Through Your BS*. #ShamelessPlug

Getting a mentor or coach who can help give you specific advice is the safest bet.

The directions I would give to someone wanting to get to Los Angeles if they're coming from New York would be different than if they're coming from London. This is why I'm hesitant to offer one-size-fits all advice because great advice for one person could be terrible advice for another. This is why it's critical to get a great coach or a mentor who can see your blind spots so they can help you find your own path to success which is different for everybody.

LEARN MORE ABOUT DEREK'S BUSINESS:

You can learn more about the work I do with authors and download a free copy of *Why Authors Fail* at EbookBestsellerSecrets.com/FreeBook

Find my books on Amazon at: Amazon.com/Derek-Doepker/e/B0086IEHDY.

SCOTT GINSBERG OF HELLOMYNAMEISSCOTT.COM

HOW DID YOU COME UP WITH THE IDEA FOR YOUR BUSINESS?

I started wearing a nametag 24/7 just for fun. The idea went viral in college. Then I wrote a book about it, which went viral on the Internet. Then people asked me to give speeches, consult, etc., so I asked them for money and suddenly, I had a business.

WHAT WAS YOUR FIRST MAJOR BREAKTHROUGH?

I met a stranger on a bus who passed my business card along to his wife, who wrote a four-page feature article about me in a local paper, which went out on the news wire and went viral and essentially launched my career.

HOW LONG DID IT TAKE YOU TO REACH 100% DIGITAL FREEDOM?

Five years.

WHAT WAS YOUR BIGGEST MISTAKE?

Failure was trying to launch an online television channel to compete with YouTube. Waste of time was having coffee with every stranger who wanted to pick my brain. Waste of money was printing way too many books that nobody wanted, including myself. Most embarrassing mistake was insulting the homeless on CNN in front of 10 million people.

WHAT IS THE SINGLE MOST EFFECTIVE TACTIC YOU DISCOVERED?

Blog every single day. Writing is the basis of all wealth.

WHAT ADVICE WOULD YOU GIVE SOMEONE WANTING TO ACHIEVE SIMILAR SUCCESS?

Blog every single day. Writing is the basis of all wealth.

LEARN MORE ABOUT SCOTT'S BUSINESS:

Just Google the word "Nametag Scott." It's a way to find me, but more importantly, a lesson in brand recognition. Because I never paid for a single advertisement in my life. Writing is the basis of all wealth.

EMILY GOWOR OF
GOWORINTERNATIONALPUBLISHING.COM

HOW DID YOU COME UP WITH THE IDEA FOR YOUR BUSINESS?

I was working in retail at age 19 selling books when a contact of mine who was in the franchising industry asked me a question that literally changed my life: "Did you know you can get paid to write?" He had recognized my talent for and love of writing and saw a greater potential for me than what I was currently doing. I wrote an article for him that was published in a business magazine, and I was off and running!

Fast-forward 10 years to today and I've now written and published eight books, founded a publishing company, written for many entre-preneurs globally, won the 30under30 Anthill Award for young entrepreneurs twice in 2012 and 2014, created global projects uniting people from 15 countries, and inspired thousands from around the world to live a greater life.

WHAT WAS YOUR FIRST MAJOR BREAKTHROUGH?

For me, it was the moment where I was offered the opportunity at age 20 to be an editor on Dr. John Demartini's best-selling book, *Inspired Destiny*. It was a *huge* opportunity for me at the time, and I still feel blessed for it today. It was then that I realized I had the potential to do something BIG in the world and leave a legacy in my own name. I realized my words mattered to people and that I could play a significant role in other people's lives. After working for Dr. Demartini in early 2009, I found the confidence I needed to begin publishing my own books and sharing my original, unique inspiration—my gift of writing—with the world. I believe this was where my life and business really began to take off.

HOW LONG DID IT TAKE YOU TO REACH 100% DIGITAL FREEDOM?

I began writing professionally for people at the age of 19. By the time I was 20, I had left my job to pursue my newfound love of writing for clients, but as I was only earning around $22,000 a year back then, a friend was assisting me with living expenses. But, by age 21, I was earning enough from my writing jobs to fund my journey of traveling around the world and blogging, which I did from age 21 to 23—and it has grown steadily from there. Today, I have several revenue sources including my online life planning trainings, sales from products and my books, publishing services through Gowor International Publishing, licensed consulting methods, one-to-one mentoring on book writing and more.

WHAT WAS YOUR BIGGEST MISTAKE?

Oh, this is a good one! In late 2013, my marketer and I tried (ha ha) to run a week-long campaign called "Authorfest" where we would share content about book writing with people every day and have a 24-hour offer running each day on an author product or training. It was essentially designed as a content-focused upsell fest, and it failed—dismally! But it was a blessing as it showed me what I *really* wanted to focus on: launching my publishing company. I quickly bounced back, sent out an initial offer and enrolled more than $10,000 worth of clients the next week. This proved to me yet again that every failure is an opportunity to become clearer: you just have to have the courage to get up out of the dust and keep going.

WHAT IS THE SINGLE MOST EFFECTIVE TACTIC YOU DISCOVERED?

Continually inspiring and connecting with people! People are where the sales, service, and revenue exist and so nurturing a brand that touches, moves and informs people every day is crucial to the success of a business in today's world. This is the essence of marketing: the more people you meet, the more people you can serve. Also, every single achievement, opportunity, and success I've had in the past decade has come from someone I knew. Either someone mentioned me to someone else for an opportunity, I met the right person at an event, I attracted clients through speaking from stage, or a business colleague nominated me for an award. I've also received countless business advice and spiritual support along the way from my incredible network of contacts and friends. Moral of the story: who you know matters!

WHAT ADVICE WOULD YOU GIVE SOMEONE WANTING TO ACHIEVE SIMILAR SUCCESS?

The most important thing to do is to connect—deeply—with a) what you ultimately love to do and b) what you would love to achieve in the world. Then, build a business around that. For example, my entire business and all my trainings today were built from my love of writing and bringing inspiring messages to the world. So, whenever we are working hard to improve the business or facing an obstacle, this love—the inspiration for the business—remains a strong reminder of *why* we do what we do. If you don't love the business you're in, you're unlikely to see it to its success, but if you do? You'll take it to the world and achieve all of your heartfelt dreams.

LEARN MORE ABOUT EMILY'S BUSINESS:

Follow me on social media, to start with! Many people follow my personal profile: Facebook.com/EmilyGowor and my fan page: Facebook.com/EmilyGoworPage. My personal website is EmilyGowor.com where you can find a lot of inspiration and writing!

You can also find out about my publishing company on GoworInternationalPublishing.com and even book a call to talk with me about your book and future as an author!

STEPHEN GUISE OF STEPHENGUISE.COM

HOW DID YOU COME UP WITH THE IDEA FOR YOUR BUSINESS?

I started writing because I wanted to do it. I found it to be a powerful way to explore life's possibilities. After two and a half years, I finally had a bit of a breakthrough and had about 4,000 subscribers, which I thought was enough to think about making a business of it.

Around that same time, I stumbled upon a powerful strategy I began to call "mini habits" and that ended up being my first book. With my group of loyal followers and a great idea, the book got traction and is now in 17 languages. The success of this book has allowed me to write more books and create without deadlines or worrying about paying rent. The greatest thing about success is gaining freedom to do what you REALLY want to do. I want to write books and create courses to help people change their behavior. And later, I might try my hand at fiction.

WHAT WAS YOUR FIRST MAJOR BREAKTHROUGH?

After more than two years of blogging, I had 400 subscribers and very little hope. I almost quit the blog six (yes, six separate) times. But I enjoyed it, and I had varying times of vigorous guest posting. I wrote a post for Dumb Little Man called "Six Unconventional, Scientific Ways to Be Happier" that was picked up by LifeHacker. From that one post alone, I got 250 new subscribers. Then I started writing regularly for Dumb Little Man and gained a few thousand more subscribers over the next few months. That gave me enough of a following to launch a book.

When I launched the book, it started pretty well, and then I got a Bookbub promotion for it. With the massive spike in sales and even more visibility, I started receiving offers for foreign translation rights and everything kind of took off.

HOW LONG DID IT TAKE YOU TO REACH 100% DIGITAL FREEDOM?

I started blogging in March 2011. I first made money when I launched my book in December 2013. That's about two and a half years.

WHAT WAS YOUR BIGGEST MISTAKE?

I had a failed business idea called "Review My Post." The idea was to give bloggers professional feedback on their posts. I thought it was a good idea and I worked hard to make it compelling, but it didn't really take hold (or else I gave up too soon). Other than that, my first two years of blogging was pretty unimpressive from a business standpoint.

WHAT IS THE SINGLE MOST EFFECTIVE TACTIC YOU DISCOVERED?

Everything changed when I adopted my own "mini habits" strategy that allowed me to be consistent. Before that, I don't think I ever put in enough time in the right places to succeed. But I've been writing every day for probably three years now. Not only is that great for honing your craft, but the sheer increase of content output makes you more visible and gives you more chances to write those home run books or posts.

Other than consistency, persistence is obviously key to my success. So many other bloggers who were far more successful than I was quit before I quit. Some might call me lucky, but you have to be persistently "in the game" to even have a chance at luck.

WHAT ADVICE WOULD YOU GIVE SOMEONE WANTING TO ACHIEVE SIMILAR SUCCESS?

Be consistent. Be persistent. Develop habits in the areas critical to success in your field. The way I develop habits is to shrink the behavior down to something so small I can't say no to it, like writing 50 words per day. Then, once I start, I'll often continue, but even if not, I still did *something*. Too many people try to do too much, and they sacrifice consistency to do it. Consistency is far more valuable than any mega work session, so it's a poor choice. Trust me, I tried the "get motivated and reach your dreams" way for all of my life. My breakthrough happened when (and because) I minified my daily targets to ensure I was consistent. Consistency made my behaviors habitual, which means they're second nature, I don't resist them, and it's *weird* if I *don't* do them. It's a lot easier than having to get motivated every time I need to work.

Your habits define who you are. Don't leave them up to chance like so many people do.

LEARN MORE ABOUT STEPHEN'S BUSINESS:

My online home is StephenGuise.com. My best work is my book collection, which can be found on Amazon: Amazon.com/Stephen-Guise/e/B00HGY6WPA/

JESSE KRIEGER OF LIFESTYLEENTREPRENEURSPRESS.COM

HOW DID YOU COME UP WITH THE IDEA FOR YOUR BUSINESS?

For my current business, Lifestyle Entrepreneurs Press, the idea was birthed after writing my book *Lifestyle Entrepreneur* and working with two traditional publishers, in Asia and America. After seeing how publishing worked from the inside, I had some ideas on how to build a publishing company that is marketing-focused and author-centric. Most authors expect that they'll receive marketing support by signing with a publisher but it's rarely the case. We provide extensive marketing strategy and support in addition to expertly attentive publishing services. It's not a model I see anyone else doing and I love working with interesting authors.

WHAT WAS YOUR FIRST MAJOR BREAKTHROUGH?

Well, in regards to publishing, before I made any big announcements about starting a publishing company, I worked with one of the "lifestyle entrepreneurs" I featured in my book, Jasper Ribbers, who had been traveling the world 10 months of the year and making money from renting his place out on Airbnb. He wrote a book called *Get Paid For Your Pad*, which has become the #1 book for Airbnb hosts and sells consistently month after month. Perhaps without that early success I wouldn't have pursued publishing as much and got interested in something else. After the first couple books I was hooked and decided to really scale this as far as I can

HOW LONG DID IT TAKE YOU TO REACH 100% DIGITAL FREEDOM?

I've been an entrepreneur my whole adult life. My first business was starting a record label at age 21 to support my rock band's career. We raised $100,000, enlisted some mentors and hired a team to support our band Harsh Krieger's debut album, which went on to have nine songs on MTV and music on hundreds of radio stations. Once I saw the connectivity of creativity and commerce I was hooked and have founded or co-founded seven businesses in the last 12 years. Now, that being said, there have certainly been times when I've had more cash than others. There were plenty of times when I invested most of what I had and wasn't sure if I'd run out of money, but one way or another I've found a way to have a pretty interesting life and some cool business opportunities.

WHAT WAS YOUR BIGGEST MISTAKE?

I am resistant to categorizing any of my entrepreneurial experiences as failures or wastes of time and money because I always seek to extract lessons, especially when times seem particularly rough. Instead, I see tough times, failing businesses or seemingly embarrassing moments as preparatory experiences to undertake something greater. I know it's probably not the answer you'd expect but it is the way I look at it. Finding the opportunity in what feels like failure is at the heart of entrepreneurship.

With that said, one of my first "biggest failures" was a $20m investment banking project I worked on for close to a year collapsing at the 11th hour.

The project was to develop an ethanol dehydration plant in Kingston, Jamaica to take ethanol produced in Brazil and blend it for export to USA. I had developed a relationship with the two principals for the project over months, they had flown me down to Jamaica and we even met with the Minister of Energy, who said he supported the development and would even provide tax credits to the developers.

I had fought hard to win this client and was on phone calls, sometimes for hours a day, for months on end putting the deal together. What started off as a long shot started to come into focus and we eventually had support from all the constituents needed to put the deal together. If successful, this would have generated hundreds of thousands of dollars in commissions.

The one missing piece was to get a final approval from the former owner of the site—a major international oil company–- that the development site was clean and ready to build on. We had every assurance every step of the way that this was the case and proceeded to put everything together for the deal.

Imagine my surprise when we finally received the environmental impact report and the site was so polluted and toxic that people shouldn't even be near it.

Very quickly months of work unraveled, everyone involved became increasingly frustrated, and ultimately I made $0.00 for working crazy hours for months.

It was a very difficult lesson to learn—and internalize—that despite giving my best effort and diligently working to put every piece into place, that in some cases that is not enough. I took it very personally, and ultimately that was my lesson: To have better boundaries and expectations for projects so I don't wind up so invested and so involved that I lose perspective on what is realistic to accomplish, and a better idea of when it makes sense to walk away.

WHAT IS THE SINGLE MOST EFFECTIVE TACTIC YOU DISCOVERED?

I proactively build relationships with people I would like to learn from and partner with. By proactively, I mean seeking opportunities to add legitimate value to them and their business or brand, then doing so without asking for anything in return. Once that value has been delivered and acknowledged, there is usually an opportunity to share what would be valuable to me. Then we can discuss it from a position of mutual respect and determine how we could collaborate. One example of this would be joining a course or training program from someone you admire, actually doing the work and engaging with the other students. Help make the leader look good and he or she will definitely pay attention. I've become case studies, spoke on stages in front of hundreds and developed powerful JV partnerships from taking this approach.

WHAT ADVICE WOULD YOU GIVE SOMEONE WANTING TO ACHIEVE SIMILAR SUCCESS?

1. Make a decision to take action THIS YEAR

2. Decide an initial direction you want to go. Don't be married to this, just choose and know you can change

3. Take action every day. Consistency builds momentum, and at a certain point momentum becomes unstoppable.

4. Stay humble. When you have a success, celebrate it and move on.

5. Read Lifestyle Entrepreneur :-)

LEARN MORE ABOUT JESSE'S BUSINESS:

I am always interested in meeting authors and entrepreneurs who want to publish a book they can be proud of for years to come. Learn more about the Lifestyle Entrepreneurs Press approach to publishing here: LifestyleEntrepreneursPress.com and my personal site is JesseKrieger.com

SHAWN MANAHER OF BOOKMARKETINGTOOLS.COM

HOW DID YOU COME UP WITH THE IDEA FOR YOUR BUSINESS?

The cool but crazy story behind Book Marketing Tools starts a little over four years ago. Back in 2012, the noise around new authors who were experiencing remarkable success publishing through Amazon. com was becoming increasingly loud. Each month, a royalty check brought in a tidy little income that eventually allowed many of these writers to create fully-fledged, profitable book businesses. Who wouldn't want in on that? So, it wasn't long before I decided to join the game and test things out for myself.

With several book concepts in mind, I outlined the content and then worked with a ghostwriter to pull everything together. Within 45 days, I had my first book published on Amazon. Full control over the process. No rejection letters. It was an author's dream.

After researching how to market effectively on Amazon, I knew that I needed to enroll in the site's KDP Select program if I wanted access to a powerful suite of marketing tools that would allow me to promote my book on the platform. The reality was a little different, though. In order to attain the reach I wanted, I had to leverage KDP's promotional tools along with free and bargain book promotion sites. I submitted my book to almost 100 sites and...it worked! Within the first month of publishing, I was earning $400 in income, which only continued to increase as the months rolled by.

While stepping into the realm of self-publishing, I quickly realized a few things: marketing a book on Amazon is hard work, it's incredibly time intensive, and it's not an easy thing to do. That's when I knew I had to help simplify this process. I wanted to create tools and services that wouldn't only help me as an author but others, too. Shortly after, Book Marketing Tools was birthed.

WHAT WAS YOUR FIRST MAJOR BREAKTHROUGH?

Our first major breakthrough only came when we launched The Author Hangout Podcast. Taking six months to chat with authors one-on-one, we heard their struggles and took note of their pain points. It gave us a strong idea of the type of content authors both needed and wanted.

The success of our first episode was mind blowing. More than 400 people tuned in to listen and that was when I knew we had an audience to serve. With the right products, we would find success.

Before we launched the podcast, we knew that building an email list was crucial. So, we created The Ultimate Author Checklist, (BookMarketingTools.com/Free-Checklist-Guide/) an initial opt-in offer that has generated more than 6,000 downloads since the show launched.

HOW LONG DID IT TAKE YOU TO REACH 100% DIGITAL FREEDOM?

Here's where I tell you that I used my list to make enough money to quit my job and go digital full-time, but I had actually done that three years prior thanks to my first online business, The Content Authority. It did take me three years to become 100% digitally free, though.

WHAT WAS YOUR BIGGEST MISTAKE?

With all my experience and subsequent accomplishments, I wish I could tell you that Book Marketing Tools was a success right off the bat—but it wasn't. My biggest failure when starting the business was creating a product no one wanted. Even though my team and I had listened to authors, spent time getting to know them, and learned about their pain points, I got it stuck in my head that what they really needed was something not as vital as what they said they wanted.

So, I spent $15,000 (ouch!) building a stats dashboard for authors to keep track of the results from their marketing efforts. As you can imagine, it completely bombed because I didn't have the discipline at the time to know the difference between what I thought authors needed and what they actually wanted. In the end, we recouped $1,000 in sales—a significant loss.

WHAT IS THE SINGLE MOST EFFECTIVE TACTIC YOU DISCOVERED?

Our forethought in building our email list paid off big time. We managed to turn our losses around with solid author-centered products people wanted. Besides Book Marketing Tools, we built out Reading Deals, as well as other popular offerings to help authors get their book in front of targeted readers. We've also made sure to grow our list continuously by producing new opt-in offers our subscribers genuinely appreciate.

The real power in actively growing our email list is that we can market and sell the products and services we now have to offer without limitations and to people who want to hear about them. Their response to a particular offering quickly lets us know whether it's hot or not. And because we know how much each subscriber is worth, we can now make a close estimate of future sales based on how many people are on our list. These days, we do $150k+ in annual sales.

WHAT ADVICE WOULD YOU GIVE SOMEONE WANTING TO ACHIEVE SIMILAR SUCCESS?

If there's one piece of advice I'd give to someone wanting to achieve similar success, it would be to be patient. Be persistent, but be patient as well. As someone who has been there multiple times, I get the mindset of an entrepreneur. You want results yesterday. The reality is it doesn't work that way. Results only come with a patient approach to doing things right in business:

1. Identify the needs of your audience.

2. Build products to meet those needs.

3. Grow a targeted audience to buy your offerings. (Start early!)

4. Test every part of a product's creation so that you produce the most value for your customers while making healthy margins for your business.

Patience is key.

LEARN MORE ABOUT SHAWN'S BUSINESS:

One of our bestselling products today is our Reading Deals Book Promotion service. (ReadingDeals.com/Submit-Ebook) With the click of a button, it tackles the very thing I wanted when I first published to Amazon—reach. With a Reading Deals promo, authors can put their free and bargain books in front of more than 35,000 genre-specific readers who are eager to find their new favorite authors. It not only creates phenomenal exposure, but it also has the potential to increase download volume and drive your book up bestseller lists. Pretty awesome, right?

To find out more about us or to get in touch, visit BookMarketingTools.com.

DEREK MURPHY OF CREATIVEINDIE.COM

HOW DID YOU COME UP WITH THE IDEA FOR YOUR BUSINESS?

I've had lots of business ideas that weren't that great. When I was doing my master's degree in literature I started an editing company, which taught me a little about web design and online marketing. Then I started doing book covers for my own books, and offered them to my editing clients. Then I just started offering cover design, which paid better. I think the trick to business is trying to find something that people in your community want or need, and giving it to them—in a cooler/better way than anyone else is doing.

WHAT WAS YOUR FIRST MAJOR BREAKTHROUGH?

The shift I talk about on my main site, Creativindie, is going from self-fulfillment to providing value. A lot of people want a business that reflects what *they* want to do, and expect people to just pay them for existing. You need to have something of value that people want. The easiest way to do that is by *making things of value*. Most people, especially creatives like artists and authors, make what they want first and then try to convince people to buy it. I did that for a decade and was a starving artist. Then I "gave up" and started learning how to make money online by helping people achieve their own goals. Ironically, now that I can make money easily and don't have to spend much time working, I have a lot more time to focus on my creative projects.

HOW LONG DID IT TAKE YOU TO REACH 100% DIGITAL FREEDOM?

This depends a lot on where you live. For about the past ten years I've been living in Taiwan, and it's crazy cheap. I remember being an English teacher and earning $2,000 a month, and feeling good because we were making twice what locals made, with half the hours. Then I met a guy with an import business that made $5,000 a month and played video games all day. Once I was making that much, I felt like a rock star. But that can also be dangerous—if you're in a cheap country and are making more than enough to live well, you may stop hustling to build your business. Last year I made just enough for my wife and I to travel full time, rent a castle in France for a month, and take a 14-day cruise, but I was still making less than the year before. However I have some bigger goals now, and am ready to build my business to the next level. Someone asked recently on Facebook if I'd rather have $2,500 in passive income a month or $10,000 in active income working 60 hours a week... I chose passive, because I've already gone down the other road—making $10K a month but working all the time, and I don't want to do it again. Instead I want to build passive assets and funnels that make $10K a month without all the work.

WHAT WAS YOUR BIGGEST MISTAKE?

An embarrassing mistake I made recently was failing to upload a final copy of my book, *Guerrilla Publishing*, before the publishing deadline. So over 200 people got the shitty rough draft that I'd uploaded months before. But I'd do it again, because the preorders force me to finish a lot of writing quickly. I just emailed my list and apologized and sent them a full PDF version—it sucks to be so unprofessional, but actually I don't think it'll hurt my credibility at all (it just humanizes me), and I uploaded the right file as soon as I could so it's fine now.

Some authors don't like the way I do things, because it's so rough and unpolished, but I get a lot done and they can't argue with my results—most authors don't make any money with their books and I earned almost $1,000 this week. Now that I'm writing fiction (which sells much better), I'm aiming to get just my book income up to $10K a month by the end of the year.

I've also said some stupid things on my blog, and sometimes someone will dig out an old post and lead an internet crusade against me. It doesn't happen often, but it's happened more than once. Don't forget, when you're writing something, to consider whether it's going to alienate or piss off a lot of people. One of these was an article on choosing an editor for my editing company. At the time, I was a 24 year old trying to get business away from 60 year old publishing veterans, so I said things like how younger people have better eyesight and mental focus. I got a lot of hate mail for that, edited the post, removed most of the incendiary content, posted an apology and removed the harshest reviews. And actually, I've learned that "hate traffic" is just as good or better than real traffic. So it's OK to piss some people off, but I wouldn't fuel the flames or continue to stir the controversy if people are angry. Just diffuse the tension as best you can and move on.

WHAT IS THE SINGLE MOST EFFECTIVE TACTIC YOU DISCOVERED?

In the beginning, I reached out to influencers and tried to see whether I could help them with something; or I asked if they'd add me to their resources list. Now I use a combination of giveaways and Facebook advertising to build lists, which is effective, but more work than getting natural traffic with SEO and guest posts. I also try to make pretty epic content that's useful for my audience (big case studies, lots of screenshots, tons of details).

I use KingSumo giveaways and offer something attractive, like a free month long writing retreat in a castle, or a $2,500 publishing package. Something practical, and something amazing. People will sign up to win, but they share more if the prize is awesome. I get those people on a list and try to provide value quickly, establish myself as an expert, and keep showing up so they get familiar with me. Eventually I may try to sell them a course or something. I'm still working on improving my funnels to be more profitable... but basically I'd get them on my site, get them to sign up for something for free, add a tripwire (cheap product or service) and a one-time offer (upgrade to a course at a discount) and then shower them with free and amazingly useful content and resources for a few weeks. Then I'd ask if they need more help and support, or are ready to take it to the next level... and let them know about my course (then I'd use a full course launch funnel, 7 or 10 steps). This is tricky stuff but I'll be doing evergreen launches so I can test a lot of things out quickly.

I also do well with books, which is my main business—I put out permafree books that rank at #1 in several categories in the free store. There's very little competition because few nonfiction authors are using permafree books. Those books take zero promotion and show up in search results; I turn the books into Powerpoints for SlideShare, make a video series talking about each section, and put all of that content up pointing back to my lead gen offer. I can repeat that process with multiple topics or books, and it works well for fiction or nonfiction.

WHAT ADVICE WOULD YOU GIVE SOMEONE WANTING TO ACHIEVE SIMILAR SUCCESS?

Focus on design, branding and positioning. After you have something people want, you need to give it to them in a better/new/prettier way. So you need your offer, and you need traffic to get people to see it—but that's not enough. You can increase your conversions a lot by having a great brand. But also, you should always be trying to make more and work less. A lot of people get overwhelmed just trying to keep things running and boost sales to make more money; but more money won't solve all the problems if your business isn't scalable. This year I've chosen to make significantly less money, so I can finally fix some of my platforms and make them more profitable. Once I have my time back, I can build more passive assets, or focus on increasing traffic, because it'll make a much bigger difference.

LEARN MORE ABOUT DEREK'S BUSINESS:

My main hub site is CreativIndie.com, but I recommend you grab *Guerrilla Publishing* for free here: CreativIndie.clickfunnels.com/optin79kfixln—although it focuses on book marketing, almost all the same tactics can be used to build any online business.

KARY OBERBRUNNER OF KARYOBERBRUNNER.COM

HOW DID YOU COME UP WITH THE IDEA FOR YOUR BUSINESS?

I had been writing books since 2004. It was a side hobby because I didn't understand how to turn books into a business. Like most people, I was taught that a book is a business card. Although there are major differences between business cards and businesses, most authors don't know them. Sadly, this is why most authors are also broke. Here are just a few of the differences:

BUSINESS CARDS	BOOKS
Cost Money	Create Value
Are an Expense	Are an Asset
Decrease Space in your Wallet or Purse	Increases Influence, Impact, and Income
Get Thrown Away	Last Forever
Change Landfills	Change Lives

WHAT WAS YOUR FIRST MAJOR BREAKTHROUGH?

I started out as a poor author and I stayed a poor author, despite being a traditionally published. Put it this way, although I wanted to be a full-time writer I kept my day job. I made three critical mistakes in the beginning.

Poor Authors	Smart Authors
1. My book is a business card.	1. My book is a business.
2. My book is the end of a relationship.	2. My book is the start of a relationship.
3. My book is a single product.	3. My book is a suite of products and services.

In 2010 with my fourth book I started to get smarter. I changed my perspective and created 18 Steams of Income© from my books. My influence, impact, and income began increasing. I turned each of my next four books each into six-figure+ businesses. This switch helped my dream of becoming a full-time writer become a reality. Since many people ask me about these 18 Streams of Income© I've included them below:

1. AUDIOBOOKS

Audiobooks are the Fastest-Growing Format in Publishing. If your books aren't on audio you are missing a huge opportunity.

Here are three reasons why audiobooks are exploding in popularity:

» Audiobook players (a.k.a. smart phones) are always within our grasp.

» Audiobooks create an entirely different experience. (The spoken word adds a new dynamic.)

» Audiobooks allow us to do two things at once (1 cognitive and 1 non-cognitive).

2. EBOOKS

Similarly to audiobook players, ebook readers are now as close as your smartphone. The average person touches their smartphone over 2,600 times a day. Reading an ebook can happen while standing on a subway, sitting in a doctor's office, or waiting in line at the grocery store. The deal sweetens rather quickly when most ebook royalties now pay authors 70% of the retail price.

3. HARDCOVER

Hardcovers make a statement unlike any other format. They scream expensive and they are. They often retail at more than twice the price of the paperback version. However, self-published authors and top selling traditional authors can benefit from getting massive discounts for their hardcover books when they order in bulk.

4. SOFTCOVER

Softcovers (also called paperbacks) are still hot sellers. This format gives your readers the benefit of your book without the higher cost of a hardcover.

5. EPUB

EPUB is an ebook file format with the extension .epub that can be downloaded and read on devices like smartphones, tablets, computers, or e-readers. Why not maximize your book sales by making it available in every format possible?

6. MASTERMIND GROUP

Napoleon Hill defined a mastermind as, "Two or more people, who work in perfect harmony for the attainment of a definite purpose." Masterminds can range in price from free to over $100,000 per person per year for high end versions. I've built yearlong masterminds around several of my books including *Day Job to Dream Job*. (Amazon.com/gp/product/0801015227)

7. SELF-STUDY ONLINE PROGRAMS

Many readers want to experience your content on a deeper level. As a result, we've created an online coaching program (DayJobToDreamJob.com/Dream-Job-Bootcamp-Join/) for each of my last four books, including my fiction book too. Clients can access the content 24/7. Best of all, you only need to create this once and then you can increase your influence, impact, and income for the rest of your life.

8. LIVE COACHING PROGRAMS

I love the rush I get from coaching clients through my books in a live setting. Although I started in 2012 with in-person coaching programs, after a few months I quickly moved these coaching programs to include a live virtual programs too. This is easy to do with Zoom for as little as $15 a month. You can even record the session and send the video to clients who had to miss. It's as easy as connecting with your phone, tablet, or computer.

9. CERTIFICATION PROGRAM FOR SPEAKERS, TRAINERS, COACHES

One of the smartest ways to increase your influence, impact, and income is to certify other people to speak, coach, and train on your content. We began this process in 2011 and today we now have over 100 team members in over a dozen countries.

10. PAID WEBINARS

You can run free webinars through GoToWebinar or many other platforms. These webinars can be live or recorded. It's a great way to bring in some extra income and extend your reach.

11. PAID CONFERENCE CALLS

Paid conference calls are cheaper and just as effective. I ran dozens of conference calls several years ago. With free tools like Eventbrite and FreeConferencing there is no reason not to. We use Eventbrite monthly and have for the past five years.

12. KEYNOTE SPEAKING

Getting paid to share your message is an incredibly rewarding experience. Why not? You're the expert...and you literally wrote the book! You should be the one to speak on your subject matter. Keynote speaking often involves traveling to breathtaking places and connecting with amazing people.

13. LIVE SEMINARS

I've done over one hundred live seminars on topics from my books. These ranged from 30 minutes to several hours. I love this format because it gives people the opportunity to experience you and your content in a small way without a high level of commitment. Don't forget to have a table in the back where you can make your books and coaching programs available.

14. CONFERENCES

The past five years we've had an annual event called the Igniting Souls Conference. (IgnitingSoulsConference.com) People come from all over the world come to attend. Think of it as a family reunion chock full of practical content. Last year we designed the entire conference around my most recent book—*Elixir Project*. Attendees learned how to become unhackable in work and life.

15. WORKSHOP IMMERSION

Don't think your event needs to take place within the four walls of a hotel or conference center. My book *Day Job to Dream Job* uses a *Shawshank Redemption* metaphor to describe how the prison of our day jobs keep us institutionalized. In the book I teach people how to go from Prison to Plan to Payoff.

I thought it would be cool to have an event called Escaping Shawshank at Shawshank Prison. We taught people how to escape the prisons holding them back. Every attendee said this event was life-changing.

Think outside the box. Maybe your immersion experience could be at a castle, a bed and breakfast, a museum, or some other exclusive location relevant to your book.

16. HIGH-END BOOK CREATION CONSULTING

Once you create a few of these streams of income, people begin to take notice. They look to you as an authority who can help them in their own author journey. If you like you can begin consulting with individuals or organizations. I call these 1/2 day experiences Igniter Sessions. I find them incredibly fulfilling for me and the author alike.

17. HIGH-END BOOK MARKETING AND LAUNCH CONSULTING

Again, at this point you're creating an amazing enterprise. I document everything I do in my own launches so I can help others save time and money when it comes time to create their own launches. Marketing the book is as important as writing and publishing the book.

18. AUTHOR PROGRAM

After creating 17 streams of income you might want to think about creating your own author program.

HOW LONG DID IT TAKE YOU TO REACH 100% DIGITAL FREEDOM?

I earned money immediately and about two years later I was able to more than replace my income and leave my day job.

WHAT WAS YOUR BIGGEST MISTAKE?

In the beginning I didn't have the courage to say no to the "can I pick your brain?" lunch invitations. I wasted a few meetings with less than interested paying clients. However, I quickly learned how to filter those requests and qualify prospects.

WHAT IS THE SINGLE MOST EFFECTIVE TACTIC YOU DISCOVERED?

Clarity attracts. Confusion repels.

WHAT ADVICE WOULD YOU GIVE SOMEONE WANTING TO ACHIEVE SIMILAR SUCCESS?

Start with a side hustle first. If you can't make time for your passion in the margins then you won't be able to make it when it's your full-time gig either. Your dream job is earned when you become the person worthy of your dream job.

LEARN MORE ABOUT KARY'S BUSINESS:

I've helped over 300 authors write, publish, and market their book the right way. Each of them started by watching the free training. On the webinar there is no click to buy anything. Rather, you'll receive a webinar guidebook that will help you on your author journey. Every minute is designed to bring you value. I've reduced the most important lessons I've learned in my 13+ year career as a six-time traditionally published author, including how to turn a book into a business. KaryOberbrunner.com/Book

JYOTSNA RAMACHANDRAN OF HAPPYSELFPUBLISHING.COM

HOW DID YOU COME UP WITH THE IDEA FOR YOUR BUSINESS?

I used the hedgehog concept from the book *Good to Great* by Jim Collins to arrive at my business idea.

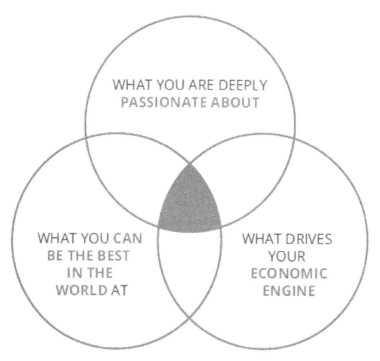

THREE CIRCLES OF THE HEDGEHOG CONCEPT
JIM COLLINS - GOOD TO GREAT

Source: Good to Great by Jim Collins:
http://www.jimcollins.com/books.html

During 2014-2015, I published over 50 Kindle books written by ghostwriters, which was giving me a decent passive income. While it was great to make money on Amazon, I wanted to build a sustainable business on my own platform. That's when I was interviewed by Ani Alexander on her podcast Write to Be Read. She suggested that I should start a service for authors who want to self publish, as I had the perfect skills, network, and expertise. I tried to fit this idea into the Hedgehog concept and realized that it would work as I was very passionate about books. My team of freelancers and I had the competence to produce great work, and I was part of many author's groups on Facebook who were looking for designers, formatters, editors, etc. all the time. Therefore, I partnered with Ani and started the business. After a few months, we both felt that the partnership was not working; we parted ways, and my current business Happy Self Publishing was born.

WHAT WAS YOUR FIRST MAJOR BREAKTHROUGH?

Publishing my book, *Job Escape Plan,* has been my biggest breakthrough so far. The minute my book hit the bestseller charts, I got the confidence to call myself an authority in my niche. I then got the opportunity to showcase my personal brand, build connections with successful people, speak at conferences, and get noticed. I don't think Happy Self Publishing would have happened if I had not become an author in the first place!

HOW LONG DID IT TAKE YOU TO REACH 100% DIGITAL FREEDOM?

I actually quit my job five years ago to have the freedom to be my own boss. My first business was a staff recruitment agency, which was doing well but was taking too much of my time and energy. After my first child was born, I decided to have a business that would give me the freedom of time and the ability to work from home. I found publishing books on Amazon a good method to make money online. It took me six months to start earning enough money through royalties so that I could shut my other offline businesses.

WHAT WAS YOUR BIGGEST MISTAKE?

Before I started my online businesses, I was under tremendous pressure to grow my staff recruitment agency. So, I borrowed money from my dad to recruit some full-time employees, even before I had built any systems in the business. I finally had to shut the business as I couldn't afford to pay my staff when the revenue dropped. Thankfully, my Kindle business had started to pick up by then. But, this failure taught me a lesson which I still use at Happy Self Publishing. I have a team of 15 talented people from across the world, and the number is growing every month. However, none of them are on my company's payroll. They all work on a project basis, and this decision has lifted a lot of pressure from me. I can now grow the business at my own pace without incurring a lot of fixed monthly costs.

WHAT IS THE SINGLE MOST EFFECTIVE TACTIC YOU DISCOVERED?

I realized that people like to do business with people whom they know, like, and trust. Therefore, I am quite active inside author communities and masterminds. I go out of my way to help fellow authors as much as I can by sharing my knowledge, giving feedback, directing them to the right tools, etc. As a result of this, many of them come back to my company when they need publishing related services. This gives me an edge over other freelancing websites.

WHAT ADVICE WOULD YOU GIVE SOMEONE WANTING TO ACHIEVE SIMILAR SUCCESS?

I have suffered the shiny object syndrome for a very long time, until I read the book *The One Thing* by Jay Papasan and Gary Keller. I decided that I should singularly focus on one business till I can completely automate and scale it before I jump into another idea. There was a time when I was managing four businesses and felt miserable. The moment I decided that I should devote myself to Happy Self Publishing, it created a momentum to grow the business. Therefore, my advice to other entrepreneurs would be to FOCUS: Follow One Course Until Successful.

LEARN MORE ABOUT JYOTSNA'S BUSINESS:

If you've been thinking of writing a book for a long time, I would recommend you to take up my 7 Day Book Kickstart challenge that will prepare you to finish your manuscript and publish your book in 60 days or less: HappySelfPublishing.com/Challenge

If you just don't have the time or skills to write, you may want to check out my Angel Writing services (this is *not* the typical ghost-writing!) : HappySelfPublishing.com/Angel-Writing

If you've already finished your book's rough draft, congratulations! You can now head over to the publishing packages we offer: HappySelfPublishing.com/#Packages

RICK SMITH OF RICKSMITHBOOKS.COM

HOW DID YOU COME UP WITH THE IDEA FOR YOUR BUSINESS?

I was desperate, to be honest. I'd crashed out of my high-flying, high-earning executive career when a company I'd been hired to turn around suddenly lost its investor. At 55, I knew I was done with big business, I knew I wanted to work alone—preferably online— but after months of false starts—blogging, e-commerce, the usual stuff—I couldn't come up with a viable idea. So I wrote a book about something I already knew and stuck it up on Amazon to see what would happen.

WHAT WAS YOUR FIRST MAJOR BREAKTHROUGH?

It was a niche book, but it started to make steady sales. I was hustling on some Facebook groups, and in the second month I sold over a hundred copies. These were the first dollars I'd ever made online, and it smelled like a real business. So, I thought of something else I didn't need to research very much, and wrote another, then another.

HOW LONG DID IT TAKE YOU TO REACH 100% DIGITAL FREEDOM?

I'd already quit, so I was full time from the word go. It took me about a year before I was covering the bills, but I could see it growing month by month. It was a simple equation; the harder I worked, the more money I made. I'd always written, but during my previous career I'd never had time to do anything serious. I don't think I'd have made it that way.

WHAT WAS YOUR BIGGEST MISTAKE?

Collaborations. Based on my own results on Amazon, I took on a bunch of projects for other first-time authors, everything from deep editing, cover design, formatting, to publishing and promotion, on a royalty-split basis. Sadly, most of them didn't do any promotion of their own, so the books didn't sell. I don't do that anymore!

WHAT IS THE SINGLE MOST EFFECTIVE TACTIC YOU DISCOVERED?

Content is king, but marketing is King Kong. Once I understood how Amazon's search works, I focused on mastering keywords. There are two traffic sources for Amazon; the clicks you generate yourself through advertising and promotion, which can cost a lot of money, and Amazon's own organic traffic, which is essentially free if you can figure out how to hijack your fair share. So, visibility is paramount, and relevance drives visibility. Hence, for me, effective keywords are the single most important factor in optimizing your product on Amazon.

Running a close second is building your "base." I waited a couple of years before I got serious about building my mailing list, and I wish I'd started much earlier. Now, I have thousands of opted-in subscribers, so when I publish new products or content, there's a ready-made, easy-to-reach audience to launch to.

WHAT ADVICE WOULD YOU GIVE SOMEONE WANTING TO ACHIEVE SIMILAR SUCCESS?

Firstly, focus on your work ethic. The concept of passive income works fine in theory, but it's important to create a critical mass of revenue streams, using multiple products or services, before you can sit back and watch the cash accumulate. Create a structure around yourself which enables realistic deadlines, and work hard to achieve them.

Second, embrace outsourcing. Learn how to write short, accurate briefing documents. The internet offers every possible kind of service, enabling you to offload tedious or repetitive tasks very easily. Focus your own efforts on the most important tasks: creating and marketing content, the essence of revenue generation. There are thousands of low-cost freelancers out there who are only too happy to take on your grunt work and complete it more quickly than you can ever do.

Third, choose your tools wisely. Invest in reliable hardware, and get the right software for the job. Everything is available on monthly subscription (Microsoft Office, Adobe Creative Cloud, Grammarly, Canva, aWeber etc.) so it's easy to keep your costs under control.

LEARN MORE ABOUT RICK'S BUSINESS:

If anyone's interested in my books, simply search for "RickSmithBooks" on Amazon, and take your pick. If you are interested in producing your own book you can check out "Createspace and Kindle Self-Publishing Masterclass, a step-by-step Author's guide to writing, publishing and marketing your books on Amazon, or visit me at my site: RickSmithBooks.com

AMANDA TURNER OF VAGABONDINGWITHKIDS.COM

HOW DID YOU COME UP WITH THE IDEA FOR YOUR BUSINESS?

I self-published a parenting humor book called *This Little Piggy Went to the Liquor Store* after struggling to break into the traditional New York publishing houses. When it did well, I realized I was on to something. I followed it up with *Mommy Had a Little Flask,* and *Hair of the Corn Dog.* By that point my husband, two daughters, and I were traveling more and for longer periods of time, really testing out the digital nomad life, and I realized that I wanted to transition my work into travel humor. I'm a big fan of Rolf Potts, Tim Ferriss, Bill Bryson, and Anthony Bourdain. But there weren't any women's voices in there, and certainly no stories of families on the road. My husband helped me put together VagabondingWithKids.com and from there I published *Vagabonding with Kids* and *Vagabonding with Kids: Australia.* The series continues with forthcoming books on Brazil, Alaska, Mexico, Spain, and other locations around the world.

WHAT WAS YOUR FIRST MAJOR BREAKTHROUGH?

I signed up for an editor evaluation at a writers' conference in San Diego. I was paired with an editor from Penguin who read a chapter from a draft I'd written. She loved it and asked to see the full manuscript. I was on cloud nine! She gave me invaluable tips to improve the book and really helped me identify my focus and my voice. I was devastated that I never got a contract to publish the book with Penguin, but looking back, I can see now that it was still a pivotal time in my writing career. The manuscript would become *This Little Piggy Went to the Liquor Store*, which I self-published and which eventually went on to become a *New York Times* best seller.

HOW LONG DID IT TAKE YOU TO REACH 100% DIGITAL FREEDOM?

It wasn't long after self-publishing my first book that I transitioned to writing full-time, probably less than a year. But being a writer, like any artistic profession, is a very uncertain business. There are big paychecks and other times when you have to take on debt and hope for the best (most entrepreneurs are accustomed to this.) My husband is an entrepreneur as well, and he's been extremely supportive of me in my career. We work together to advise each other on our respective businesses and manage the income and expenses of them to keep the whole machine running.

WHAT WAS YOUR BIGGEST MISTAKE?

Early on I tried various forms of advertising, most of which turned out to be a waste of money. The biggest waste of time by far is reading negative reviews and fretting over them. As long as the vast majority of my readers are giving five-star reviews, there's no point in getting distressed over the occasional troll. Like most writers, I had to learn this the hard way, and early on I wasted time and energy stressing about bad reviews. Sometimes these reviews had nothing to do with the actual book. For instance, I received a one-star review from a reader because he couldn't figure out how to access the book on his e-reader. Eventually I learned that there are always going to be people like that. The best thing to do is to not worry about them, focus on producing a quality product, and when I do devote energy to my readers, I focus on my fans and let them know they are appreciated. (My fans rock!)

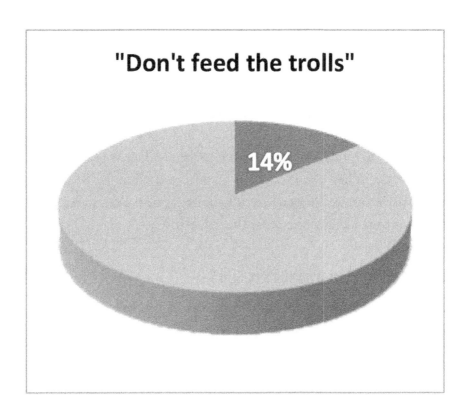

"Don't feed the trolls"

14%

WHAT IS THE SINGLE MOST EFFECTIVE TACTIC YOU DISCOVERED?

Scheduling my time! For an independent author, the most effective tactic to grow readership is to consistently produce high quality content. This means harnessing your energy and consciously focusing it on writing. People hate to hear this, but that often means turning off the television and the Internet. You must own your time and refuse to be a slave to things like email, social media, and the compulsion to constantly check your phone.

WHAT ADVICE WOULD YOU GIVE SOMEONE WANTING TO ACHIEVE SIMILAR SUCCESS?

Outline your book, set deadlines, and meet them. Never attempt to design your own cover or do your own editing. Hiring professionals in those areas is non-negotiable. For a first book, a critique group can be very helpful. Learn to accept criticism and use it to make your book better. When you think your book is ready, find five or six beta readers who are willing to take a look and give feedback, and take the time to really listen to what they have to say.

LEARN MORE ABOUT AMANDA'S BUSINESS:

I write as AK Turner and all of my books are available on Amazon, Barnes and Noble, Google, and can be ordered through bookstores if they're not already on the shelf. You can find me at VagabondingWithKids.com, where I include a free download on how we work, travel, parent, and maintain sanity along the way.

I'm also on social media:

Vagabonding with Kids on Facebook: Facebook.com/VagabondingWithKids

AK Turner on Facebook: Facebook.com/AKTurnerAuthor

Twitter: Twitter.com/VagabondingKids

Instagram: Instagram.com/VagabondingWithKids

Pinterest: Pinterest.com/VagabondKids

TYLER WAGNER OF AUTHORSUNITE.COM

HOW DID YOU COME UP WITH THE IDEA FOR YOUR BUSINESS?

After I launched my first book, tons of people started reaching out to me with questions on how to write and market books. I created my business based off that need in the market.

WHAT WAS YOUR FIRST MAJOR BREAKTHROUGH?

The success of my first book, *Conference Crushing*. It hit bestseller in multiple categories on Amazon and was featured in *Inc. Magazine*. After that, I began writing more books, public speaking, helping others write and market books, and helping people grow their business online.

HOW LONG DID IT TAKE YOU TO REACH 100% DIGITAL FREEDOM?

I actually dropped out of school and wrote my first book within six months of that decision. I had jobs previously, but not during my launch, so I didn't have to quit a job. I became financially free after my company's first launch to help others write and market their books. The first class did really well and now my business mainly runs on referrals.

WHAT WAS YOUR BIGGEST MISTAKE?

One of my first public speeches was to a group undergrads for my business fraternity. At the end of the talk I had everyone do a 15 minute guided meditation that I put on. This group was not ready for this, to say the least. They thought it was extremely weird and I felt uncomfortable after the interaction. My lesson here was to make sure you know your audience before you do something like this.

WHAT IS THE SINGLE MOST EFFECTIVE TACTIC YOU DISCOVERED?

To play the long game. I over deliver on everything. I truly love helping others, whether they are paying me or not. I continuously deliver value to everyone I come in contact with. This naturally gives you leverage. A referral based business is the best business. When clients come to you, it makes things a lot easier.

WHAT ADVICE WOULD YOU GIVE SOMEONE WANTING TO ACHIEVE SIMILAR SUCCESS?

I would tell them to write a book, ASAP. Get a book out there in a field that you want to be an authority in. Then deliver massive value to everyone possible in that field. Build your business around this.

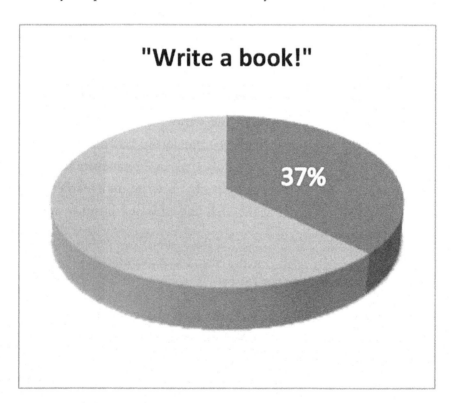

LEARN MORE ABOUT TYLER'S BUSINESS:

If you want to write a book, grow your business online, and have fun while doing it...hit me up!

AuthorsUnite.com

Facebook.com/tywagz

Instagram @tywagz: Instagram.com/tywagz/

VISUAL ARTISTS & GRAPHIC DESIGNERS: SEEING IS BELIEVING

JACOB CASS OF JUSTCREATIVE.COM

HOW DID YOU COME UP WITH THE IDEA FOR YOUR BUSINESS?

My graphic design and branding business is not an original idea; however, what differentiates my business from others is my style of work and my niche of focusing on branding for small to mid-sized businesses. Clients are attracted to the knowledge and articles that are provided on my website.

WHAT WAS YOUR FIRST MAJOR BREAKTHROUGH?

Rebranding and redesigning my website according to my actual goals was my biggest breakthrough. Traffic skyrocketed, work requests doubled as well as my fees, and I had to start turning work away.

HOW LONG DID IT TAKE YOU TO REACH 100% DIGITAL FREEDOM?

Becoming a free digital nomad was a gradual progression and it was not an actual goal of mine. At the time, I enjoyed working at high end agencies with the big brands; however, as an avid traveler, this lifestyle was tying me down and the draw of seeing the world before having kids was too much.

I gradually convinced my wife (travel themed presents helped) and before we knew it we had already circled the globe twice, while visiting 55+ countries. On a side note, we share our travel tips and adventures on our travel blog, **Just Globetrotting**.

WHAT WAS YOUR BIGGEST MISTAKE?

My biggest mistake was underestimating work culture in the USA, especially in New York City. As soon as I graduated university in Australia with my design degree, I moved to New York to work for a digital agency. This move was intimidating in itself, but I soon found out exactly how hard New Yorkers work. It was inspiring but a big wake up call. It really put me in to gear, inspiring me to become bigger and better. I just wish it had been sooner!

WHAT IS THE SINGLE MOST EFFECTIVE TACTIC YOU DISCOVERED?

The single most effective tactic for growing my business is by blogging or what is now called "content marketing." I've never spent a cent on advertising and all my traffic and leads are organic due to the resources and articles provided on my website.

WHAT ADVICE WOULD YOU GIVE SOMEONE WANTING TO ACHIEVE SIMILAR SUCCESS?

Learn SEO (search engine optimization). It's the single most important factor for driving traffic to your website

LEARN MORE ABOUT JACOB'S BUSINESS:

Visit my design blog JustCreative.com and check out my design portfolio (JustCreative.com/Portfolio/)

Sign up to my newsletter (http://bit.ly/2rM7Cts) for great design resources and a free Logo Design Inspiration eBook.

DAMON FREEMAN OF DAMONZA.COM

HOW DID YOU COME UP WITH THE IDEA FOR YOUR BUSINESS?

Out of desperation! I had major debt in the form of a huge overdraft that needed to be paid up within a year. I was on the brink of bankruptcy. I started looking online for ways to use my graphic design skills to make money, and came across a crowdsourcing website called 99designs.com. That site allowed me to bid against other designers for design projects by first doing the work, and then hoping to win the reward of payment for that job. I did this for around six months, just barely keeping my head above water. I started to notice that my win rate was higher on book cover designs than other forms of design, so I started to concentrate only on those. I got paid on around a third of the projects I attempted. This eventually led to my own website offering book cover design exclusively.

WHAT WAS YOUR FIRST MAJOR BREAKTHROUGH?

I happened to find another crowdsourcing type website, although for this one, I could bid for projects using my existing portfolio, and be awarded the job (and later the fee) before doing any actual work. The site was called Elance. Because I had attempted (and won) so many book cover designs by this point through the other website, I had a pretty extensive book cover design portfolio. This allowed me to leverage that portfolio, competing against other designers without having to the design work up front. This was clearly far more time effective.

HOW LONG DID IT TAKE YOU TO REACH 100% DIGITAL FREEDOM?

12 months.

WHAT WAS YOUR BIGGEST MISTAKE?

I made many mistakes before starting this business, which was why I was in so much debt and desperate to earn some additional income. I would say the biggest mistake I made was living beyond my means in the beginning. I had a semi-successful business that grew nicely over the first three years. As it grew, I started to take more profit out of the business, bought more stuff, incurred more debt (which I was confident I would be able to pay off through the business), until gradually my spending outgrew the income of the business. Eventually, I was up to my eyeballs in debt and searching all over the place for loans from any financial institution that would give me money, just to service my lifestyle. I'm now completely debt free.

WHAT IS THE SINGLE MOST EFFECTIVE TACTIC YOU DISCOVERED?

I have two that affected different stages of my business:

1. Become an expert in your field (through research), and then share that expertise far and wide. Become the go-to guy for whatever it is you're selling or the service you're providing by giving away information and advice for free. Write articles, make YouTube videos, be on social media, etc. Websites are always looking for content. If you can provide the content for those websites, you increase your credibility and build trust in your own brand.

2. I was selling my design skills in the form of time. It took me time to create something for a client. The biggest jump in my income came when I started to outsource that time. I used my own skills and expertise to train up other designers and sell their time to my clients. It increased my income four-fold within a few months.

WHAT ADVICE WOULD YOU GIVE SOMEONE WANTING TO ACHIEVE SIMILAR SUCCESS?

You need to give something away for free in order to get paid later. Whether it's your knowledge, your skills or your time, that's what builds up trust and brings you clients in future.

LEARN MORE ABOUT DAMON'S BUSINESS:

Check out my website (Damonza.com) or Facebook page (Facebook.com/DamonzaDotCom)

CRAFTERS AND OTHER MAKERS: BUSY HANDS

HOLLY CASTO OF HOLLYCASTO.COM

HOW DID YOU COME UP WITH THE IDEA FOR YOUR BUSINESS?

I started a blog while working at a boring receptionist job after college, and it instantly sparked something in me. I had been trying to deny my creativity and do the "practical" thing for years, but the more I fed that creative part of my brain, the more it grew. I taught myself Adobe Illustrator, started designing stationery and art prints, and opened an Etsy shop. From there, I started doing freelance design, grew my blog, started a YouTube channel, and the rest is history!

WHAT WAS YOUR FIRST MAJOR BREAKTHROUGH?

There was a span of a few months in my second year of business where my products were featured on some of my favorite blogs that I had been reading for years, and I could not believe it. They were like celebrities to me! The traffic to my shop was obviously amazing, but more importantly, it was a sign to me that I was on the right track.

HOW LONG DID IT TAKE YOU TO REACH 100% DIGITAL FREEDOM?

About 2-3 years.

WHAT WAS YOUR BIGGEST MISTAKE?

In the early days, I was way too quick to delete everything and start fresh (with blogging, products, branding, etc.). In my effort to do things perfectly, I lost a lot of website traffic and sales in the long run.

WHAT IS THE SINGLE MOST EFFECTIVE TACTIC YOU DISCOVERED?

Branding has always been important to my business, especially because I relied heavily on social media marketing. I tried to carefully craft out my target customer and reverse engineer my products from there to a certain extent. I really think that gave my business a competitive edge in the beginning because most Etsy sellers were just creating what they liked without much attention to their brand.

WHAT ADVICE WOULD YOU GIVE SOMEONE WANTING TO ACHIEVE SIMILAR SUCCESS?

Having a successful creative business is a delicate balance of passion and strategy. Find something that you love to create, but make sure there is also a market for it. Then just work hard and put in the time!

LEARN MORE ABOUT HOLLY'S BUSINESS:

You can follow me on YouTube at YouTube.com/HollyCasto or check out my blog at HollyCasto.com

TALITA ESTELLE OF ESTHER.COM.AU

HOW DID YOU COME UP WITH THE IDEA FOR YOUR BUSINESS?

I saw a continuous a gap in the market for women's evening wear, specifically dresses. I realized there was an amazing business opportunity! I've always loved fashion and knew it was the perfect time to launch my own company in the industry. From there Esther was created.

WHAT WAS YOUR FIRST MAJOR BREAKTHROUGH?

Initially, the challenge was establishing brand awareness, which is key for establishing trust and credibility among consumers. To overcome this we utilized our social channels, specifically Instagram, Facebook and Pinterest to get our name out there. While people loved our clothes, once they saw them on our digital platforms, the next issue we faced was getting customers to the stores. This was ultimately what led to the decision of going completely online—I didn't want Esther to be kept within the walls of a brick & mortar store. Esther can now be found in homes all over the world.

HOW LONG DID IT TAKE YOU TO REACH 100% DIGITAL FREEDOM?

I've been very fortunate in that I started working for myself straight out of high school.

WHAT WAS YOUR BIGGEST MISTAKE?

When we moved into our new warehouse/office premises we experienced a major flood. Unfortunately we had a lot of stock and property damaged and had to stop trading for a short period. It was a huge setback for the business.

Looking back, our mistake was moving into new premises and not checking any existing condition thoroughly for issues that should have been addressed or noted upon signing of the lease. I also should have made more consideration when organizing the insurance for the business. Had I looked into the potential risks, we could have saved a lot of time and money.

WHAT IS THE SINGLE MOST EFFECTIVE TACTIC YOU DISCOVERED?

Social media—in the early days of establishing Esther's online presence we used all channels of social media, before there were paid posts and algorithms. This was and still is an amazing way we connect to our target market. Pinterest was the biggest for us—we were very early adopters of utilizing Pinterest to generate exposure to our website. In fact, one pin alone managed to get 80,000 repins, which really gave us a nice push into the U.S. market.

At the beginning we followed similar brand Instagram accounts. We collaborated with influencers who had the market we were after, which allowed us to get exposure via their audience.

WHAT ADVICE WOULD YOU GIVE SOMEONE WANTING TO ACHIEVE SIMILAR SUCCESS?

You need to be passionate about the idea you're pursuing, completely committed and willing to sacrifice. From my experience it's putting your company first, and in saying that you also need to be conscious not to burn out a as result of this.

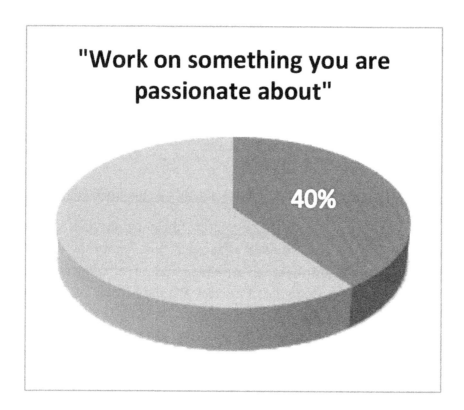

"Work on something you are passionate about"

40%

Surround yourself with an amazing team who share similar values. Remember, you can't do everything yourself, so trust and listen to your team, and don't micro manage.

Stay healthy—physically and mentally, plan ahead, be diligent. In retail you need to be one step ahead of the game, and in an age of constantly evolving technology you need to look at ways to keep up. Listen to feedback, from your staff and your customers. Don't be complacent even when your business is performing well; keep striving for more. We've managed to continually evolve—launching into the U.S. market was huge for us and we have plans to further expand globally.

LEARN MORE ABOUT TALITA'S BUSINESS:

Our site can be found at: Esther.com.au

Instagram: @esther.com.au: Instagram.com/Esther.com.au/

Personal Instagram @health.and.
me: Instagram.com/Health.And.Me/

Pinterest: Pinterest.com/EstherBoutique/

Facebook: Facebook.com/Esther.com.au

Twitter: Twitter.com/EstherBoutique

JAMIE LEWIS OF JLEWBAGS.COM

HOW DID YOU COME UP WITH THE IDEA FOR YOUR BUSINESS?

I have toyed with the idea of starting a business on and off since graduating from an honors entrepreneurship program at DePauw University, the Management Fellows program. Then I toyed with it again during Columbia Business School when I was trying to decide what career to pursue after investment banking. With that being said, I never really got excited about an idea that I thought would work, so I never pursued anything. Much like a number of start-ups, JLEW bags just kind of happened. I never set out to start a business. I saw a gap in the market, put one foot in front of the other to try and address that gap, and here we are. Truly, I needed a bag big enough and nice looking enough to carry all of my workout and work gear. When I couldn't find one, I decided to make my own.

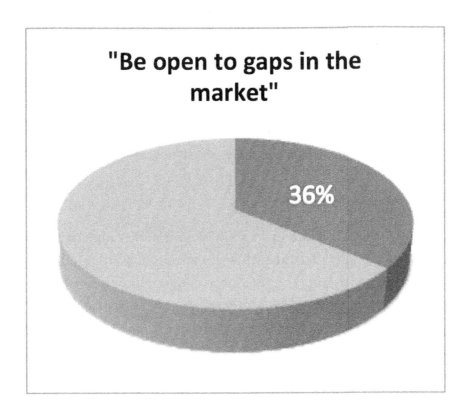

WHAT WAS YOUR FIRST MAJOR BREAKTHROUGH?

Every day I feel like we take two steps forward and one step back, and many days it feels like we take one step forward and two steps back! It's a process and a journey and I can't point to one break-through per se. I get excited every time we improve our product, get positive feedback from customers, land new accounts, grow our community of like-minded #GirlsWithGuts, etc. When I reflect on all we've accomplished in such a short period of time, I think the success comes from a lot of cumulative wins rather than one pivotal "breakthrough." Hard work and passion truly drive us.

HOW LONG DID IT TAKE YOU TO REACH 100% DIGITAL FREEDOM?

Um, does one ever earn enough to quit? I think it's more like when did I gain enough confidence to take the plunge? That too sort of happened. I'm a risk taker at heart, but this is definitely the biggest risk I've ever taken. I feel lucky to have so many supportive family members and friends who helped push me to take the plunge.

WHAT WAS YOUR BIGGEST MISTAKE?

A lot of the mistakes and/or wastes of time or money came from not really trusting myself. I listened to or outsourced to others because they purportedly had more experience or exposure than me, even when my gut instinct indicated otherwise. Nearly every time, while I thought I was spending money to help make money, they cost more to fix in the end, both emotionally and financially. These mistakes frustrate me the most, but have helped me gain confidence and avoid similar pitfalls going forward. I'm lucky to have learned these lessons on my own dime, primarily because I feel the impact directly, but also I would feel incredibly embarrassed had I made such expensive mistakes at the expense of investors' funds and good will.

WHAT IS THE SINGLE MOST EFFECTIVE TACTIC YOU DISCOVERED?

Don't get distracted comparing yourself to competitors or get hung up trying to be all things to all people, because you can't! Be authentic and have patience (insert advice: do as I say, not as I do, as I'm *so* impatient). I do think there's an over-emphasis on growth for the sake of growth. I get caught up in this race and have to remind myself to pause—there's good growth and there's hasty growth; make sure you know and appreciate the difference.

WHAT ADVICE WOULD YOU GIVE SOMEONE WANTING TO ACHIEVE SIMILAR SUCCESS?

Stay flexible, nimble, open minded *and* remember why you started. Believe in yourself. A dear friend and former boss, Ron Christie, texts me this message almost weekly and I thank him for it every time: "Own your brand Jamie. You are your best spokesperson." He's right but it's easy to forget. Having a great support system, belief in yourself and building a dynamite team are critical components of success.

LEARN MORE ABOUT JAMIE'S BUSINESS:

For more, visit JLEWBags.com and follow along on social at @ JLEWbags

PERFORMING ARTS:
FOR THE LOVE OF THE DANCE

SUZANNE VENNARD OF DANCECLASS.COM

SUZANNE VENNARD OF DANCECLASS.COM

HOW DID YOU COME UP WITH THE IDEA FOR YOUR BUSINESS?

It was a simple gap in the market—but, crucially, it wasn't a service or product that I lacked or longed for. It was something I already had access to but could see that others didn't.

I'm a lifelong dancer, but I noticed that although people are fascinated by dance, and may confess a longing to be able to dance, many won't ever sign up for classes—the fear of embarrassment keeps them away. Meanwhile, dance teachers always want to teach adult beginners, but if no one ever comes to the classes, what's the point of holding them? So I brought the two together by filming the best dance teachers I could find, so that beginners could have their first class at home, in private—no embarrassment, problem solved.

I become the first person in the world to offer full length dance classes online, and to date I have had over 25 million views of my videos. That demonstrates a market, right..?

WHAT WAS YOUR FIRST MAJOR BREAKTHROUGH?

Taking control of my company—no longer relying on web designers and consultants, but taking on every single aspect myself brought a natural cohesion to the operation that had been lacking. I stopped being pinged around a bunch of other people's ideas of what I "should" be doing and took full control. That's a nice way of saying I became "chief cook and bottle washer" but it wasn't until I fully understood every aspect of my business that I could really push it in the right direction.

No one is ever going to be as invested in or excited by your business success as you are—yes, I really did need to actually learn this.

HOW LONG DID IT TAKE YOU TO REACH 100% DIGITAL FREEDOM?

I was one of those nutters who quit my job first and set up my company second. That produces a special kind of panic and does focus your mind somewhat. However, during the first few years I did occasionally take on freelance work to keep body and soul together, working for someone else during the day, and at my company evenings, weekends and holidays. And actually, I did some of my best work then as it was such a pleasure to do it, compared to the day job.

WHAT WAS YOUR BIGGEST MISTAKE?

Ugh, by far the biggest time and money suck was having other people code my website for me. Bless them, they meant well, but I landed not one but two websites in a row that looked lovely but the search engines hated with a passion. It wasn't until I decided to take control, learn about what ranks, what doesn't and why, and then learn how a CMS works, that I launched a site that was finally ranked and started to receive organic search engine traffic. And I haven't looked back since.

WHAT IS THE SINGLE MOST EFFECTIVE TACTIC YOU DISCOVERED?

Sticking with it. Just keeping going. Look, we all hear these amazing stories of people who seem to have had one simple idea, flung up a basic website or video, and apparently overnight, have virtual queues around the block, making them a fortune in a week and a half. That's nice. But rare indeed. (And often, although that's their story, there's a lot more to it that you don't get to hear.) And although these stories can be inspirational, they can also make you feel that your business idea isn't worthy because that hasn't happened to you. It took me years, absolute years, to build up my business. It took real sustained effort and now earns what it does because of the genuine momentum all that effort made. Not glamorous or trendy, but taking a gently long-term view paid dividends for me. So just keeping going was the single best thing I did.

WHAT ADVICE WOULD YOU GIVE SOMEONE WANTING TO ACHIEVE SIMILAR SUCCESS?

Keep going (as per above) but keep recalibrating, too. Test, tweak, test again and never, ever, think that you have all the answers. You've got to keep your eye on the prize while realizing that the path there may not take the route you anticipate. I really, really thought that the partner dances, especially the Latin dances such as Salsa, would be my biggest sellers—I put the most money into their development. And was totally wrong.

My ballet program sells more than all my other titles put together. But, instead of doggedly pushing the Latin stuff, I've sidelined it slightly to make much more room for the ballet program, which now has by far the biggest section on my website, and gets 90% of my attention and investment. So you'll have to be OK with letting go of things you love and focusing on lesser or related areas that do have the market demand. Keep an open mind. If what you do is all about you, it's a hobby. It's only a business when it's about your customers.

LEARN MORE ABOUT SUZANNE'S BUSINESS:

Do an adult beginner's dance class online, and be taught by the best dance teachers in the world. Ballet, modern, hip hop, waltz, foxtrot, swing/jive, cha cha—there's something in there for everybody. So if you want to get fit, or just get up off your sofa, want to dance at a wedding, or just want to try a dance class because you've always wanted to, you can. It's all on DanceClass.com—the home of the original online dance classes.

Chapter Four

30 SKILLS AND LESSONS LEARNED

INTRODUCTION

The percentages in these tips and in the graphs throughout this book measure how many contributors mentioned each one. Sometimes it's not completely clear whether a contributor specifically mentioned a particular skill, so the percentages are approximate. The point is, these tips came up repeatedly from the contributors.

We suspect (and in many cases know) that many more contributors are practicing a particular skill. Take "start an email list" as an example: it is likely that all 100% of the entrepreneurs in this book use this particular strategy, although only 15% actually directly tell us to do so. This just goes to show the importance of getting information from many sources. Sometimes a strategy can seem too obvious to mention because it has been so ingrained in us. Yet the beginner might not know it.

You may notice that some of the lessons are very similar, sometimes crossing over. They could be placed under one general umbrella lesson such as "have a positive attitude," or "do marketing," but this leaves too much room for error in exactly what the contributors were trying to say.

We have tried to sort the lessons into a logical order, and you might want to start developing these skills in that order. However, many of these skills will be needed at many stages in your projects, so keep an open mind. You are likely already practicing some (or many) of the skills listed, so you may want to dive in, find areas of weakness, and try to develop these areas in particular.

Finally, our goal was to pick out the lessons which came up over and over again, as these are likely the areas that will help the most people. If you think you are taking a short cut by jumping straight to this section, you may miss out on the many gems contained in each of the 101 contributions. They may be lessons that are just as valuable to your specific circumstance or industry, so be sure to read the actual interviews as well as this lessons section. I guarantee these fascinating people will have something to new to teach that I have failed to summarize in these 30 lessons.

With that said, enjoy—take what you need and run with it, but don't try to do everything at once!

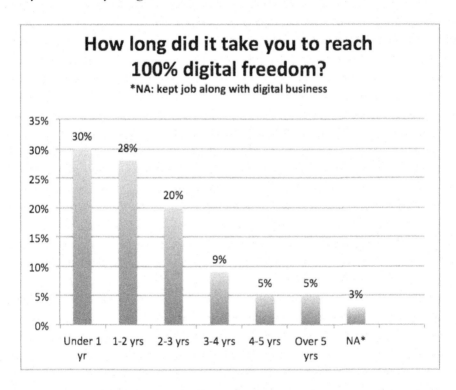

LESSON 1

"Just begin and the mind grows heated; continue, and the task will be completed!"

– Johann Wolfgang von Goethe

Just begin! (24%)

Reading through all the contributions to this book may have left you reeling with ideas, but where do you start? At the beginning, of course!

Start thinking of the goal you want to achieve and then take action. It may sound simple, but our first lesson is "Just begin!" Dr. Martin Luther King, Jr., sums this up with his quote:

"Faith is taking the first step, even when you don't see the whole staircase."

"Until one is committed, there is hesitancy, the chance to draw back. Concerning all acts of initiative (and creation), there is one elementary truth, the ignorance of which kills countless ideas and splendid plans: that the moment one definitely commits oneself, then Providence moves too. All sorts of things occur to help one that would never otherwise have occurred. A whole stream of events issues from the decision, raising in one's favor all manner of unforeseen incidents and meetings and material assistance, which no man could have dreamed would have come his way."

– William Hutchinson Murray

You can look at "providence" as "divine providence," or, in a more scientific mindset, if you go down a certain path you will start finding solutions. It's up to you how to interpret this lesson, but just begin!

LESSON 2

"Nothing great in the world has ever been accomplished without passion."

– Georg Wilhelm Friedrich Hegel

Work on something you are passionate about. (40%)

So we know we should "just begin," but if you don't have an existing idea, this is a good place to start looking for one.

What do you love to do with your time, and how can you use this knowledge to help others? This alludes to another of our lessons, but while it's great to work on something you are passionate about, will others value this information or service and be willing to pay for it? As Benjamin Franklin said:

"If passion drives you, let reason hold the reins"

If you are in a position where you are working on something you feel negative about, it may be time to look at what you are doing and go back to the drawing board. Look for your passion in big, bold things that improve the lives of others by giving them value.

If you have yet to experience passion for your work in this way, how will you know it when it comes up? As T.S. Eliot puts it:

"It is obvious that we can no more explain a passion to a person who has never experienced it than we can explain light to the blind."

When you feel it you will know, and that is when you will also know you are on the right path.

LESSON 3

"Don't try to create a product or service that you know nothing about. Find a problem that you yourself are having, and solve that problem with an amazing product. You will already know everything that the product needs and will feel passionate about creating a solution for yourself and many others like you."

– Tim Ferriss

Scratch your own itch. (28%)

Sometimes it is difficult to find your passion, and you end up working on things that just seem like a good opportunity. While it isn't definite that you will fail under these circumstances, it is a whole lot more difficult to stay the course and produce outstanding results if you don't love doing what you do.

One way to find a passion project is to look at your own problems and try to come up with a solution that will benefit not only yourself, but others too.

This need not be an actual product or service. As somebody who has been reading with great interest about successful people for over twenty years, this is what this book is to me. I'm scratching my own itch to dig into this area for myself and find evidence of what people *really* say about success.

Scratching your own itch is a fantastic way to find your passion project. Every time something bugs you, or something isn't working for you, write it on a notepad and mull over possible solutions. You might be surprised at what your subconscious starts throwing back out when you feed in problems while considering solutions.

LESSON 4

"You can't be all of the people you're influenced by, so you make your own filter and create your own beautiful, unique thing in the world. Soak up the world, man, and make something of your own."

– CeeLo Green

Be open to gaps in the market. (36%)

Is there a gap in the market for your idea? This can be looked at in one of five ways:

1. If there are already solutions out there, can it be done in a different, better, or alternative way? Don't knock an idea off the table just because other people are already doing it. You can consider existing ideas part of your market validation and improve on them. (Especially if those ideas are not completely solving your problem!)

2. More than one idea can be combined to come up with something totally new. Take James Heller's example from this book. James took advertising and put it on public vehicles, allowing drivers to make money in the process. I like to call James's brainchild "Wrapify—the Uber of advertising." (you heard it here first!)

3. If you are really creative, you can totally disrupt the market. In this book, John Pollock is a great example. He understood tax planning on a deeper level than the advisors in the industry and, in Johns words: "...instead of joining the CPA industry I instead decided to disrupt it."

4. Can you create something that complements an already existing service?

5. Finally, can you spot a niche where people are being left behind? To quote Fred Stutzman:

"...what I've learned is that when the market is entirely moving towards a business model (e.g. mobile first), there are big opportunities for those forgotten consumers. So my advice would be to look for your opening—and those openings are often non-obvious because all of the market and your peers are moving in a single direction. But if you can figure out your underserved area and gain a foothold, you can grow reliably from that position."

Keep an open mind when looking for ideas and be aware of what other businesses and solutions are not yet doing in the services or products you are using, or industries you work within.

LESSON 5

"If you can't measure it, you can't improve it."
– Peter Drucker

Measure results and be prepared to pivot. (37%)

You might think this would belong deeper into the lessons, and you would be right. It also belongs here too, however, as you also have to measure your initial idea to see if there is a market for this product or service.

When you have a product or service in place, measure results when you implement new things and don't break the bank spending until measurement has determined the usefulness and profitability of this implementation. Measure again as you move forward. Even if something is working, sometimes the law of diminishing returns will kick in, and this is when you can change focus.

Finally, remember that if you are unhappy in your work, or if stress and overworking are affecting your health or family life, then it may be time to make a change. Take stock of your personal needs and make changes if things don't feel good to you personally. Although making money is of course desirable, it isn't everything. Your health and happiness are a priority too! Are you taking time to measure this?

LESSON 6

"A genius in the wrong position could look like a fool."

– Idowu Koyenikan

Know your strengths. (21%)

Allow yourself to work on the things you enjoy and excel at. You are far more likely to produce outstanding results if you do this. Then surround yourself with others whose strengths lay in the areas where you are weak.

Could I have edited this book myself? Sure, I could have! I also could have created a cover, proofread, and formatted it for paperback and digital reading. I could do all of that, but the results would be average at best. These are not my strengths. By spending my time on them I would be doing you, the reader, a disservice by delivering a product I could have made better by allowing experts to take control. I would also not be using my time optimally by doing other things that don't revolve around my strengths.

Although it is a good idea to have a working knowledge of all areas of your business, you should concentrate your efforts on developing your strengths. Through practice and learning more in your area of strength, you will become one of the best in your field.

LESSON 7

"Essentialists see trade-offs as an inherent part of life, not as an inherently negative part of life. Instead of asking, 'What do I have to give up?' they ask, 'What do I want to go big on?'"

– Greg McKeown, Essentialism: The Disciplined Pursuit of Less

Focus on few things. (24%)

This lesson can be put to work many different levels. It concerns you as an individual, and if you ignore it, you are almost certainly not going to achieve much. Stephen Guise put it best when he wrote:

"Too many people try to do too much, and they sacrifice consistency to do it."

The more projects you work on, the less likely you are to finish any of them. You are also not focusing your full attention and are going to produce suboptimal results even if you do eventually finish.

Think of it this way. Let's say it takes you six months to create one product. You have ten ideas and begin work on all of them. It would take you five years to complete them all, and in the meantime you would have made no money at all. If you had taken one project at a time, after six months you would already be making some money, after a year you would double that, and you would be adding to your income regularly every six months. Still want to begin work on several of those great ideas you have?

Focusing on just a few things is the optimal way to get things finished and out the door. Both the quality and quantity of your work will improve if you follow this rule.

LESSON 8

"When you stand alone and sell yourself, you can't please everyone. But when you're different, you can last."

– Don Rickles

Don't try to be everything to everyone. (23%)

With regard to both your business and yourself as a figurehead for and within that business, don't try to be everything to everyone. This is closely related to the previous lesson, "focus on few things," but has separate connotations.

With regard to your business, specialize. Focus on being the best you can be in a smaller niche, rather than producing mediocre results in many different areas. This isn't to say you can't expand once you have accomplished your mission of being a leader in a niche—you can, but specialize first! How did Jeff Bezos and Amazon start out? Selling books! In other words, they specialized first. Had Jeff Bezos began by trying to build a website that sold "everything" right from the beginning, we might not have "the everything store" today.

This lesson also concerns you personally as the figurehead and personality of your business. You should also allow your true self to shine through. Don't try to be the squeaky clean guy on your competitors' website, the one whose teeth gleam in the sunlight (unless that is really you!). "Compare and despair," as John Lee Dumas often says! There will be lovers and haters whoever you are, so be genuine!

Don't try to keep everyone happy in every way. Don't be afraid to say "no" if another person's agenda is going to pull you away from your own course.

LESSON 9

"You must acquire the habits and skills of managing a small amount of money before you can have a large amount. Remember, we are creatures of habit and, therefore, the habit of managing your money is more important than the amount."

– T. Harv Eker

Manage your money carefully. (43%)

This may sound like simple common sense and you might even be thinking of skipping it, but there are lessons to be learned on this subject.

When you are spending your money on products and services to help either yourself or your business improve, are you really doing your homework before you click that "buy now" button just because that sales page is convincing? This is a good point to stop and think: could you find recommendations on what you need from people in your network?

Another red light can be the pricing: if the price seems too good to be true, it likely is. Although there is great information out there for a small price or even free, it is often true that if you buy cheap, you buy twice. Likely more than twice. Take Dave Perdew's example:

"I spent $22,000 on $27 products before I made a nickel online. I thought that I could get the answers and the skills that I needed without investing in real solutions. That was a huge mistake."

This lesson also ties into a previous lesson on measuring results. Validate new products before beginning that project in a big way. On existing projects, test first before massively investing money into something to see if it will actually have a positive impact. Never just hope that something will work because it did for somebody else and go all out. You may end up throwing away a lot of money on something that may not work in your particular circumstances. Worst case scenario, you might actually do damage to your business. As an example, most coders have little knowledge of search engine optimization, so you might spend a bucket load on making your site look great, but the search engines may hate it and never send another visitor your way!

Finally, and maybe most important of all, be aware of cash flow in your business. Are things moving in the right direction? Does everything check out? If you don't understand this side of your business, or somebody else deals with it, then it is a good idea to get educated, at least in the basics, so you can make regular checks on these figures.

LESSON 10

"If people believe they share values with a company, they will stay loyal to the brand."

– Howard Schultz

Make branding a priority. (31%)

What do you or your company stand for? It is vital that your customers understand exactly why your company exists and who it exists for. Give customers something they can associate with, and they are far more likely to build an emotional bond with you or your company.

Don't fall into the trap of thinking of marketing and branding as the same thing. With branding we are telling the public "This is what I am and what I stand for." Your branding might disqualify certain potential customers, just as it will act as a magnet to the customers you want to attract.

Are you running the website for young, hungry entrepreneurs, selling information that will help beginners get off the starting blocks? Or are you catering to the older, experienced entrepreneur who understands the bedrock of business and needs deeper, more specialized information that is more suitable to help existing businesses?

You can see how these two groups of entrepreneurs would need to be communicated with in a different way—not only because of a potential age difference, but also because you can't use the same terminology with a beginner as you can with a seasoned veteran. Selling to the wrong group in this example will only result in unhappy customers.

You should also think about making your message stand out and be unique. Do things people will remember, whether in person or virtually. Nobody remembers the grey man who simply drones his message or sits quietly in the back of the room.

A logo may be something that springs to mind when you hear the word "branding," and for good reason. Logos are often associated with a company's brand. In your logo you can reflect back aspects of your customer's ideal self and keep this message alive throughout all of your interactions, products and services.

LESSON 11

*"Overdeliver on promises and deadlines. Show up early,
deliver your product early, and deliver more than you promised.
Overdeliver now, and in the future, you will be overpaid."*

– Clay Clark

Over-deliver. (50%)

This was the second most mentioned lesson from our contributors at 50%, which should give you some idea of its importance in helping you to succeed. The idea is simple: give more than is expected of you in all interactions and transactions.

Go the extra mile to help people. Deliver outstanding free information in whichever media you choose to present it. Make sure your customer service is second to none. Got a complaint? Put things right and give even more value to make up for the inconvenience.

Don't look at this as extra work on your part. Think of it as an investment. It will pay you back in spades when your customers come back and share your service with others because they trust you to deliver. The more you are prepared to give, the more you will receive in return.

Here is an example of this in action from Ben Tristem:

"When a student has an issue with understanding or following something, our ideal response is "'Thank you, we have improved this content. Now take a look."

LESSON 12

"Email is the Jason Bourne of online: somebody's always trying to kill it. It can't be done."

– Luis Hestres

Start building an email list. (15%)

Surprisingly, this lesson was only mentioned by 15% of our contributors, perhaps because it's one of those easily forgotten things you had to learn when starting out. Even experienced people seem to put off starting an email list for much too long, which is a huge mistake.

An email list can become one of your biggest assets. With it, you can once again deliver knock-your-socks-off information that is valuable to your followers and build a solid relationship with them. When you ask for the sale, email marketing shows its power once again. When it is done well, it has a very high conversion rate. Even if you are not selling products just yet, it is a reliable method of getting people back to your site to read new material.

Finally, you have total ownership of your email list. While other methods of interacting with your followers like Facebook and Twitter might be helpful, you have no control over these sites. If they shut up shop tomorrow, you lose all those followers you have built up. Not only that, how much of the stuff you put out there is actually seen by your followers without you having to pay for some extra service? The results are minuscule compared to your email list.

LESSON 13

"Every human being is entitled to courtesy and consideration. Constructive criticism is not only to be expected but sought."

– Margaret Chase Smith

Accept and even seek out constructive criticism. (14%)

Just what you need, right? More people telling you what you should be doing! Well, in this case the critics will be useful. Listen to those around you who have input regarding your service if they are customers or have a direct interest in seeing you succeed.

This could not only be feedback from mentors, partners or mastermind groups. Your existing customers are also a resource: you'll get spontaneous feedback, and you can seek constructive criticism via short questionnaires or surveys. The feedback can help you to improve on your product and even get new ideas.

Creating a new product? You can use the same principle to help you validate the idea and to see what potential customers want.

While we don't want to listen to the trolls who tend to come out of the woodwork, it's a good idea in general to listen to constructive feedback. If the message carries a valid point rather than just an insult or accusation, it might be time to take notice. If you aren't getting this feedback now, then go out and find it. It could save you a lot of time and make you money if you allow others to point out things you may be blind to.

LESSON 14

"First they ignore you, then they laugh at you, then they fight you, then you win."

– Mahatma Gandhi

Don't feed the trolls. (14%)

Whoever you are and whatever you are doing, there are going to be haters. Don't let idle chatter from negative critics deter you from your path.

Get it into your head right now that you can never please everyone. Hell, it's probable that some people are going to downright hate you or what you do! When these trolls emerge, in whatever form, you will be prepared.

Don't confuse trolling with constructive criticism. Sometimes you are going to hear truths that you may not like. Learn to judge whether this feedback holds any information that you can learn from, or if it's simply an attack. If it's the latter, let it roll off your back. Don't get involved or interact with these people—you will simply feed the fire and perhaps negatively impact your own integrity.

LESSON 15

"Mentorship is an incredibly huge responsibility. And you need to choose your mentors carefully, just like mentors choose their apprentices carefully. There has to be trust there, on a very deep level."

– Jimmy Chin

Find a mentor. (45%)

Mentors can come in many forms. You may be able to find an individual within your network who understands your business or personal goals and can help you, but there are other options.

Consultants, a mastermind group, angel investors, a business partner or even friends or a family member with relevant knowledge can act as mentors in some way.

If you are just getting started, it is likely you know few people in your industry, or perhaps you do not yet have a budget for paid mentorship. If this is the case, you can use virtual mentorship via online courses, read all you can on the subject and contact those who have seen success in your area. Seek out podcasts and websites that give out valuable knowledge and resources. Reach out and ask questions—this will also help you to build your network.

There is nothing wrong with learning all you can with these methods, but nothing will replace having a good mentor. He or she will accelerate your success, help you avoid problems and bring out the best in you. They will also make you more productive and help you follow through on things because accountability has now entered the equation.

In the words of Derek Doepker:

"... it's critical to get a great coach or a mentor who can see your blind spots so they can help you find your own path to success..."

LESSON 16

"Sometimes, idealistic people are put off by the whole business of networking as something tainted by flattery and the pursuit of selfish advantage. But virtue in obscurity is rewarded only in Heaven. To succeed in this world you have to be known to people."

– Sonia Sotomayor

Network. (37%)

Building a network that includes trustworthy individuals, companies and communities who share similar struggles, interests or goals to you is an underrated, sometimes overlooked and sometimes even shunned way to accelerate your success. Affiliates and influencers in your industry can help you with joint ventures and cross promotion so that both of your tribes benefit. However, this isn't the only way your network can help you.

Individuals in completely different fields from yours may also possess valuable information that can be brought over to your field. More experienced entrepreneurs may be able to help you make choices about solutions for your business that are suitable across a variety of fields.

Your network might also include those you perhaps consider competitors. Viewing those in the same industry as yours as competitors is flawed thinking. They might be potential promotional partners, and they certainly hold valuable knowledge about your industry that they can share with you, and you with them.

This doesn't mean you should be out trying to get hundreds of business cards from people whose name you likely won't remember the next day. Although you may meet a lot of people, it is likely you will only click with a small amount of them, and this is great. The idea is to build lasting relationships with people who will come to actually care about you, as you come to care about them. Networking is not to introduce yourself to every person in the room briefly and then just as quickly forget about them.

There is also a dark side to networking. Fred Stutzman warns us of doing too much of this as opposed to taking action. John Bura also mentions that this can be a problem for some entrepreneurs. Utilize networking, but don't let it take over too much of your time.

LESSON 17

"The greatness of a man is not in how much wealth he acquires, but in his integrity and his ability to affect those around him positively."

– Bob Marley

Practice honesty, patience and integrity. (27%)

Always treat the people you come into contact with in a manner that you would like to be treated yourself. Be patient and understanding with others and let honesty guide you. Even if you manage to find success short term, it will not last without the assistance of others, and others will not help you to realize your dreams unless they see within you a strong internal moral and ethical code.

Your integrity is something you should guard closely. It will help you build genuine relationships with your network, great working relationships with employees, and trust with your customers. Word will soon spread that you are not a good person to associate with if you cannot be trusted to deal with others in a manner that results in a positive outcome for all involved.

LESSON 18

"Nothing in the world can take the place of Persistence. Talent will not; nothing is more common than unsuccessful men with talent. Genius will not; unrewarded genius is almost a proverb. Education will not; the world is full of educated derelicts. Persistence and determination alone are omnipotent. The slogan 'Press On' has solved and always will solve the problems of the human race."

– Calvin Coolidge

Don't give up! (53%)

53% of our contributors told us that you should never give up when it feels like you are going nowhere fast, or you become discouraged. Learn to keep striving for your goals. Just keep putting one foot in front of the other and remember that success takes time.

"Winners never quit and quitters never win."

– Vince Lombardi

Make consistent productivity a habit that can help carry you through the times when you just feel like quitting and find a way to avoid that "stinking thinking."

Change your mindset back to positivity in whichever way works for you so you can get your show on the road again. This might include a quick blast of listening to motivational talks, reading a book that set you off on this journey in the first place or looking into the success of others who have overcome difficulties to achieve their goals in the form of biographies. (My suggestion: The Art Williams "Just do it" speech—if that doesn't pick you up, nothing will!)

Being persistent doesn't mean you have to continue on a path you find you have no desire to follow. Persistence means actually continuing to search for the work you will enjoy being a part of. Many of our contributors had several attempts at creating a business and either didn't enjoy it, or it failed. But they persisted in searching for the thing they loved doing, rather than quitting and settling for a "normal" job for the rest of their days.

Don't give up looking for the side hustle that is right for you, and don't give up when you start facing problems on the path to making that work, whether it be internal struggles or external obstacles.

LESSON 19

"It is impossible to live without failing at something, unless you live so cautiously that you might as well not have lived at all, in which case you have failed by default."

–J. K. Rowling

Look at failures and adversity as opportunity. (44%)

You are going to make mistakes and things will go wrong—it is inevitable! You must train yourself to see any adversity or "failures" that you go through as learning experiences that will help you grow, learn, and do things better in future.

You should of course plan ahead to avoid problems, but always keep in mind that things will go wrong at some point. When things inevitably do go wrong, you will be mentally prepared and less likely to be deterred from sticking with your goal.

I am wary of even using the word "failure" here. Many of our contributors refused to even acknowledge the word failure in the context of their businesses or their lives in general. Several didn't even answer the question until I rephrased it!

Finally on the subject of failure, admit to and own your failures— use this opportunity to get feedback where possible. Letting allies see you stumble will not cause them to see weakness. Rather, they will see both the strength you possess in getting back up, and the integrity you possess in your ability to admit your shortcomings and correct them.

We also need to cover adversity here, and I can't think of a more shining example than Mark Goblowsky. When he was only three years old, Josh, Mark's son, was involved in a hit and run accident that left him with a traumatic brain injury. I'm sure you will agree that this is every parent's nightmare! As a parent myself, it brings a tear to my eye every time I even think about it!

This was devastating for Mark and his family. But in the end, he used this traumatic experience in his "Strength Through the Struggle" podcast, as a way to connect with and help others who are fighting through their own struggles.

If Mark can use such a devastating experience to help those around him, what's your excuse?

LESSON 20

> *"Study hard what interests you the most in the most undisciplined, irreverent and original manner possible."*
>
> – Richard Feynman

<u>Keep learning and developing new skills. (35%)</u>

This seems like a no-brainer, but 35% mentioned that you should keep on educating yourself and developing new skills that will help you run your business. This is especially true in the areas where your strengths lie, but it also applies to your business as a whole. You should have a good working knowledge of your entire business so that you are able to see if something looks wrong.

Although this rule may apply to learning via courses, mentors and your network, there is also plenty to be learned by experimenting on your own. If you are particularly creative, you might come across an idea that may not have been tried before. How else can you make it work unless you learn through trial and error?

If you truly want to accelerate your learning on a deeper level, remember to do two things. Teach what you know, and get involved in *doing* what you don't know. Merely reading about subjects never allows you to connect with that knowledge as deeply as utilizing it and then teaching it.

LESSON 21

"The biggest risk is not taking any risk. In a world that's changing really quickly, the only strategy that is guaranteed to fail is not taking risks."

– Mark Zuckerberg

<u>Get used to being uncomfortable. (13%)</u>

It is likely you can think of something you could do to take your business to the next level, yet you don't because the thought of it scares you. This fear might be there because you don't yet hold all of the information you think you need to begin, or it could simply be a fear of putting yourself out there in a way you are unaccustomed to, such as interviewing somebody for audio or video rather than a simple written set of questions. (I'm guilty as charged here!)

Brad Wilson summarized this idea in the following way:

"...fears are the barrier to entry and they keep most people from truly realizing their fullest potential. Do what the others are unwilling to do and bust through that barrier."

If you willing to take steps to get past your fears, it is probable that you will accelerate your success, and in the process you will be delivering more value to people. If you mess up, or make mistakes, what the hell? Learn, keep trying and you will eventually succeed.

LESSON 22

"You become financially free when your passive income exceeds your expenses."

– T. Harv Eker

Don't exchange time for money. (10%)

While it is arguable whether you can ever make your online income truly passive, it is a truth that you can certainly make your income more passive.

The idea here is to stop exchanging time for money in the traditional sense. To put this into practice, you wouldn't work for an hourly rate. Instead you work on something for free up front, and then you put that product on the market where it can sell over and over again without you having to do much work on it ever again.

Ebooks, online courses, or recorded webinars might fall into this category. To take the example of an online course, as long as the material is evergreen (see below) it could continue to sell for years and years. If you were to take the same material and teach it to a live class, you only get paid one time and then you have to do it all over again to earn from this material again.

Once you have a suitable product, you can utilize value packed automated email auto-responders and funnels that guide potential customers through to a point where they can finally buy, and it's almost all hands off once it has been tweaked and tested.

It also bears mentioning that you might want to think about whether your material is "evergreen" or not. For example, if you create a course on using Windows 10, it may sell very well while Windows 10 is current but how many people do you think are buying informational products on Windows XP these days? A product dealing with anger management, on the other hand, will likely have a much longer shelf life and bring you passive income much longer.

LESSON 23

"In today's uncertain economy, the safest solution to be wealthy, be in total control and enjoy freedom for you and your family is to have multiple streams of income."

– Robert G Allen

Create multiple streams of income. (23%)

Building on the previous concept of not exchanging time for money, creating multiple streams of income will help you hit that stage where you have enough money coming in to take your online endeavors to a full time gig.

This needn't involve creating dozens of different types of products. (Although there is nothing inherently bad about that.) Often you can simply repurpose existing information in a new way that will give you access to a new audience. So you wrote a book? Why not put the course version on your site or on Udemy? You organized a live event? Record it so others can make a purchase and enjoy the information.

Another benefit of this strategy lies in the security it brings. With many different streams of income coming in, if one dries up you are not going to feel the effects so much as if you had put all your eggs into one basket. And remember, once you have a nice stream of income coming in, there are also places away from the internet where you can make investments to bring in passive income.

Need ideas for stream of income? Check out Kary Oberbrunner's contribution again.

LESSON 24

"The old mantra of 'be everywhere' will quickly be replaced with 'be where it matters to our business."

– Mike Stelzner

Be everywhere. (18%)

One of the best sources I have found to get this point across comes from Pat Flynn of Smart Passive Income. While I won't go into detail on the story of "the God bless you man," I do suggest you go take a look at this lesson for yourself at SmartPassiveIncome.com/podcasts/how-to-be-everywhere/

The idea behind this lesson is that if you limit yourself to only your own website, you are limiting your reach. By putting yourself out there in different forms of media, you can grow your following exponentially.

This needn't be a whole lot of extra work or cost a lot of money if you are just starting out. Although it will reduce the quality of your messages somewhat, WordPress websites, for example, can be set up to automatically post newly released material to places like Facebook and Twitter. Have a podcast? Why not put up the audio on YouTube too?

This doesn't just apply to social media. You can appear on other people's podcasts, guest post on other peoples sites, and speak at live events. Learn at least the basics of search engine optimization so you can structure your articles to appear in Google's search results.

There are numerous different ways to do this, but be sure that your target audience actually frequents the places you promote on. If possible, measure results to see what is working best and double down in this area.

Finally, I'll leave you with the words of one of our contributors just in case nothing seems to be working for you:

"If you get the feeling that 'we've tried everything, and nothing works,' then maybe it's a product problem."

– Ryan Kulp

LESSON 25

"Don't undersell yourself. Instead, write your own price-tag."
– Lisa Messenger

Don't undersell yourself. (5%)

Although this lesson was only spotted in 5% of the contributions, it is nonetheless very important to your success. Are you charging too little for your time, services or products? While this may come across as greedy on first look, you should understand that as well as taking great care of your customers by giving them good value, you also have to take care of yourself.

If you are working every hour God sends yet you are still struggling to make ends meet, then you might be missing the fact that your services are in high enough demand that you could likely charge more and work less. Think of your own health and welfare as well as that of your customers, and if the service you are providing is second to none then people will be more than happy to pay you extra for a job well done.

This also applies to the products you sell. Are you selling a similar item to a competitor's at a far lower price because you are under-estimating the worth of your work? Maybe it's time to measure that theory by testing a price increase on new incoming customers. Raising your prices can often not only result in more income, it can also result in a better quality of customer.

Sometimes we forget what we went through to develop the skills we have and assume that others have just as much knowledge. This often isn't the case. The things you know and do, day in and day out, are likely the skills that others will pay you handsomely, and happily, to learn or develop.

LESSON 26

"To me, book writing is fun, and I basically just write about things that are entertaining to myself."

– Chuck Klosterman

Write a book! (37%)

37% of the people in this book have themselves written their own books. It is a great way to get your message out to interested parties, it is an excellent marketing tool, and it can also help you cement yourself as an authority in your niche. As if this wasn't enough, if you put your book up for sale on sites like Amazon, they also provide an avenue of passive income.

As mentioned elsewhere, do not try to take on all aspects of the book creation process unless you are trained. Editing, book covers, formatting, promotion and marketing, etc. should all be left up to the professionals if you want to produce a quality product that actually sells!

If you decide this is an avenue you would like to pursue, there is more than one person in this book who can help you out, so hit them up!

"Writing is the basis of all wealth."

– Scott Ginsberg

LESSON 27

"It is far better to be alone, than to be in bad company."

– George Washington

Be careful of bad partnerships. (25%)

25% of our contributors warned against getting into bad partnerships. This goes beyond just your business partner. It could include employees, subcontractors, or even needy clients or customers!

A bad partner doesn't necessarily mean they are a bad person. It could just be that you both went into partnership with different goals and visions for your business moving forward. At some stage this is going to lead to problems.

"If you are going to go into a business partnership with anyone, make sure you both agree to a contract that specifically states what the objective of the partnership is, what your ownership and payment terms are, what your respective roles and responsibilities will be in the business, and what your exit strategy will be."

– John Lagoudakis

Whichever type of partnership we are talking about, it is important to make it clear what is expected of each party involved, in writing when possible, to protect both parties. Although *your* word may be your bond, bear in mind that misunderstanding can and will happen, and the fact that unfortunately, not everybody holds to the same level of integrity as you.

LESSON 28

"Come on, come on! And there'll be no turning back! You were only killing time and it can kill you right back. Come on, come on! It's time to burn up the fuse. You got nothing to do and even less to lose."

– Jim Steinman

Burn your bridges. (10%)

Think you should just quit your job and work digitally right away? That's just what 10% of our contributors did! Think twice before you do this. It might be an option if you have a financial safety net or if there is a second income coming in. But it's risky.

The benefit of burning your bridges lies in the motivation and urgency it will give you to succeed. If you go down this route, leave your current position in an amicable way as you never know if you might need to go back. Negative motivation is also a factor here. Do you really want to go back, cap in hand, to your old boss and admit you were wrong? I didn't think so!

Although not included in this 10%, some of our contributors were forced into this position when their jobs were lost through no fault of their own. If fate deals you a similar hand, look at it as an opportunity to buckle down and make things happen.

LESSON 29

"It's rare for a startup to make money immediately, so you need to make sure that you have enough saved or that you have another income stream that can support you."

– Richard Branson

Keep your job or existing businesses. (45%)

While burning your bridges may evoke urgency and motivation in you, it isn't the only way to succeed. 45% of our book contributors either stuck with their job while building their side hustle, or recommended doing so.

As you build up your side hustle, you can move into a part time position at your job when money is coming in consistently from your online endeavors. Save as much money as you can from both your job and the side hustle. When the time finally comes to set out on your own, this safety net will help to see you through any rough patches you might encounter.

This also applies if you are in full or part time education. Just because you have read all these stories about high school dropouts turned millionaires, don't think you have to do it this way too. It seems that these dropout stories are the exception rather than the rule.

BONUS - LESSON 30

"I believe in this concept that you learn by teaching."
– Stephen Covey

Teach what you have learned.

Although this is not really mentioned by the contributors in this book to any great extent, I believe it bears mentioning. The vast majority of the contributors are also teachers in their industry, and this is a great way to build trust and give value to your customers.

I am not fond of the term "fake it 'til you make it" with regard to teaching in general. To me this implies that you are lying or pretending that you possess knowledge that you don't have. This is not the way forward if you want to create something valuable. This ties closely in with passion and integrity, so if you want to teach, make it in an area where you are truly interested and knowledgeable. In some cases, however, you do not need to be an expert. You can document your own trials and discoveries for others if you believe it will be of value. This book is the perfect example of this method of teaching in action.

Whenever you successfully complete something, ask yourself: "Would others find value if I were to document what I have learned?" If the answer is "yes," you might have your next product idea right there!

Finally, teaching is also a fantastic method of accelerating your own learning. It helps you to deeply absorb information when you have to lay it out in a logical manner for others to learn from.

Chapter Five

QUOTES OF NOTE

BUSINESS IDEAS

PERFECTION IS DESIRABLE BUT OPTIONAL

The important part is to just start doing something, and once you're in that world and learning and soaking things up, only then will opportunity and chance become apparent to you. You can't figure out the end form of your business on day one.

– Patrick King of PatrickKingConsulting.com

Those of us who have made it have an obligation to share with others how we did it and what we learned.

– Beate Chelette of BeateChelette.com

When I started to find success I went ahead and started teaching other people how to do what I was doing.

– Debbie Drum of DebbieDrum.com

All good businesses solve problems. Otherwise, there's no business there.

– David Perdew of MyNAMS.com

Every business I create all come from trying to solve the problems I personally experience.

– Chris Guthrie of UpFuel.com

The greatest thing about success is gaining freedom to do what you really want to do.

– Stephen Guise of StephenGuise.com

BREAKTHROUGHS

THIS BIRD WILL FLY

Eventually you reach a certain point in your business where the scales suddenly start weighing in your favor, and all the work you put in finally pays off.

– Adam Sicinski of IQMatrix.com

Success is really hard to define. I assume most people want to hear about financial windfalls but, for me, it was the realization that my time and knowledge is absolutely worth the cost of the lessons that I give. Life is about adding value to fellow humans so, whatever your gift is, start sharing it with the world and money will be created as a side effect.

– Brad Wilson of EnhanceYourEdge.com

You have to decide if you want to put it all in or let it all go. To be clear, this happens to all entrepreneurs and it is extremely uncomfortable.

– Beate Chelette of BeateChelette.com

My greatest breakthrough was to watch what people were responding to in order to give them more of what they wanted.

– Nicole Dean of NicoleOnTheNet.com

Once I realized that my market was not limited to my local geographic area, and that with technology I could reach the world and maximize my efficiencies in communication, I was on the road to success.

– Dave Fuller of ProfitYourselfHealthy.com

A lot of times when you're first starting out and you have to do everything, that can be very overwhelming, so if you have somebody that has complementary talents, that's a perfect dream team because while you're over here doing one set of tasks they're over there doing another set of tasks. Then you bring it together and something very magical happens.

– Debbie Drum of DebbieDrum.com

The most important thing I ever did was get honest about my skill level.

– David Perdew of MyNAMS.com

Lots of people have good ideas, [but] ultimately your success is all about execution.

– Fred Stutzman of Freedom.to

THE SWEET, SWEET TASTE OF DIGITAL FREEDOM

With experience came competence, and with competence came self-confidence.

– Adam Sicinski of IQMatrix.com

Creating my website, for me, wasn't about "quitting my job"—it was about creating a balance in my own life and giving me the opportunity to serve other people.

– Brad Wilson of EnhanceYourEdge.com

Don't just build a business that makes money. Instead, build a business that becomes a salable asset.

– Barbara Findlay Schenk of Bizstrong.com

The freedom that comes from working *when* you want to work, *where* you want to work, and *never worry about money again* is amazing!

– Bill Burniece of HighPayingAffiliatePrograms.com

Entrepreneurship is not for the faint of heart.

– David Perdew of MyNAMS.com

Nothing is worse then realizing you wouldn't have financial problems today if you wouldn't have bought that expensive car a year ago.

– Mark van Stratum, Author

I quit my job about three months after the launch of my first successful book. Not from the book royalties, but from creating an online course teaching other authors what I had discovered.

– Derek Doepker of EbookBestsellerSecrets.com

MISTAKES WERE MADE

AND LESSONS WERE LEARNED

Never think that you fully understand your audience, and keep striving to discover what makes them happy or sad. It will indirectly and directly affect your bottom line.

– Patrick King of PatrickKingConsulting.com

I don't really look at anything as failure. Failure only happens if you stop.

– Jason Treu of JasonTreu.com

The biggest failure and waste of time in general is not doing your homework before you invest money in either software, equipment or educational paths.

– Sherry Thacker of SherryThacker.com

At the end of the day, the most important project that any of us can work on is ourselves. The absolute biggest mistake that I have made was waiting so long to get started. Ignore the bells, whistles, and random tactics people will try to sell you in order for you to "get rich." There is no substitute for pouring your heart and soul into a piece of content and sharing it with the world. Believe me, if your content is awesome and you are diligent about creating it every single day, the masses will show up.

– Brad Wilson of EnhanceYourEdge.com

In my not-so-humble opinion, perfection is just a nice word for procrastination. Done is better than perfect and done makes money and helps people. So done is the path to profits.

– Nicole Dean of NicoleOnTheNet.com

The only real mistake is a misstep you learn nothing from.

Emphasize, explain and deliver value and don't sell yourself short.

– Barbara Findlay Schenk of Bizstrong.com

My most embarrassing and frustrating mistake was failing to build an email list.

– Dennis Becker of Earn1kADay.net

You should start building your email list from day one even if you have no clue what you're doing yet.

– Bill Burniece of HighPayingAffiliatePrograms.com

You just have to make a decision and that decision is sometimes not the best decision, but ultimately when you do make a decision you reflect back and you kind of see, you try to pick out the great parts of the direction you ultimately took. You can always think about the direction you didn't take and think of the potential outcome, but don't harp on it and just move on.

– Debbie Drum of DebbieDrum.com

The hardest working (and most persistent) guy always wins.

The lie of passive online income is just that, a lie.

– Quinton Hamp of CubicleHoudini.com

Whenever I didn't trust my intuition and did something against my gut feeling, I lost money. After a few of those incidents, I learned to trust my intuition.

– Britt Malka of GetMoneyMakingIdeas.com

Failure is an ugly negative word for awesome opportunities to learn positive steps in negative situations. Every problem I've ever had was the stepping stone to the next big win. Too many people see a challenge, and quit. That's the only failure that anyone can make that counts because it's permanent.

– David Perdew of MyNAMS.com

If you treat every obstacle as an opportunity to better yourself then you can never really fail. If you slip up three times with the same mistake then yes, I consider that a "failure," not in the task but in the opportunity to grow from it the first and the second time.

– Jamie Stenhouse of JamieStenhouse.com

Getting traffic, while important, isn't the most important thing to do. Getting the right traffic is far more important.

– Chris Guthrie of UpFuel.com

Find out what works and focus on that. Spreading yourself too thin—especially in the early days—can be really distracting and counter-productive.

– Adam Rotman of GetStencil.com

A big part of being an entrepreneur is making mistakes and learning from them.

– Fred Stutzman of Freedom.to

It's hard for me to even see things as mistakes at this point because it all seems so necessary looking back.

– Derek Doepker of EbookBestsellerSecrets.com

I am resistant to categorizing any of my entrepreneurial experiences as failures or wastes of time and money because I always seek to extract lessons, especially when times seem particularly rough. Instead, I see tough times, failing businesses or seemingly embarrassing moments as preparatory experiences to undertake something greater. I know it's probably not the answer you'd expect but it is the way I look at it. Finding the opportunity in what feels like failure is at the heart of entrepreneurship.

– Jesse Krieger of LifestyleEntrepreneursPress.com

There's no point in getting distressed over the occasional troll.

– Amanda Turner of VagabondingWithKids.com

TACTICS

BATTLE TESTED IN THE FIELD

Find amazing mentors and surround yourself with highly motivated individuals. We like to surround ourselves with people who complement our strengths and strengthen our weaknesses.

– Cody Barbo of Industry.co

If you are trying to run any type of business without copywriting knowledge or experience, you're selling yourself massively short and leaving a lot of money on the table.

– Patrick King of PatrickKingConsulting.com

To successfully grow an online business you need to be consistent for an extended period of time. Consistency is the key to absolutely everything that eventually turns out to be successful. You hear all the time about people becoming overnight successes. However, things are never really that easy. A lot of work, thought, experimentation and failure goes on behind the scenes. In fact, it typically goes on for many years.

– Adam Sicinski of IQMatrix.com

Invest in yourself by getting coaching and help. You speed up the learning curve by 10X. Someone out there has achieved the success you want, so model what they did and put your specific touch on it. It is imperative to build out your network. Go to conferences. Join groups or a mastermind. Get a mentor. [But] you need to come from a place of giving, helping and inspiring other people. If you go around trying to get things from other people to be successful, you will fail. Successful people can see "takers" and they don't want to be around them.

– Jason Treu of JasonTreu.com

It's all about offering as much free content as you can. You have to really give in order to receive.

– Sherry Thacker of SherryThacker.com

You don't know everything; others have plenty to impart and allow you to better understand your ultimate goals.

– Al Spath of AlSpath.com

If you do not put your time, energy, and soul into creating awesome content that will impact lives, then you better just close up shop. Everybody and their mom has their own website or blog but what are you going to do that can really change lives? Start with trying to change a couple of people's lives and let them be your ambassadors to the world. Brand ambassadors are a uniquely powerful tool. Fears are the barrier to entry and they keep most people from truly realizing their fullest potential. Do what the others are unwilling to do and bust through that barrier.

– Brad Wilson of EnhanceYourEdge.com

If we can focus on what we do best by playing to our strengths, we can be much more successful and get there faster.

– Beate Chelette of BeateChelette.com

The single most effective tactic is not really a tactic, but a strategy. It's leverage. I love to leverage other people's audiences. I love to leverage what's already working for me to work even better. Leverage is like magic pixie dust. It makes your traffic numbers go up, your lists grow faster, your conversion spike, and your overall profits soar.

– Nicole Dean of NicoleOnTheNet.com

Do what you love and what you are good at and hire the rest!

– Dave Fuller of ProfitYourselfHealthy.com

Never be afraid to share what you do with as many people as you can.

– Christina Nicholson of MediaMavenAndMore.com

Set yourself apart from others with similar offerings and then develop your business or personal name into a brand that people believe is different, better, more trustworthy and of higher value than competitive alternatives.

– Barbara Findlay Schenk of Bizstrong.com

Don't be afraid to do things you've never done before.

– Dennis Becker of Earn1kADay.net

If you're not incorporating email marketing into your online business strategy you're making a big mistake and leaving a ton of easy money on the table.

– Bill Burniece of HighPayingAffiliatePrograms.com

The single most effective tactic to grow your business is having assets that you own and that you sell. Having your own stuff to sell, having your own assets, your own products that you control is very important and that takes a long time to build up. The more you can strive to get that done, the better off you will be for sure.

– Debbie Drum of DebbieDrum.com

Focus on those channels that are creating the most profit.

– Quinton Hamp of CubicleHoudini.com

Building relationships via networking is an absolute must. If I hadn't gone out in the real world and built strong relationships, the business would be nowhere near where it is today.

– Daniel Knowlton of KPSDigitalMarketing.co.uk

In a world of social media and feel good projects hardly anyone is doing the number one thing that a business needs to survive. And that is to sell, to generate sales. Sales can fix any problem in any business at anytime anywhere in the world.

– Jamie Stenhouse of JamieStenhouse.com

I strongly believe in treating others in the same way I'd like to be treated.

– Akshat Choudhary of BlogVault.net

Strategic partnerships can be incredibly powerful. Trying to come up with cool cross-promos to do with brands in a similar space can be a win-win for everyone and a great way to tap into a new audience.

– Adam Rotman of GetStencil.com

Form genuine relationships with others and see my competition not as competitors, but as collaborators. It's much quicker to network with 10 influencers and have them share my work with their thousands of followers than to try to build up tens of thousands of followers of my own from scratch.

– Derek Doepker of EbookBestsellerSecrets.com

I don't think I ever put in enough time in the right places to succeed. But I've been writing every day for probably three years now. Not only is that great for honing your craft, but the sheer increase of content output makes you more visible and gives you more chances to write those home run books or posts. Some might call me lucky, but you have to be persistently "in the game" to even have a chance at luck.

– Stephen Guise of StephenGuise.com

I proactively build relationships with people I would like to learn from and partner with. By proactively, I mean seeking opportunities to add legitimate value to them and their business or brand, then doing so without asking for anything in return.

– Jesse Krieger of LifestyleEntrepreneursPress.com

Content is king, but marketing is King Kong.

Visibility is paramount, and relevance drives visibility.

I waited a couple of years before I got serious about building my mailing list, and I wish I'd started much earlier.

– Rick Smith of RickSmithBooks.com

The most effective tactic to grow readership is to consistently produce high quality content. You must own your time and refuse to be a slave to things like email, social media, and the compulsion to constantly check your phone.

– Amanda Turner of VagabondingWithKids.com

Become the go-to guy for whatever it is you're selling or the service you're providing by giving away information and advice for free.

– Damon Freeman of DamonZa.com

The best way to achieve big results is by partnering with a mentor who can help you to reverse engineer your goals. Create a clear plan for action, create the steps to achieve those goals, and then take action every single day.

– Rachel Pedersen of RachelPedersen.com

ADVICE FROM THE MOUNTAINTOP

TELL ME, OH WISE ONE

Keep doing what you love, keep learning, stay humble, stay open minded, challenge yourself and when the time is right your moment may come.

The fear will never go away, but the opportunity will. Building the habit of acting despite discomfort is like building a muscle: the more you do it the better you'll get.

– Ben Tristem of GameDev.tv

Don't ever let the haters get in the way of your opportunity to succeed. Be so dedicated to the vision and mission of your company that nothing can stop you from making your dream a reality.

– Cody Barbo of Industry.co

It's really really hard to create an audience from scratch. Its much easier to piggyback off of an existing audience.

– Matt Bodnar of ScienceOfSuccess.co

There is something to be said for outsourcing things that are your weaknesses, but you must at least understand them at first.

– Patrick King of PatrickKingConsulting.com

It's of course important to learn and develop yourself in ways that help you grow your business over time. However it's also important to be very flexible and to adapt whatever you learn to your specific situation and business. Don't just accept that something will work. Question absolutely everything, be willing to experiment, and adapt what you learn to what you're doing. Measure your results and make adjustments until you figure out the best course of action for your business moving forward.

– Adam Sicinski of IQMatrix.com

Find at least three people doing what you want to do and speak to them. Really understand their business, what they love, what they dislike, etc. It will help you understand what's involved with the business and if you really want to put years of sweat equity into it. Find a person and business you admire and model it. You can't copy anything completely, but you can take many of the parts and leverage them to design your business. Get help, coaching and a support system (i.e. mastermind group or other groups). You can't go it alone. That's a recipe for failure or very slow growth.

– Jason Treu of JasonTreu.com

Some days, I don't feel like I have a confident, decided heart, and I have to put my cloak of courage on. What scares you is usually what will give you the most results, so if it scares you, good. Doing what you said you would long after the feeling has passed is the fine line that separates winners from losers.

– Samantha Davis of SammyD.tv

Love what you do first and foremost, then put the required and necessary effort into building whatever it is you are attempting, into the finest product or service available. Customer service is #1, make sure your audience, client, user, are *more* than fully satisfied. Provide "knock your socks off" service!

– Al Spath of AlSpath.com

Most people severely overestimate what they can do in a year and severely underestimate what they can do in 10 years. If you keep showing up day after day then, in however sense you define it, you will become a success. Most people focus on tactics like SEO or website design. Who really gives a shit about having the prettiest website? If your content is remarkable then nothing can stop you.

– Brad Wilson of EnhanceYourEdge.com

Perfectionism doesn't work, but getting stuff done does. Consistent execution and a strong belief in our own success will get you to the goal. Learn to move on from mistakes as quickly as you can.

Just because you don't fulfill certain criteria or someone else's blueprint doesn't mean you will be a failure. There is no chance of extraordinary success without an equal chance of extraordinary failure.

Always, always set up your business so that you could sell it if you want to.

– Beate Chelette of BeateChelette.com

Baby steps in the right direction is still progress. When it all feels overwhelming and you think of quitting, I encourage you to look back in order to see just how far you've come. I don't know about you but this has happened to me a few times. I've been paddleboarding or canoeing and I get into the groove and keep paddling and paddling. All of a sudden, I go to turn around and I'm so much further from the shore than I even realized. I had *no* idea. I was too busy paddling to take the time to look back to appreciate my own hard work. Take a break to look back and give yourself a big hug and a high five for all that you've accomplished.

– Nicole Dean of NicoleOnTheNet.com

Stepping out of your comfort zone with little things on a daily basis helps prepare you for those situations where you are going to really have to be uncomfortable on the road to success. Success doesn't happen overnight and if you take the time you can learn from your failures. Taking time each day to meditate or pray and reflect on what is happening around you and to you can be huge in this regard. It allows you a different perspective and helps you understand that you are not the center of the universe, that you are achieving something and that when you follow your heart, you can make a difference in the lives of so many other people, and make a living doing it.

– Dave Fuller of ProfitYourselfHealthy.com

Be relentless, be persistent and don't take "no" for an answer from anybody.

– James Heller of Wrapify.com

Don't worry about failure. You will fail, because everyone does. It's not only the best way to learn, but the best way to move forward and succeed.

– Christina Nicholson of MediaMavenAndMore.com

Don't be afraid to fail. You can just pick yourself up, dust yourself off, and learn from your mistakes. As I say often: Failure is your friend.

– Dennis Becker of Earn1kADay.net

There is a common misconception that the internet is already too crowded and all of the great ideas have been fulfilled. That's BS.

Trust is the only thing that matters online and if you lose it you may never get it back. Keep things real and treat every site visitor and customer as if they were a million-dollar client.

– Bill Burniece of HighPayingAffiliatePrograms.com

You need to have that go-getter mindset because no one else is going to pick up the pieces for you when you're in a business and you're trying to grow your business. That's what it takes to really make it, by being relentless and not giving up and experiencing that failure and picking yourself back up and just keep doing and doing and doing and doing. That is the attitude that is going to get you very far.

– Debbie Drum of DebbieDrum.com

Your goal is to identify and name the problem that is holding you back so that you can find a solution.

– Quinton Hamp of CubicleHoudini.com

If you want something to happen, only you can make it happen. Don't wait until the stars are aligned, the children have moved out, or for other ideal conditions. Make it happen now.

– Britt Malka of GetMoneyMakingIdeas.com

Don't handcuff your success by limiting the investment you put into your business, health, relationships, money, and your spiritual well-being. I spent $22,000 on $27 products before I made a nickel online. I thought I could get the answers and the skills that I needed without investing in real solutions. That was a huge mistake. I needed a coach and mentor to guide me along the way, and when I discovered that, I never looked back.

– David Perdew of MyNAMS.com

You don't want to go and try and force yourself to develop a skill set based on a weakness. Develop a skill set based on a strength.

– Yaro Starak of Entrepreneurs-Journey.com

If you learn how to treat people with respect you have a great edge over others.

If you become a more valuable person, you'll start making more money.

– Mark van Stratum, Author

Follow your passion and work your face off to achieve whatever it is you want to achieve.

– Daniel Knowlton of KPSDigitalMarketing.co.uk

When you go "all in" and follow through, people feel the difference and respond accordingly.

– John Ruhlin of RuhlinGroup.com

The power of a single focus is incredible.

While money isn't everything, it's everything in business.

Too many people pick something up and put it down when it doesn't give a result after 15 months. This is your life's work, be patient, show it respect and focus on the one thing.

– Jamie Stenhouse of JamieStenhouse.com

If you're good, not only will customers stick around, but they'll talk about you to their friends, and everybody else as well.

– Akshat Choudhary of BlogVault.net

Persistence pays off. The temptation to give up can sometimes be totally overwhelming, but the trick is to charge through.

– Adam Rotman of GetStencil.com

There is such a vast gap between those with ideas, and those who actually execute on ideas. So you need to start doing the work - actually executing on ideas. Your first few ideas won't work out, so you also need to prepare for that and learn from it. Eventually, you will execute on a successful idea, but only if you do the work.

– Fred Stutzman of Freedom.to

Getting a mentor or coach who can help give you specific advice is the safest bet. It's critical to get a great coach or a mentor who can see your blind spots so they can help you find your own path to success which is different for everybody.

– Derek Doepker of EbookBestsellerSecrets.com

Writing is the basis of all wealth.

– Scott Ginsberg of HelloMyNameIsScott.com

Develop habits in the areas critical to success in your field. The way I develop habits is to shrink the behavior down to something so small I can't say no to it. Too many people try to do too much, and they sacrifice consistency to do it. Consistency is far more valuable than any mega work session, so it's a poor choice. My breakthrough happened when (and because) I minified my daily targets to ensure I was consistent. Consistency made my behaviors habitual, which means they're second nature, I don't resist them, and it's *weird* if

I *don't* do them. Your habits define who you are. Don't leave them up to chance like so many people do.

– Stephen Guise of StephenGuise.com

The concept of passive income works fine in theory, but it's important to create a critical mass of revenue streams, using multiple products or services, before you can sit back and watch the cash accumulate. Create a structure around yourself which enables realistic deadlines, and work hard to achieve them.

– Rick Smith of RickSmithBooks.com

Learn to accept criticism and use it to make your book better.

– Amanda Turner of VagabondingWithKids.com

You need to give something away for free in order to get paid later. Whether it's your knowledge, your skills or your time, that's what builds up trust and brings you clients in the future.

– Damon Freeman of DamonZa.com

CONCLUSION

Overwhelmed? Excited? Confused? Scared? Inspired?

You should be a little bit of all of them.

Making a living online is complex but simple. It's hard work but it's easy. And that's just the doing part. The hardest and most complicated part of the process is just getting started!

You've seen those skiers and snowboarders at the X-Games right? They fly and spin and twirl through the air doing outrageously complicated tricks. Now, if you ask them to do a simple backflip, they can do it no problem. It's easy. Almost automatic. They've trained with the best their whole lives, and they are world-class athletes. This is a piece of cake. It probably feels foolishly silly for them to think that fewer than 1% of the people in the world can actually do something that is so easy for them.

That's what most successful internet entrepreneurs feel like.

You see, what we do is easy for us. It's hard for us to even understand why those who haven't done it feel so intimidated by coming up with a decent idea, creating a product or service, driving some traffic to the offer, and watching the money come rolling in. I mean, on the surface, it's pathetically simple.

But when you haven't already been there and done that, it does seem hard doesn't it? It seems almost like a foolish dream to even consider that YOU, measly ol' YOU, could earn a substantial and reliable income online.

But the thing is, you can. You don't have to be a world-class anything to do it either. It's much easier than doing flying tricks on a pair of skis. It's much easier than trying to make the same amount of money with the same amount of hours invested in the regular job market. It does, however, take the accumulation of enough knowledge and skill for it to be effective and start to feel fun and easy.

Whatever you are feeling after reading this book, please don't convince yourself that this is too hard or complex for you. It's not. Pretty much everything that you do now and find to be simple, routine, easy-to-comprehend, and almost automatic once was a great enigma to you. You couldn't walk. You couldn't talk. You couldn't even tie your shoes.

But, you clumsily started, learned enough to become proficient, and eventually achieved mastery as you kept after it. The art of internet business—real, authentic, well-intentioned internet business, not that scammer crap—is just a learned skill. And once you get good at it, you'll be able to take good ideas and turn them into a nice source of income with ease.

Therefore, it's a skill and language that everyone should learn. You never know when that great idea will strike you. And you also shouldn't expect to be all that good at it when you start. None of the contributors to this book were, and you won't be either. But that's not a reason to assume it's too hard and give up before you even start.

Start. There's nothing you're doing in your spare time more useful than learning this, I promise you that.

Whether you are just starting out or well on your way, we hope this book served as a nice addition to your education.

For more like this, including a course, live internet business case studies, and more, visit: QuitN6.com

ABOUT THE AUTHORS

CHRIS NAISH

Like yourself perhaps, Chris Naish has seen his online income rise and fall many times over the past few years but has never quite hit that stage where a consistent, reliable income has allowed him to quit his day job.

Tired of listening to advice from many sources and not quite knowing what is most important, or even true, he set out to find this information by getting the stories of many different entrepreneurs to see what was *really* working for others. Partnering with Buck Flogging from the get-go, they built the ideas behind this book into what you now hold in your hands.

Chris is also currently in the process of both removing all traces of his odd sense of humor from the manuscript so the over 100 people involved are not mortified, while struggling hard not to type the overused phrase "... and likes to write about himself in the third person."

You can read more from Chris on Amazon:
amazon.com/author/chrisnaish

His personal site is ThinkClickRich.com

BUCK FLOGGING

Buck Flogging, also known as Matt Stone, has had tremendous success online—turning himself into not one but TWO minor internet celebrities with six-figure incomes.

You're most likely to have heard of Buck Flogging, who has had big, highly-publicized appearances on: Your Mom, Your Aunt, Your Sister, Your Other Sister, Your Girlfriend, and Your Wife.

The internet is a giant playground for Flogging (also known as The Flogfather and/or the Godflogger). He launches several new ventures every year, and almost all of them find instant success.

A small sampling of his successes include:

100Covers.com

BuckBooks.net

QuitN6.com

BookAds.co

ArchangelInk.com

Success wasn't always easy for Flogging though. He spun his wheels aimlessly for four long years with virtually nothing to show for it. Out of desperation, he was forced to figure out what worked, and in just 30 days he was able to go from $300 per month to nearly $3,000, never to return to the workforce again.

His primary focus these days is helping people avoid the costly and time-consuming mistakes he once made, launching efficiently-designed internet-based businesses to quick success. As he says, "If it takes you longer than six months to carve out a full-time living online, you're doing something wrong."

He also often says, "Argh! No matter how much I scratch it won't stop itching!" "It burns!" and "What's that smell?"

Learn Buck's successful fast-start methods, get more of his crude and irreverent humor as he parodies the typical egomaniacal internet marketer sleazebag, and even communicate with him directly after watching this short video at QuitN6.com

CPSIA information can be obtained
at www.ICGtesting.com
Printed in the USA
LVOW03s2022080118

562248LV00001B/226/P